Student Activism and Protest

Alternatives for Social Change

student activism and protest

Edward E. Sampson,
Harold A. Korn, and Associates

Jossey-Bass Inc., Publishers
615 Montgomery Street • San Francisco • 1970

STUDENT ACTIVISM AND PROTEST
Alternatives for Social Change
Edward E. Sampson, Harold A. Korn, and Associates

Copyright © 1970 by Jossey-Bass, Inc., Publishers

Jossey-Bass, Inc., Publishers
615 Montgomery Street
San Francisco, California 94111

Library of Congress Catalog Card Number 77–92898

Standard Book Number SBN 87589–052–0

Manufactured in the United States of America
Composed and printed by York Composition Company, Inc.
Bound by Chas. H. Bohn & Co., Inc., New York

JACKET DESIGN BY WILLI BAUM, SAN FRANCISCO

FIRST EDITION

Code 7001

THE JOSSEY-BASS SERIES IN HIGHER EDUCATION

General Editors

JOSEPH AXELROD, *San Francisco State College*

MERVIN B. FREEDMAN, *San Francisco State College and Wright Institute, Berkeley*

Preface

Edward E. Sampson

Harold A. Korn

The 1960s were a time of national turmoil and crisis. Forces released in the individual and in society gave rise to outbursts of mass discontent and led many to question seriously the legitimacy of the authority of social institutions and established leadership. Not since the Civil War had the system of government been so sorely tested. Now, in the 1970s, we still do not have the full returns by which to evaluate the outcomes of that test.

Many social scientists became psychological newsmen, analyzing the day's events that same evening and preparing their reports for publication the next day. A nation watched in awe as television brought to everyone who cared to watch—and if you cared not, it was damn difficult to avoid—wars, natural disasters, poverty, starvation, assassinations, and protest, and protest, and protest.

"Scholarly" pieces, hastily turned out, interpreted what was happening and why. Puzzled and fearful, citizens and professionals alike reached for anything that might provide an explanation. Instant volumes explained the family origins of the protestors and the inner layers of their psyche. Occasional volumes left the protestors alone and concentrated instead on the faults in society that created the human earthquakes of demonstration.

None of us, even now, have had sufficient time away from the battle lines to take stock of the numerous changing events. We all suffer from a lack of the perspective that the passage of time provides —the guide that permits the analyst to gaze backward and to see clearly and in perspective the key events and turning points that mark a given era.

Yet, a new decade is now upon us. We can ill afford the academic luxury of waiting for things to cool down before putting our multiple heads together and attempting to arrive at some answers, however tentative. Nor can we feel secure in adopting the view that the sixties are simply a replay of some earlier historical era and thereby permit ourselves to return to complacency in the eye of the hurricane.

Today never was before; it is not merely an extrapolation of the past. Contemporary combinations of technology, population, and social organization are unique. So with some sense of urgency we have joined with our colleagues in this effort to understand the events of the 1960s. Perhaps we are naive, but we hope that *Student Activism and Protest* will allow the voices that called out so loudly in the sixties to be heard more effectively in this new decade.

The events of the 1960s had no innocent bystanders; nor can there be any in the decade now upon us. Standing pat, remaining silent, keeping out of it, and not choosing sides are active positions on the issues. Day after day students, faculty, and others have to make choices: crossing a picket line and going to class are acts of decision and choice as much as are standing on that picket line and refusing to attend or teach a class. When the cry goes up for no business as usual, continuing with business as usual is a committed position. We present this volume to those often unwitting coconspirators in the processes of social change—those who protest and those who do not.

Berkeley   EDWARD E. SAMPSON
Tallahassee   HAROLD A. KORN
January 1970

Contents

The Authors

Christian Bay, Ph.D., *professor of political science, University of Alberta*

Donald R. Brown, Ph.D., *professor of psychology, The University of Michigan*

Richard Flacks, Ph.D., *professor of sociology, University of California, Santa Barbara*

Mervin B. Freedman, Ph.D., *professor of psychology,*
    San Francisco State College

Paul Kanzer, Ph.D., *professor of psychology, University of*
    Massachusetts, Boston

Kenneth Keniston, Ph.D., *professor of psychology, Yale*
    University Medical School

Harold A. Korn, Ph.D., *professor of psychology, Florida*
    State University

Edward E. Sampson, Ph.D., *professor of psychology,*
    University of California, Berkeley

James W. Trent, Ph.D., *professor of psychology,*
    University of California, Los Angeles

Student Activism and Protest

※※※※※※※※※※※※※※※※※※※※※※※※※※※※

Alternatives for
Social Change

CHAPTER I

Student Activism and the Decade of Protest

Edward E. Sampson

Sometime in the future, when historians write about the domestic scene of the sixties, one of the major themes that will emerge undoubtedly will focus on the related issues of general unrest, dissent, organized activism, and mass protest. Somewhat *surprisingly,* a select group of students from a few universities will emerge as having been of major importance. Youth has always been a period of restlessness, of searching, of unbounded energy. When the students on the Berkeley campus of the University of California committed themselves to action in 1964, they became the triggers that released a barely tapped reservoir of national energy. They were fed from a stream which flowed out of the civil rights movement, and they gave impetus, direction, and a base of identification for the new and growing force of the under-thirty youth.

That the university has become a major vehicle of organized dissent is surprising for several reasons. Given the relatively quiet campus years of the fifties, with the silent generation, born in war, bred in war, participants in war, seeking only security in income, home, and career, one would not think to look to the university campus for leadership in national protest and dissent. We had become accustomed to the more frivolous outbursts of youth on the rampage in panty raids, football riots, and faddish activities such as flagpole sitting, phone-booth stuffing, and hula-hooping. Silence and seriousness were seen by many to be appropriate behavior for the mature collegian. The campus activism of the post-depression and pre-World War Two years had faded from our memories. We no longer expected any organized political, headline-grabbing activist movement to emanate from the college community. It was *surprising* when students rose up in protest over their education, their society, and their world.

In this country the subversive function of the university—subversive in that it seeks to bring into its view all manner of thought, questioning the foundations upon which the society is based—had been minimized in comparison to its technical, applied social service functions. The latter, so we are told, will increase as we move into a more technologically demanding social system in which the role of the university involves turning out students skilled in running the complex machinery of our increasingly planned, programmed, and

2

rationalized society. It is *surprising* when a university begins to take on the character of a dissent-producing and maintaining vehicle. For some it is surprising when the university and some of its occupants appear so blatantly to bite the hand that feeds them. This is especially the case when that food comes from the taxpayer and the dissent is focused on the very society that foots the bill. It is at moments like these that the taxpaying citizen calls for the quashing of what he considers to be extreme dissent and excessive protest. At times, he even calls for a change in the financing structure of the university itself.

Some think of the mind of the intellectual as being incapable of moving from the realm of ideas and abstract thought into the world of power politics and action. It is *surprising*, therefore, to find the university campus housing not only dissenters in thought, but also dissenters in action. The modification of the ivory-tower image of the academician and his growing function in servicing society has placed him in positions of political—that is, action-oriented, program-determining—power. Gradually members of the intellectual and academic community have been getting their hands dirty in arenas far away from the laboratory and the library. The conflict between the two worlds remains with us: the contemplative world of scholarly thought, rooted deeply in history and tradition and viewing a permanence not granted to those who must act with immediacy in that outside world; and the world of policy and decision making, of choice before all the facts are in, and of choice made in terms of values in spite of those facts. The pendulum appears to be swinging toward the side of more active participation in the day-by-day business of national and international decision making.

To understand these developments, it is not enough merely to examine the dissenters in thought and action that the university campus houses. The protest-prone personality described by such writers as Flacks, Keniston, Trent, and others is not sufficient to account for the development of contemporary activism without the context and triggering mechanism provided by the institution. The role of the institution in this regard is rather varied and complex. Although it would be possible to write an entire chapter which dealt with each component of the institution's contribution to activism, I will address myself to a brief description of each.

One of the contributions of the institution to the occurrence of organized student activism is the congregation of a select group of protest-prone, intelligent persons who share equalitarian familial backgrounds. It is just such propinquity that provides one of the essential bases for the evolution of an activist subculture or contraculture (to use Yinger's term).[1] These students are able to meet others who share similar feelings about life and the world, and who reinforce and support each other's beliefs, developing values and codes of personal morality and ethics which stand apart and often in sharp contrast to other students' values *and* to the kind of education which the activists see themselves receiving.

Another institutional factor involves the presence in academically select, large institutions, of a ready body of persons of especial leadership caliber: the perennially disadvantaged graduate teaching assistants. The teaching assistant occupies that awkward and marginal position between the status of undergraduate which he has recently left and the status of faculty to which he often aspires. In some universities, not only is he part of this in-between generation in which both worlds are unavailable to his full participation, but in addition he is often cast loose in his role of teacher with few directives or guidelines. After the assistantship has been used to lure him to the university, he is told essentially, "go in there and teach." His contact with the undergraduate student, while serving in the capacity of assistant to the professor, gives him a new, often rather shocking perspective on the entire educational process. He becomes privy to the realities of the professor's role, ambition, concerns—and sometimes lack of concern for his class and his students.

While living in that limbo land between both worlds, the teaching assistant is accorded extreme degrees of responsibility from the professor and often deferent high status from his undergraduate students. He has a flock ready to be led and colleagues who share his grievances. At Berkeley, this group of teaching assistants formed into a labor union after the 1964 FSM. As a legitimate union within the AFL-CIO, this group occupies a somewhat novel position for negotiating with the university administration. Were they to support a student strike over issues involving their working conditions—a legiti-

---

[1] J. Milton Yinger, "Contraculture and Subculture," *American Sociological Review*, 1960, *25*, 625–635.

mate union grievance—and were this strike to gain central union recognition, the power of this body of teaching assistants would become something which could not be taken lightly.

Another factor best included under this institutional rubric concerns the history of relationships and techniques of conflict resolution within the institution. One upheaval soon attracts to the university *both* students who seek further confrontations *and* administrators who have reputations in the area of conflict resolution. These new members enter a situation in which complaints have been settled by mass action: a setting which fosters paranoia. One could argue that where mass action has proved effective in the past, it will be turned to again. Students know this, administrators know this, and faculty know this. So the students' demands and claims sound to the administrators like blackmail threats—even if they were not intended as such by the students. In turn, the administrators give in to these perceived threats, leading eventually to new demands on a newly escalated level. So upward spirals the threat-counterthreat-give-in sequence until finally the seam in the gas pipe bursts and all hell breaks loose. One thinks most easily of a family that has managed a rough accommodation to one another through mutual threats, retreats and counterthreats, until one day the reservoir of distrust and fear breaks into a volcanic upheaval. Return to normal under such circumstances cannot ignore the history of prior conflict resolution and the vicious cycle of mistrust that lies barely beneath the surface.

The rationalization of education in the multiversity contributes significantly to contemporary student unrest and activism. *Rationalization* is used here in the sense in which Donald Michael uses it:

> a state of affairs in which "much greater effort will be put into applying the methods of science and engineering to set all sorts of goals and to organize men, work methods and administration so that those goals can be attained by the most efficient means.[2]

Flacks points to the conflict which exists when the more democratically socialized student faces the realities of such a rationalized education. If one is trained at home to play an active role in making the decisions

[2] *The Next Generation* (New York: Vintage, 1965), p. 34.

which affect one's behavior, how difficult it must be to face up to the impotent life one is asked to lead in many universities. Furthermore, as Bay suggests and as Trent demonstrates in his data comparing a college-educated sample with a comparable group of non-college-educated, the process of education itself, though it may be rationalized, has a certain liberating influence on the individual. The student is taught, even urged by some, to question, to think, to be critical. The mark of the success of his education occurs finally when he focuses his keenly honed mind on the institution that sought to sharpen it.

We sit upon the horns of a dilemma. As the university increasingly becomes a rationalized tool for producing essential human components for societal functioning, it seems that it must place students (and faculty as well in many cases) into a position of decreased personal power. Yet at the same time, it still seeks to instruct in the classical academic values of inquiry and critical thought. When that critical power is turned toward an examination of one's personally diminished ability to influence outcomes even in the narrow confines of the university, let alone to produce change in the larger society and world, something in the system must give. It is possible to imagine a delicate balance being maintained; but undoubtedly that kind of balance would require a more stable outside world or an entirely closed and cloistered academic world in order to work effectively. Without that, there is little doubt that upheavals will continue. You cannot socialize democratic, participatory values in the home and teach one to question and to be critical at school without allowing for the possibility that these values and these learnings will be turned toward the very institutions themselves.

The modern large university in this country, having historical roots which can be traced back to the classical academic institutions of Europe, exists today as a complex collage of the new plastered hastily and tenuously over the old. The traditional model of the university as a community of scholars and learners with a common set of shared intellectual values exists side by side with the modern big business university of faculty entrepreneurs, administrative managers, and scores of preprofessional students, who often have more conflicts of interests than sharing of values. Clark Kerr's description of the multiversity documents this present state of affairs. Through its contractual arrangements with government and business, the university itself has often taken on roles and functions which depart from the usual values of the classic academic tradition. Members of the faculty, particularly in those fields in which federal grants come most easily, are the last surviving small businessmen. Though big grantsmanship is not inevitably at odds with more academic values, large-scale projects which demand a visible product (often of the research-and-development sort) for one's labors often produce interest conflicts between professor and student and professor and professor. In this picture of a large heterogeneous academic community, however, one can still find the "real" scholar of old who wishes to examine enduring truths by methods of inquiry that have changed little from the time of antiquity.

Given these divergent perspectives, communications which issue from both the faculty and the administration have a double-bind quality that strikes the students with confusion, ambivalence, frustration, and often episodes of eruptive hostility. Discussions build around a theme of shared common values while lives are more apparently and noticeably built around themes of conflicts of interests. The administrator talks about common values shared by all, then enacts his role as mediator between various campus community interest groups, playing more the role of the politician that he must be than the academician he claims to be. The faculty tell their students about the pursuit of knowledge and truth as an academic value, then submit a proposal for another research-and-development grant, negotiate over several contracts to write another popular, money-making text, and manifest about as much of the image of the scholar as the president of some mini-corporation. There are certain concrete realities of the modern university. Their denial and the substitution of the verbiage of shared values clouds more than it clarifies, arouses anger more than it pacifies.

Not only do communications have this double-bind quality, but also the institutions themselves serve as perfect models of archaic organizations surrounded by the best in new business management. Lines of communication and authority frequently have both the surviving features of the old with the realities of the new, sitting in conflict, side by side. At Berkeley, the office of the Dean of Students, which once had an important function in student life, has gradually lost that function as student activities have shifted from fraternity and dorm pranks to political action. In this latter arena, which is seen to be a greater threat to the organizational stability of the entire enterprise, decisions must be made at the top. The authority of those in the dean's office is thus undercut; they serve in the role of policemen or as sometimes useful agents called on to be the buffer between the students and those who are really in charge of decision making. Much of this institutional struggle with communications and lines of authority has direct personal relevance for the people involved. When students have a grievance, to whom can they turn? Suspecting that they can get real answers only by going to the top (where other obligations and matters of personal style make direct contact problematical), they find nowhere to turn except to noisy displays of frustration and discontent.

On the reciprocal side of this overall institutional picture, one finds as fully complex an array of conflicting student motivations, interests, and investments as befits the diverse and often divergent models of the university itself. Some have come for preprofessional and pre-career training. They want to learn the three R's, but now at a higher level. Education means getting a degree, and getting a degree means getting more money. They want their institution to give them the straight facts and technical training they will need when they get out. They are often hard and highly competitive workers in class. They learn what the professor wants them to learn; they would memorize the Koran backwards if required for an assignment and give it back verbatim on the final examination. They get upset when the university is in a state of turmoil because it makes studying more difficult (which it does) and threatens the achievement of their own educational goals (which it undoubtedly can do).

Some have come to learn about themselves. They hate courses that ask them to memorize the periodic table, the periods of history, the names and dates of people, places, and events. They are seeking a sense of community; really a place in which they will find (or be given) a personal ethic.

Some have come to hear people tell them about the world in which they live, with the hope that they can change that world. Many of them arrive with a bag filled with notions about life and their world and wait to hear them validated or challenged by their professors. They want a campus that is active, community- and world-directed; a platform for both the exploration of ideas and for the generation of action to produce change.

Still others have come out of the more pure, classical motives of the scholar who enjoys playing the games of the intellect whether or not these have any immediately evident results. Peace, tranquillity, and isolation, mixed with philosophical discussions around a table over beer, have an appeal for them.

The resultant in such an institutional situation comes to look more like a highly complex modern urban community than a simple community of academicians and learners. One part calls for students and others to adhere to rules of thought and to an ethic of common academic values. Another part calls out in many voices for the achievement of many diverse and divergent goals. Accordingly, the role of the university administration, especially at the top levels, has changed from one of leadership with new and visionary ideas about education to one of leadership emphasizing political and organizational skills. There are few dreamers and innovators on top; there are few exciting new ideas in education which they seek to impart through their skillful leadership. Rather, the goals of the administrators appear to be to maintain the multiversity system as a smoothly running machine. They are most adept in their role of crisis managers.

Where then comes the leadership in the broad issues of education? If administrators are busy mediating conflicting interests within their campus and between their campus and external groups, and if faculty are busy marketing their research and writing, who has the time or the inclination to examine and to work to change higher education? Some of the activist students have taken this role upon themselves. It seems that they have interpreted their first step in this student-led educational campaign to be one of awakening the others in the academic community out of their apparent complacency.

For many of the activist students, to use a phrase which first appeared in the Berkeley campus paper, the administration is seen as the *enemy in residence*.[3] They are given this role as immediate targets of the frustration of students who have sought and repeatedly felt failure in producing quick change in their university and their society. The administration takes a view of the students as a basic threat to the peace of their campus. They view the students as seeking a total

[3] Mark Schechner, article in the *Daily Californian*, November 22, 1966, p. 2.

takeover of their campus with the consequent relegation of their role as administrators to groundskeeping and maintenance functions. In their turn, the activist students view the administration (their enemy in residence) as a group of evil sorts who have no business at all in making any kinds of policies dealing with education, theirs or anyone else's. They tend to see each action of the administration as being calculated to stifle their freedom and to deny them access to any important decision-making roles. They feel that the administration does not trust or respect them and looks upon them as highly impressionable youth, easily manipulated by outside influences.

One further integral part of this student activist-administrator confrontation concerns the cues used by the activists to gauge the success of their actions. The problem in general is how to determine if one's dissent is effective. Often it is felt that dissent which does not provoke an intense reaction on the part of members of the Establishment is dissent which is in-system and thereby ineffective. One is successful to the extent to which the Establishment is roused to angry reply. In fact, one suspects that several of the activist leaders assume that any action which does not bring on a negative administrative response is by very definition a failure. For such persons, the more the Establishment accommodates itself to their activities, the more extreme must their actions become. In simple outline, the preceding describes one significant component of the kind of confrontation politics that marks many of the student activist-administrator contacts on the Berkeley campus and perhaps elsewhere as well.

As one who both watches and participates in this scene, I cannot help feeling that without the administration, the intensity and at times unbounded energy of the student movement would falter and perhaps fail. It would be foolish in fact to underestimate the important role played by the administration in helping to maintain a state of student unrest and activism. This student activist-administrator relationship has a somewhat symbiotic quality about it: if the student activists need an active administration to keep them going, an active administration that would make its importance known and visible for all to see, requires a good core of student activists. With a good group of limits-testing activists around, every administrator, regardless of how generally ambivalent he may feel, can at least sense the importance and meaningfulness of his own administrative role. For after all, without him, who would keep the place in order and running smoothly? A theorist interested in organizational equilibrium could find endless moments of pleasure in examining in more depth and detail this fascinating though perhaps peculiar activist student-administrator symbiosis.

Whereas the administration has taken on a set of managerial functions, the faculty is almost as heterogeneous as the students. Their role in the institutional dynamics of student unrest and activism is potent, but complex. If the activist students view the administration as the enemy in residence, they view the faculty as their colleagues in the process of education. The more entrepreneurially oriented faculty view the administration as the saviors of a peaceful working environment and see many of the students (primarily the undergraduates) at best as being mildly annoying when they are around and disturbing when they make their presence vigorously known. Many faculty, through not fitting the modern grantsman image, have the more ivory-towered view of their role as educators, and cannot understand what all the ruckus is about. They are not offended as much as they are confused by what is happening. They sense that the noise from the activist students will be heard out in the community and that their protected status will be jeopardized. Still other faculty view the students as children needing the kind of mature guidance that only they can provide. Their condescending paternalism rankles the early maturing activist and adds fuel to a fire that needs little to make it burn brightly.

One sympathetic group bears special attention. Part of this group is composed of the old, still disillusioned rebels of the thirties. They see in the present student movement their own life replayed, now life-sized, on a screen outside their offices. Though their heart is with the movement, their minds tell them that failure is all that faces these new activists. Their message is filled with the fond reminiscences of the old guard watching the new young bucks try their hand at this most difficult and failure-filled game of social change. You get the feeling in watching many of them that they wish their professional position would permit them to walk the picket lines, sit in, and hurl sloganesque invectives toward the administration. The other part of this faculty group is composed of the younger, just Ph.D'd, instructor and assistant professor (with a marginal sprinkling of tenured staff as well) who rose from the ranks of the more recent protests and who now come naturally to continue their battles. These are the faculty who can be seen huddled head-to-head with the student activists at every planning session, joining together with them in preparing what they hope will be the groundwork for the wave of tomorrow.

In the scene at Berkeley, the faculty has played a rather interesting role in student unrest. During the 1964 actions, the faculty was the group the students turned to. On December 8, 1964, a set of resolutions was overwhelmingly passed by the Berkeley Division of the Academic Senate. Having passed these resolutions, most of the faculty, including the young Turks, returned to their more personal activities of research, writing, and teaching and assumed that their job had been completed. Political apathy among the faculty runs at least as high as among the students.

One can, and many do, criticize the students for not recognizing the full responsibility that would fall upon them were their programs of meaningful participation in decision making to become a reality; a similar criticism could be leveled against the faculty who find resolution passing easier than the follow-up responsibilities that such actions entail. In the events of 1966, the faculty were once again seen by the student activists to be their source of hope and salvation. The Academic Senate failed this time to produce as meaningful a document. In 1964, the students greeted the faculty with rousing applause as they left their meeting; in 1966, they formed a tensely silent gauntlet which each faculty member passed through on his way out. The tenuous coalition that had been formed between students and faculty was broken as the students suddenly awakened to the fact that their interests and those of the majority of the faculty were not as completely congruent as they had imagined or hoped. The young, rebel, activist, and liberal faculty still exists and still forms a link between the student generation and the rest of the faculty. Yet even this group is split within itself: some wish to work within the existing political framework of the Academic Senate and thus to prepare policy statements that will gain maximum support; others see their roles as lying outside the formal structure of faculty power and are willing to cast their lots more with the student activists and less with their faculty colleagues.

It is typical to view the students' apparent impulsivity and eagerness for rapid social change as being a mark of their so-called adolescent immaturity. What is often overlooked is the objective difference in time perspective between the several groups which the university comprises. The generation for the student is only four years, and as one student put it, even a revolution every two years seems like a long wait. For the faculty and for the administrators, the sense of time is extended far longer into the future. When one plans to commit a lifetime to a given university, change is seen as something that can, and, one thinks, should, come slowly. The student who wishes personally to experience the effects of a new policy has little time to wait. His impulsive actions, his eagerness for immediacy, his unwillingness to participate in a long and drawn-out movement, all speak of an understandably briefer view of time.

An ingredient which is essential to the maintenance of student activism, though not sufficient to explain the phenomenon, involves the underground community of hangers-on, part-time students, and nonstudents that exists within the academic community. Around university campuses, especially those in large metropolitan areas, is a subculture which supports the on-campus activists and provides a term-break and study-for-finals permanence to any movement which may start. It is difficult to be both a full-time student and an activist organizer, though early in the semester and at slack schoolwork periods one can devote more time to such activities. (I might add that the quarter system allows for fewer slack periods than the semester system and thus makes a time investment in political activism more costly to the student.)

This para-institutional community provides a refuge for those students who find themselves momentarily rattled by the drudge and drain of academics and who need to drop out for personal stock-taking. With such a community in existence, they can drop out formally but remain in the university culture. During the fall of 1966, a faculty member commented that we must be concerned about our students and our nonstudents. At Berkeley, at least, the boundaries of the academic community stretch beyond the land limits of the campus.

The delicate balance between the university and the general public seems shaken whenever events on a campus appear to be getting out of hand. In times of apparent crisis, some citizens, legislators, and alumni feel that their university is being endangered by a small body of difficult radicals. While the more enlightened are cognizant of the delicate balance that exists between town and gown, others have fuses as short as the ones they accuse the students of having and are quick to call for legislative investigations and mass purges to cleanse the university of its activist elements. I mention the public as an important institutional element to consider in seeking a fuller understanding of student unrest, in that they can provide a source of pressure that can magnify a situation into a major happening. Administrators, as they must be, are responsive to the demands of the public. Sometimes, however, they base their actions on their anticipation of an angry public response and therefore their response to the students is not a reaction to the students' action, but to their anticipation of the public's view of the students' action.

Students, faculty, and administrators, in their turn, may seek to use public opinion to achieve their own ends for the university. During the 1964 events at Berkeley, the faculty published a document primarily for distribution to the public which was intended to foster more favorable public opinion. Again, and more recently (April, 1967), the Berkeley faculty sponsored a full dress academic convocation whose major face was turned toward the public of the state and whose major message urged this public to support their local university. Administrators, in their turn, phrase their messages and policy statements in a manner more often designed to appease the public than to cope with an internally flammable situation. In a recent TV interview, for example, the Berkeley chancellor confessed that it was a greater problem explaining the university to the outside community than to the inside. Students, by the way, are no slouchers in this matter of working on public opinion. Their own forms of "truth squads" trip around the state seeking to talk with citizen groups in an effort both to tell their side of the complex story and to sway public opinion over to their point of view.

An often overlooked member of the total academic and community picture of unrest and activism is the communication media. Press conferences called by student groups, by administrators and even by faculty often provide one of the main but least desirable techniques of intracampus communication. Reporters from local and national newspapers pound their daily beat at their desks in the public information office of the university. They are contacted there by all sides as a sort of central clearing house for information to be leaked from official but unnamed sources. As one reporter indicated to me, the Berkeley beat is one of the best to be on; it almost always guarantees a by-line for the enterprising reporter.

All too frequently during the term one may see the noontime corps of photographers and TV camera crews waiting around Sproul Plaza for the action to begin. Eagerly, or so it begins to seem, students administrators, and faculty look forward to seeing, hearing, and reading about themselves. The person acts at noon, goes to class until four, then rushes home to watch the five o'clock news to see how he looked on TV. While the student is watching himself, the administrators and faculty are tuned in as well. Often responding to what they have just seen, one faction gets off a statement to the press which appears in the next morning's paper. This allows the student group about three hours, from nine to twelve, before their publicized noon rally, to prepare their responses to the morning paper's story: and so on around it all goes again.

It would not be stretching the point to suggest that the mass media significantly perpetuate and escalate various local conflicts both through their accurate reporting and their frequently error-filled, highly selective perspectives. One comes increasingly to respond to what was said about what was said than to what actually was said and in what context.

Apparently this situation is not entirely unique to Berkeley. A recent article in *The New Republic* reports an incident at Wayne State University in Detroit involving a "dope raid," which, according to the page-one headlines and story in the *Detroit Free Press,* implicated students and an instructor at WSU. The story continues,

> From reading the papers, the university thus got the impression that perhaps 28 of its students and an instructor had been caught with narcotics—LSD as well as pot—that there was a dope ring, and that everyone there (i.e. in the "dope den") was a bearded, booted beatnik. . . . None of these things was true. . . . Unfortunately, the university did not know these things at the time and in a moment of hysteria issued a hasty press release stating that any university employee involved would be "suspended immediately," and that students would similarly be subject to "immediate suspension

pending a hearing." . . . Some of the arrested students stopped attending classes for a short time because they had read, in the *Detroit News,* that they had been kicked out of school. Officials at Wayne have since repented of their too quick response to inaccurate and sensational newspaper accounts. . . . At first, Sells (Duncan Sells, Wayne's Dean of Students) says, the university wanted "to get off the hook that the press had put us on in the public eye,"[4]

These mass media not only serve as one of the few open channels of communication linking various parts of the campus and general community, but in addition serve to create issues which never existed and to polarize stances and intensify potential conflict. A hasty answer given by someone inexperienced in the ways of handling a news conference can create a sudden and even violent uproar in the campus community. All too easily one gets egged on by eager reporters into making extreme statements and into taking extreme stands. Since the mass media may provide a major channel of communication, we see not only a public airing of complaints and grievances, but also a public display of all or most negotiating and compromising that takes place. Where once gentlemen could gather together and seek to talk reasonably, men now face the cameras and negotiate through the mediary of the mike and the lens. Performing before the camera somehow makes everyone appear more militant and less reasonable than is possible when sitting around a table in a less public and publicized setting. No longer are there only two parties to events and discussions; the entire community and shortly the entire nation and world know. And knowing, they can and do put in their two cents' worth as well.

Parties on all sides begin to play more to their potential audience "out there" than to the people at the negotiating table. Recognition of the worth or even the legitimacy of the arguments of one's opponents or granting concessions becomes seemingly impossible in front of a TV camera. When the entire public is looking on, how can the administration feel free to act in a way which might lead one to conclude that they have given in on some point; or for that matter, how can the students feel free to take a stand that would give this same message to the public? Discussions conducted under klieg lights most

[4] David Sanford, "The Risks of Marijuana," *The New Republic,* April 22, 1967, pp. 11–12.

often get nowhere. Politically vague speeches and pronouncements that shortly solidify into formal policy too often replace reasoned and reasonable positions. This process occurs even when the reporting is minimally selective and fairly accurate. Imagine how more severe is this entire process when events become distorted by error, by intent, by selection.

I have included the issue of participation in the discussion here of the institutional context in that, at least in great part, it is within this social context that significant student participation is being sought and often not achieved. I should add, however, that according to Peterson's national survey, less than 20 per cent of student activism occurs over this matter of student participation in decision making.[5] On some campuses, however, this is one of the key themes that appears to hold together the various student action groups with their diverse causes. At Berkeley, this theme has served to join together groups on the far right with those on the far left. Although it is always a dangerous and speculative activity to read single goals into so complex a phenomenon as contemporary student activism, if one single long-range goal were to be selected, I would cast my ballot for this matter of realizing significant and meaningful participation in the processes of decision making.

It is almost a banality to mention today the increased degree to which the individual has been removed from direct access to the machinery of decision making as population, complexity of technology, and social planning and control have grown. Responses to this personal ineffectuality are varied, ranging from acute withdrawal and apathy—by far the most common response even around so highly touted an activist campus as Berkeley—through bitter resentment and open warfare, to rebellion which is designed to capture the control that appears to have been significantly reduced. A benevolent dictator who held the values and visions of today's youth could perhaps govern without the participation of those governed. However, when those governed feel that the governing are leading them "wrong," the sense of powerlessness becomes painful and efforts toward reshaping the locus of power are begun.

Today's university campus has become for many students the

⁵ Richard E. Peterson, *The Scope of Organized Student Protest in 1964–1965* (Princeton, N.J.: Educational Testing Service, 1966).

last point in their lives in which they see any hope for exercising significant influence. The activist youth have seen the bureaucratized world make older voices whisper thin. The campus seems the last stronghold for testing ways of influencing their world. They are afraid that when they leave the university, get a job, marry and raise a family, the weight of responsibilities will weaken their impetus for change. Those over thirty are not to be trusted, because of their increasing investment in the system as it exists.

They feel their time is short: their goals of significant participation are almost revolutionary in the modern American academic scene. Their frustrations are of great intensity and very likely to recur again and again. For what are they asking, and what are the institutional investments that set up barriers to their achievement?

> There are 30,000 people, approximately, that attend in one way or another this University every single day, five days a week. They spend their lives here. They eat here. They learn here. They believe here. They act here. And a community of 30,000 persons cannot be governed by fiat, but must be governed by consent. That is the basic principle upon which this republic was founded. Thirty thousand people is larger than many, many cities in the United States. We are a community and we have a right to govern ourselves and not by some Board of Regents which has proved itself to be irrelevant, immaterial, and incompetent to the functioning of this university . . . not only is it that, but it is bankrupt. And it is bankrupt because the employees, *i.e.* the faculty, are in opposition to the policies of the board of directors; and the raw materials, i.e. the students, don't like the product into which they're being molded and will not tolerate it. And when the raw material doesn't go into the machine, you can't produce any kind of a product except human beings; and that's what we are; and we are going to govern ourselves. As students, we have certain rights which no agency can legitimately grant or deny. Among these rights: the right to govern our own internal affairs, to set our own standards of conduct, and jointly with the faculty, to determine the form and nature of our education. Those are certain inalienable rights which are ours. To paraphrase it another way, certain inalienable rights to life, liberty, and the pursuit of knowledge and truth.[6]

Significant participation in making the decisions that affect

[6] Bettina Aptheker, speech made at Sproul Plaza rally, Berkeley, April 28, 1965.

their behavior sounds rather simple and straightforward, and is—like mother, God, and country, something we would all vote aye for. One thinks of the early studies conducted by Lewin and his colleagues with children's groups in which democratic leadership, which allowed member participation in decision making, proved boosting to morale while not destroying productivity.[7] Or the Coch and French study in which the full participation of factory workers in a decision which influenced their personal and financial well-being resulted in vastly superior morale and productivity than any other system of decision making examined.[8] The series of studies in changing food habits that evolved out of the Lewinian tradition are also instructive in showing how participation (even though complicated by the actual process of making a decision in a group setting) was more effective than lectured instruction in altering behavior.[9] In fact, much of the group dynamics tradition, with its origins in the work and philosophy of Kurt Lewin, lends strong support to this goal of the activist movement. The students call for no more sandbox governments in which a few campus leaders, drawn more from the organizational types, make decisions in a setting of mock legislative importance. They call for significant roles in determining the legislation that will influence their lives. This is often more a call for effective participation in establishing the rules which govern political activity than a concern for the rules which apply to one's apolitical life. This political focus does not apply to all university campuses. The call for meaningful participation, however, does appear to have an increasingly widespread appeal.

The concern for participation does go beyond the matter of rules governing campus political behavior. It stretches into the classroom as well. It is in this arena that the queasy alliance between some faculty and the student movement suffers its greatest break.

In the classroom where the professor's own sanctuary exists,

---

[7] Ronald Lippitt and Ralph K. White, "An Experimental Study of Leadership and Group Life," in Eleanor E. Maccoby, Theodore M. Newcomb, and Eugene L. Hartley (Eds.), *Readings in Social Psychology* (New York: Holt, 1958), pp. 496–511.

[8] Lester Coch and John R. P. French, Jr., "Overcoming Resistance to Change," *Human Relations*, 1948, *1*, 512–532.

[9] Kurt Lewin, "Group Decision and Social Change," in Maccoby, Newcomb, and Hartley, *op. cit.*, pp. 197–211; and Edith B. Pelz, "Some Factors in Group Decision," in Maccoby, Newcomb, and Hartley, *op. cit.*, pp. 212–219.

even an administrator hesitates to enter. Here student participation in decision making enters a new arena. The students claim that the content of their instruction is arid and is only minimally related to their concerns as citizens in a war-torn, population abundant world. They call for courses that focus on issues of immediate concern:

> The education students receive is not relevant to their felt needs. In order to understand these felt needs, it is necessary to appreciate the reality of post-World War Two America. We are now involved in a fundamental crisis in American society. The war in Vietnam shows many students that American foreign policy is all too frequently brutal and coercive. The response to the disturbances in our cities points to the fact that many whites in this country are unable to deal with their own racism. A large and growing number of university students are unwilling to live out their lives in the emptiness of middle-class America. And in the midst of all this, most of the books coming out of academia argue that America's major problems have been solved and that all we have to do now is to tie up loose ends. But students feel that America's problems have not been solved and they are searching for ways of understanding these problems and taking action that will solve them. And only in increasingly isolated instances are we receiving any intellectual or moral guidance on how to understand and deal with these issues. We want an education that will help us act; we want an education that will give us some guidance on how to live a decent life in mid-twentieth century America.[10]

Often the faculty who are trained in the more technical fields view such instruction to be of lesser relevance than the learning of details of their specialty. Those of the faculty who were trained in the more classical traditions of scholarly academics often view these immediate concerns to be of a more transient nature than the enduring problems which they trace from the antiquity of man and on which they are fond of doting. Those of the faculty who are in fields which lend themselves more readily to topics of immediate social concern (for example, sociology, political science, social psychology) try to move half-way in meeting the pressing demands of these students. However they

----

[10] Frank Bardacke, excerpt from a speech of a member of the student strike committee, read at a meeting of the Academic Senate, Berkeley, December 5, 1966.

view student demands now, for most faculty, any student say over class content is viewed as a threat to their academic freedom.

Some students call for more significant roles in determining not the content of any specific course, but rather the kinds of courses that are offered. They want some courses of a more topical nature to be established; thus on most campuses, they want some flexible mechanisms of instituting new classes to come into being which does not require long term examination before a new offering is available. As an experiment the student government at Berkeley recently voted the sum of $13,000 to pay the salary of a visiting professor hired by the students. This decision was later tempered; they decided to hire someone only if a university department would agree to take the person on the staff to teach regularly scheduled, credit courses. No department was willing to take on its staff the professor whom the students had selected. Faculty more than administrators appear to be resistant. Many believe the students want the kind of hiring and firing control that exists in some Latin American universities. Others feel that the students are not yet mature or competent enough to be important contributors to course planning and creation. Still others feel that what the students really want is plain and simple: a platform and a fortress from which to wage their war upon the society. On most of our larger university campuses no one is really certain what would happen if in fact students were brought into significant decision making, not just as a token gesture but as an institutionalized arrangement based on faith in the essential maturity and intelligence of students.

Perhaps boiled down to its most simple component, much of the confusion involves differing concepts of *education*. For many brought up on the typical grade school and high school formula, education consists simply in one person's telling facts and another person's recording, memorizing, and feeding back these facts. Lectures in college, large classes, multiple-choice exams may be a problem, then, not because they do not conform to this model of education, but rather because they may make its realization slightly more difficult. For others, education consists primarily of technical, preprofessional, and professional specialization. Still others decry the absence today of any really excellent general education programs. Even the better liberal arts colleges have somewhat redesigned their own programs in

order to enable more of their students to get into graduate and professional schools. For these decriers, education consists primarily of
coming to intimate terms with classical studies, humanistically oriented
history, philosophy, the arts, and so on, so that one may become a
more self-conscious, critic-participant of life.

When educators meet to involve themselves in a self-conscious
appraisal of higher education, they seem to churn out monographs
which either describe what is and what will always be or describe
education with such vague, broad strokes that the monograph is
filled with sweet-sounding slogans that conceal the real diversity in
viewpoints that exists. The students are then asked to accept these
generalities and to forget about the underlying diversity. Whenever
they participate in some vigorous and momentarily disruptive protest, the document is hauled out from its shrine and read aloud for all
to hear: "What you people are doing is inconsistent with the goals
of education. Go back to your classes and resume your education."

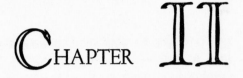

CHAPTER II

Revolution, Reformation, and Reevaluation

James W. Trent

In 1964, the student demonstrations at the University of California's Berkeley campus startled the world. Now, five years later, demonstrations of this kind have become commonplace the world over, and in the United States they are becoming prevalent in high schools and junior colleges as well as in four-year colleges. Although no campus appears immune to them, they are no less disquieting than they were a few years ago. They have shattered the administrative structure at numerous major universities, and their reverberations have affected governments both regionally and nationally.

Discussion of what has become "The Movement" of student activists is proliferated in the news and professional publications. Many reasons, from a Communist conspiracy to a castration complex, are seriously and unstintingly offered for the activists' behavior; many characteristics, from irredeemable to heroic, are attributed to the activists; many solutions to the activists' confrontations, from the fiercely repressive to the indulgent, are offered.

Behind the conglomeration of reasons, characteristics, and solutions there exists a consistent need to cut through the unceasing rhetoric on the issue and to examine the few facts that are known about activists and their movement. These are especially important to examine in the face of daily opinion that passes as fact. With enough facts and enough sifting of good implications and opinions from bad, there may exist a solid basis for suggesting positive alternatives for dealing with the present presses on the American college. Never has there been a greater need for research and evaluation of the system of higher education than under the present circumstances; thus, the proper method of evaluation also becomes a matter of concern.

The greater substance of this chapter comprises, first, a summary of several past and recent surveys pertaining to the characteristics of student activists; second, the implications the data have for the nature and roles of contemporary higher education in this context; and, third, problems of evaluating the context.[1]

[1] Judith Craise assisted with portions of an article that appeared in the July 1967 issue of the *Journal of Social Issues,* parts of which have been incorporated into this chapter.

24

Our theses are (1) that the intense activism observed in higher education is growing but remains representative of only a small proportion of students in the United States; (2) that the majority of students today largely manifest the apathy and conformity that have characterized students of the past, rather than the kind of commitment and autonomy that leads to political activism or serious intellectual involvement; (3) that, nonetheless, a considerable and growing number of nonactivists are sympathetic to causes advocated by the activists; (4) that students are increasingly affected by activists' causes and activities, regardless of their sympathies; (5) that, although activism can be destructive, it has great potential as a catalyst for improvements in higher education; (6) that the system of higher education can be reformed in the ways that activists and others are urging without having first to be destroyed; and (7) that new and consistent forms of evaluation are necessary for appropriate reformation.

STUDENT ACTIVISM

There is endless argument over what has contributed to the new student spirit which appears in such contrast to the silent generation of a decade ago. Any one or combination of factors may be involved: permissive child rearing, reaction to dehumanizing technocracy, sophistication derived from mass media, improved education leading to unprecedented critical thinking, affluence no longer making the seeking of security a dominant concern, reaction to anachronistic middle-class mores and parents, disenchantment over the war whose validity could no longer go unquestioned in the name of patriotism, equal disenchantment over the increasingly manifest disenfranchised in society, or other factors. Whatever its source, however widespread, there is a new spirit. What matters now is what forms it takes and with what effects on society.

Activism implies dissent from the status quo. But more than one form of dissent is apparent on the American college campus. There are the dissidence and general unrest found among many students who manifest an often unarticulated and uncomprehended anxiety in the face of a rapidly changing, complex, and threatening world. There is the "rebellion for the hell of it" among the few who argue that they want to be left entirely free from social and educational constraints so that they may simply "do their own thing." There is

the show of contempt for any social order found in a very few anar-
chistic students who have disaffiliated themselves from society and who
want devastating confrontation for its own sake. There are rationally
motivated intellectual dissenters who are not interested in bringing
down the social order but in probing it, testing it, and changing it.
Added to this group in the last several years are the black and
Mexican-American—or Chicano—militants who want not so much
to change the educational establishment but more to rid it of racism
and to gain a greater share of its benefits.

The activists who wish to change society may sometimes be
impulsive, noisy, and belligerent. Sometimes they even may be naive
and wrong, depending upon the standards used for judgment. They
may attract followers who find it faddish or fun to thumb their noses
at any authority. But their motives are not to be confused with those
of individuals who complain about their own uneasiness, play at independence, or disdain society out of displaced hatred.

Two hundred students interviewed by *Fortune* in 1968 explained "Our most wrenching problem is finding a place for ourselves
in society."[2] To solve the problem means to change society, a common
cry evident in the sampling of criticisms reported in the *Fortune* survey. The young critics view society as perverted, tolerating "injustice,
insensitivity, lack of candor and inhumanity." Too big and "numbed
by boredom," society needs to be infused with a "human scale"
whereby the individual can participate in the decisions that affect him.
It must become an open system, no longer controlled by engulfing,
anonymous, and immoral big business. The profit motive is questionable, and competition a "social blight" that perverts people's values.
In a world of hunger and want there is immense waste, particularly
the economic and human waste of the war. Education is not blameless;
rather than a sanctuary of free expression and thought, the university
has become a grade-race factory controlled by trustees or regents who
are actually remote from the university and whose views reflect economic and political pressures. The government, too, is ridden with
apathy, hoards power, and is remote from those most affected by its
decisions. Still, the critics urge:

[2] G. H. Wierzynski, "A Student Declaration: 'Our Most Wrenching
Problem . . . ,'" *Fortune,* 1969, 79(1), 114 ff. This comment and those that
follow in this paragraph actually represent a synthesis of the students' statements.

We are not a generation of text book revolutionaries . . . nor are we dupes, as some people suspect, of "the communist conspiracy;" the Soviet Union, with its own repressive establishment, has no appeal for us. We come to our convictions through practical experience. . . . Viewing these conditions, some of us think that the whole social system ought to be replaced by an entirely new one; the existing structures are too rotten for repair. And so, some of us advocate a revolution.[3]

There are scholars such as C. Robert Pace (in speaking to the faculty of the UCLA Graduate School of Education) who argue cogently that a cultural revolution has been under way for some time, in part beginning with the personalization of man and stress on his individual psyche launched by men like Freud. Reaction to the post-industrial depersonalization of man may be an important part of the revolution. And revolution in various forms is undoubtedly being urged.[4] This fact is substantiated in the summary of the *Fortune* survey and in many other sources. For example, Jerry Farber, a former faculty member of California State College at Los Angeles, argues in "The Student As Nigger" that the American student, like the black man, is powerless, subservient to an exploitative academic establishment, and that he must, therefore, stop prostituting himself before that establishment.[5]

Michael Rossman, formerly a member of the Free Speech Movement's steering committee at Berkeley, asserts that the entire community is divided by conflicts of interest which are also questions of power and powerlessness. In this context political advance and educational reform develop through confrontation. To Rossman it is a matter of both personal identity and violence:

To be is to confront . . . to confront in any style—by action or

---

[3] *Ibid.*, p. 116.

[4] Two major revolutions are apparent in higher education. Predominantly white middle-class activists are seeking to change higher education from what they see as negative aspects of the affluent, established society. As noted above, minority militants are seeking not so much to change higher education as to assure that they receive more of it. This chapter concentrates on the white activists' protest. (See Chapter Eight.)

[5] Jerry Farber, "The Student as Nigger," in J. Hopkins (Ed.), *The Hippie Papers: Notes from the Underground Press* (New York: Signet Books, 1968), pp. 160–168.

rhetoric—is to encounter in yourself and to awaken in those con-
fronted those emotions which are involved with doing violence:
anger, fear, guilt, creation. Thus, the act of confrontation, of articu-
lation—of identity, is psychologically very similar to the act of
violence. Liberals will not deal consciously with the terrifying
violence within them. They act it out in indirect ways, the results
of which they think they can continue to ignore, though now
America is cracking. It won't work, Charlie; you've got to let yourself get angry; you've got to watch yourself get angry—and maybe
violent as well—before you can find out who you are.[6]

Michael Vozick, formerly a founder of San Francisco State's
1965 Experimental College and currently the head of the Center for
Educational Reform at the National Student Association, rejoined
Rossman that to be is not to confront but to be. Yet he does believe
in revolution and reform of a certain type; indeed, he pointed out to
Rossman that:

You and I know that the revolution has to be lived in order to
believe in it with integrity. We find it, if only as a tone of voice, on
every campus. Students are into the beginning of the next culture.
The question is how.[7]

Vozick offers answers to his question: by teaching consciousness
through the demonstrations of the creative possibilities seen and lived,
by working for the voluntary abdication from destructive power roles
of university and other leaders, by working "to learn the ingenuity and
allow the awareness with which we can penetrate, with revolutionary
sincerity, the whole of this culture," by asking which act will empower,
best train, and best help everyone to learn what is really going on
before each situation with a choice of confrontation versus non-
confrontation.

Here, then, is revolution of complex and far-reaching dimensions. It does not center on one or a few issues; it does not take a
single form. Whether regarded as necessarily leading to the violent
overthrow of the Establishment or the Establishment's reform from
within, it cannot be explained simply or dismissed as an ephemeral

---

[6] Michael Rossman and Michael Vozick, "Dear Michael: Two Letters
on Confrontation," *Change in Higher Education,* 1969, *1*(1), 40–43.
    [7] *Ibid.,* p. 43.

phenomenon with no legitimate basis. Certainly the revolution has been prompted by far more than either sexual or generational conflict as proposed by either Farber or Feuer.[8]

EXTENT OF ACTIVISM

To say that the revolution reaches deep and far is not to say, however, that it directly involves a majority of students. The results of several studies and data from our study of high school graduates across the nation all lead to the same conclusion: that up to 1966, student activism, however defined, involved a very few select students in a very few select colleges and universities.

Peterson found that at most, only 9 per cent of any student body was reported as involved in protest movements and that protests occurred disproportionately often at select institutions of high quality. In Peterson's survey of the state of activism as viewed by deans of students and equivalent officers at 85 per cent of the country's four-year colleges, only 38 per cent of the deans reported student activism over civil rights, the issue which has evoked the most activism. Twenty-eight per cent of the deans reported student activism over living group regulations, 21 per cent over United States involvement in the war in Vietnam, 18 per cent over student participation in campus policy-making, 9 per cent over rules regarding "controversial" visitors to campus, 7 per cent over curriculum inflexibility, and 4 per cent over academic freedom for faculty.[9]

Heist observed that "strong political advocacy" has taken place since 1960 on a few campuses where this activity would least be expected but then added:

> The fact that a few institutions have had a fairly continuous mani-
> festation of such student activity and involvement, often centered
> in social problems or political issues, is not generally known. On
> several campuses in the United States, conflict and a degree of tur-
> moil seem to be taken as a matter of course; these may even be de-
> fended as part of the "design" of an effective educational program.

[8] Farber, *op. cit.;* Lewis S. Feuer, *The Conflict of Generations: The Character and Significance of Student Movements* (New York: Basic Books, 1969).

[9] Richard E. Peterson, *The Scope of Organized Student Protest in 1964–1965* (Princeton, N.J.: Educational Testing Service, 1966).

The truth is that the colleges or universities which witness considerable and frequent student activity and committed support of off-
campus causes tend to draw a student clientele that is measurably
different from the student bodies in the great mass of institutions.
In these schools a notable concentration of students of high ability
and nonconservative values often tends to set a pattern for activism
or some degree of protest.[10]

Even at schools of this kind, however, the proportion of activist
leadership was very small. In his survey of three liberal arts colleges
renowned for their liberal, aware, and activist students, Heist found
that the combined key leadership groups of the three schools comprised
only eleven students. At Berkeley, no more than 3 per cent of the
student body was committed enough to the Free Speech Movement
to risk arrest. Moreover, the Berkeley group was selective in background as well as in numbers. Heist found that half of the group had
transferred from the select colleges and universities identified by him
and Peterson as the few institutions whose students were noticeably
involved in activism.

Baird analyzed American College Survey data obtained from
sophomores in 1965 in thirty-one institutions. Even though he defined
the term comprehensively and did not focus exclusively on radicals,
he found that less than 3 per cent of the students were activists.[11]

Finally, our research on a sample of nearly 10,000 high school
graduates in sixteen communities across the United States shows that
of those graduates who went on to persist in college over a four-year
period, very few were concerned with any of the current political,
social, or educational issues that might disturb student activists. Rather,
their responses to questionnaire and interview items dealing with these
areas of concern indicated that most of them had a kind of uncritical
acceptance of, and contentment with, the *status quo* not unlike that of
the silent generation of the past.[12]

---

[10] Paul Heist, "Intellect and Commitment: The Faces of Discontent,"
in O. W. Knorr and W. J. Minter (Eds.), *Order and Freedom on the Campus:
The Rights and Responsibilities of Faculty and Students* (Boulder, Colo.:
Western Interstate Commission for Higher Education, 1965), p. 62.

[11] L. L. Baird, *A Study of Student Activism* (Iowa City: American
College Testing Program, 1968), mimeographed.

[12] James W. Trent and Leland L. Medsker, *Beyond High School: A*

A February 1969 issue of *Time* would suggest that there has been a virtual avalanche of activism since 1965. Figures charted without reference to any statistical source state that 2 per cent of American college students are "The Wreckers," 6 per cent "The Militants," and 20 per cent "The Protesters." Substantial evidence indicates otherwise.

Beginning in 1966, data obtained from a random sample of entering college freshmen, who were taken to be representative of entering American college students generally, revealed that 15 per cent of the women and 16 per cent of the men had participated in any sort of demonstration, activistic or not. Of the Anglo students, 12 per cent had participated occasionally and 2 per cent frequently. The rate of participation was higher among the black students: 24 and 11 per cent respectively.[13]

In 1968, a Harris poll indicated that only 2 per cent of college students were activists; in the same year a Gallup poll indicated that only 20 per cent of students engaged in any protest activity whatsoever, whether or not they were activists.[14]

Again in 1968, Peterson repeated the same sort of survey of student protest that he conducted in 1965. As viewed by college deans or equivalent officers, there were signs in the three-year interval that students had shifted much of their protests over civil rights to the war, educational relevancy, and governance. Also, more institutions reported student protest. However, there was no wide-scale dispute over the nature of undergraduate teaching. (Fifteen per cent of the institutions reported protests over curricular rigidity, compared with 8 per cent in 1965.) And, although more institutions reported protests and leftist groups (primarily SDS Chapters) in 1968 than they had in 1965, *proportions of activists within student bodies did not change.* This fact, however, does not belie the influence of the activists. Peterson considers an additional 8 to 10 per cent of students to be sym-

---

Psychosociological Study of 10,000 High School Graduates (San Francisco: Jossey-Bass, 1968).

[13] A. W. Astin, R. J. Panos, and J. A. Creager, *National Norms for Entering College Freshmen* (Washington, D.C.: American Council on Education, 1967).

[14] D. Seligman, "A Special Kind of Rebellion," *Fortune,* 1969, *71*(1), 66.

pathetic with the "movement for social change" and "capable of temporary activation depending on the issues."[15]

The data reviewed so far refer to students who were enrolled in college. Information pertinent to the issue of activism is also available on recent college graduates compared with those who graduated around 1950 and 1935. We conducted an intensive interview study of approximately 125 college graduates of three age groups selected to be representative of the San Francisco Bay and Los Angeles metropolitan regions; the age groups were composed of men and women primarily in their twenties, forties, and sixties. Few graduates of any age were really involved in political or community action; only a negligible number could be considered activists, even in attitude. Just over 3 per cent of the men and just over 1 per cent of the women felt they were either very liberal or radical in their political and social attitudes. Roughly 25 per cent of the men and 30 per cent of the women represented themselves to be conservative or very conservative. Proportionately, the youngest graduates were no more liberal and no less conservative than the older graduates. This was also reflected in their reading habits: 10 per cent of the men said they read magazines of liberal persuasion, regardless of age group; 5 per cent of the youngest women reported this, compared with roughly 20 per cent of the women in their forties and sixties.

Of the three groups, the youngest graduates indicated the least social concern and responsibility for others. And, although they did indicate some awareness of the nature of the needs and the basis for the behavior of today's college students, in some ways they were the least sympathetic. For example, only 4 per cent of the youngest graduates approved of college student demonstrations, compared with 18 per cent of the graduates in their forties. None of the oldest graduates approved of demonstrations, but they felt in far greater proportion that contemporary students show serious, concerned thinking about and involvement with the community.[16]

[15] Richard E. Peterson, *The Scope of Organized Student Protest in 1967–1968* (Princeton, N.J.: Educational Testing Service, 1968).

[16] James W. Trent and J. H. Ruyle, *The Educated American* (Berkeley: Center for Research and Development in Higher Education, University of Calfornia, in preparation).

The evidence is, therefore, that there is very little activism manifested by recent college graduates who live in California metropolitan areas. In this context there certainly is no evidence of conflict of opinions and values between generations. This corroborates Keniston's interview-based conclusions and Glazer's observations that there is generally a warm rapport between radicals and their parents, and that in some cases the parents have actually encouraged radicalism in their children and others through the examples of their moral, ethical, and humanist values.[17] The only difference between the generations is that the parents think their children have gone too far and the young radicals think that their parents have not gone far enough. Again, Feuer's and Farber's parent-child conflict theories of radicalism gain no credence here; and even if they are ever demonstrated, indications are that they will not be widely applicable.

STUDENT CHARACTERISTICS

But if the underlying dynamics of activism have not been clearly demonstrated, a number of personality and other characteristics have been found to distinguish student activists from college students at large. Before delving further into the important personality characteristics that distinguish the activists from other more representative college students across the nation, we offer a brief portrait based on responses to questionnaire items in 1963 by our national sample of what this more typical college student is like or at least was like in the early sixties.

The large sample of high school graduates will hereafter be referred to as the national sample. However, it can be considered national only in the sense of its geographical spread (across California, the Midwest, and Pennsylvania) and not in the sense of being a statistically representative sample of that age group throughout the United States. At the same time, it is assumed representative of a large segment of young adults in the country, especially those living in cities with a population of between 30,000 and 100,000; and it is composed of all or almost all graduating high school seniors in the sixteen

[17] Kenneth Keniston, *Young Radicals: Notes on Committed Youth* (New York: Harcourt, 1968); and Nathan Glazer, "The Jewish Role in Student Activism," *Fortune,* 1969, *70*(1), 112.

communities originally surveyed in 1959. The scope, sampling, and findings of this research are reported elsewhere.[18]

Of the original national sample, 40 per cent entered college full time in 1959 and attended approximately 700 colleges throughout the United States; about half of this group persisted for four years. When the original sample was again surveyed in 1963, over 72 per cent of the persisters, most of whom had reached senior standing, responded to the questionnaire administered to them and to scales from the Omnibus Personality Inventory.[19]

The questionnaire items inquired into the students' vocational, social, and personal values. When asked to check a list of self-descriptions applicable to themselves, 23 per cent of the students considered themselves "nonconformists"; a significantly greater proportion, 28 per cent, described themselves as a "common man" $(\chi^2 = 9.17; P < .01)$; and a little over 1 per cent considered themselves "radicals." It is not clear what these terms meant to the students or whether the terms had the same connotations for the respondents that we intended them to have. Furthermore, a majority of the students rejected the list of self-descriptions offered them altogether. But within the limits of these data, a greater tendency toward commonality was implied than toward any nonconformity or radicalism.

By 1963, a majority of the young adults in the national sample had registered or intended to register in the same political party as their father, which in largest proportion was the Republican party. Ten students in the sample considered themselves socialists. Over 500 of the youths, representative of the entire sample, were interviewed personally and for the most part were found to have very little political interest and astuteness. Typically, the interviewed subjects felt their choice of political party was prompted by the fact that it was their parents' choice, and very few could articulate any political beliefs. Unlike the activists considered later in this paper, most of the youths reported a belief in formal organized religion. But here again, in most cases their religious beliefs were ascribed to their parents, and only

---

[18] Trent and Medsker, *op. cit.*

[19] Center for the Study of Higher Education, *Omnibus Personality Inventory—Research Manual* (Berkeley: Center for the Study of Higher Education, University of California, 1962); and Paul Heist and George Yonge, *Omnibus Personality Inventory Manual* (New York: Psychological Corporation, 1968).

in rare instances were the subjects articulate about their faith or able to evince any real understanding of it.

The two factors deemed most important to a satisfying life for almost all of the subjects were job and family; and, predictably, a majority of the college persisters regarded the main purpose of college to be the development of vocational skills or talents. Forty-three per cent of the persisters saw the gaining of knowledge and appreciation of ideas as the main goal of attending college. Of this group, 11 per cent expected to get their greatest life satisfactions from interests in community and world problems, science, humanities and the arts, and scholarly pursuits.

When asked about specific issues relating to their college experiences, a majority (70 per cent) of the persisters declared that "most of the faculty are intellectually stimulating"; that "existing rules and regulations regarding student behavior are sensible and necessary" (68 per cent); and that "the faculty and administration are quite successful in developing responsibility among the students" (56 per cent). Half of the students, however, felt "too much bound by course work"; over 40 per cent felt that rules and regulations should be "more permissive"; and over 30 per cent felt that "the administration and faculty generally treat students more like children than adults."

Some students voiced some criticism of their college experience, but most, including those who had some criticism, found college basically satisfying. There was no evidence of general dissension. A utilitarian orientation toward college seemed to prevail over intellectual and social commitment. Concern over social or religious issues was seldom mentioned by the students, and political interests, awareness, and involvement were lacking in almost all of them. Very few stressed the importance of scholarly endeavor or interest in the arts and sciences. It is not yet completely known how discerning the questionnaire items are, nor therefore how valid are the data they elicited, but these data at least seem to indicate that these students had little of the intellectual, social, or political interest and involvement that concern the student activists of this generation.

ACTIVIST CHARACTERISTICS

Various appellations, ranging from "dirty beatniks" to "Communist conspirators," have been given to student activists. This name-calling has never been based on objective appraisal of the student, and it might bring surprise to some quarters responsible for this labeling to learn that many of these students are the brightest and most able students found on the nation's campuses. For example, research showed that the students in Berkeley's Free Speech Movement at the University of California were exceptionally high in measured intellectual disposition, autonomy, flexibility, and liberalism, as well as in level of ability, and that they exhibited marked qualities of individuality, social commitment, and intellectuality not observed among more representative samples of college students. They were, in fact, atypical Berkeley students and represented some of the university's most able and intellectually dedicated students.[20]

The Free Speech Movement which erupted at the University of California was one of the most notorious and long-lived of current student activist movements. And since its composition was such that it was probably similar in nature and dynamics to student movements elsewhere, certain comparisons based on Omnibus Personality Inventory data are pertinent: (a) between a sample of representative Free Speech members who risked arrest and a representative group of Berkeley seniors who were their peers at the time of the demonstrations and (b) between the Free Speech sample and those more typical college students in the national sample who persisted in college for four years. From these comparisons, it becomes apparent that few college students in general can match the positive development of those personality characteristics that distinguish student activists from their college contemporaries.

The standard mean scores obtained on the Omnibus Personality Inventory scales by the three groups are shown in Table 1. The 1965 seniors were drawn from a random sample of seniors of that year. The members of the Free Speech Movement, surveyed by Heist[21]

---

[20] Heist, *op. cit.*; R. H. Somers, "The Mainsprings of the Rebellion: A Survey of Berkeley Students in November, 1964," in Seymour M. Lipset and Sheldon S. Wolin (Eds.), *The Berkeley Student Revolt: Facts and Interpretations* (New York: Anchor Books, 1965), pp. 530–532; and William Watts and David Whittaker, "Some Social-Psychological Differences Between Highly Committed Members of the Free Speech Movement and the Student Population at Berkeley," *Journal of Applied Behavioral Science,* 1966, 2(1), 41–62.

[21] *Op. cit.*

Table 1
OMNIBUS PERSONALITY INVENTORY SCORES

Scale	National Persisters ('63) (N = 1385)	Berkeley Seniors ('65)[a] (N = 92)	FSM Arrested[a] (N = 130)
Thinking Introversion	52	55	63
Complexity	51	54	66
Estheticism	51	52	61
Autonomy	53	61	67
Impulse Expression	51	54	64
Religious Liberalism	48	58	64
Lack of Anxiety	52	51	48

[a] Source of Berkeley Senior and FSM data: Heist, *op. cit.*

two months after their arrest in December 1964, were considered representative of the entire group of arrested students with the exception of a slight overrepresentation of sophomores and an underrepresentation of graduate students.

The highly reliable scales on which these groups are compared measure the students' sensitivity and openness to ideas, beauty, and their general environment, together with their freedom from constriction of thought and overt anxiety. The scores were standardized on the basis of a large sample of public college and university freshmen. For all scales the normative freshman mean is 50, and the standard deviation is 10.

The scores of the Free Speech members on all the traits measured by the Omnibus Personality Inventory were clearly distinguishable from the scores of their own Berkeley classmates and those of the national sample of college persisters (with differences generally significant at the 1 per cent level). With the exception of the Anxiety scale, the mean scores of the activist group exceeded the 1965 Berkeley senior scores by at least 6 standard points and also exceeded the scores of the national sample by at least 10 standard points. All differences between the Free Speech Movement sample and the other samples were considerably beyond the 1 per cent level of significance.

The highest scores obtained by the Free Speech members were on the Complexity and Autonomy scales, indicating they had far more interest in intellectual inquiry, tolerance for ambiguity, objectivity, and independence of thought than the members of the other groups. But the Free Speech members compared with the other students were also marked by their much greater interest in reflective abstract thinking in the areas of art, literature, music, and philosophy (Thinking Introversion), concern with esthetic matters (Estheticism), and freedom and imaginativeness of thinking (Impulse Expression). Their high Religious Liberalism score indicated independence from long-established religious tradition and corroborated Watts' and Whittaker's finding that formal religion was not important or even relevant to the lives of most of the activists.[22]

The Anxiety scale is composed of the twenty most discriminating items selected by Bendig from the Taylor Manifest Anxiety Scale.[23] The lower scores indicate more anxiety than the other groups of students, perhaps a natural reflection of the stress imposed by the legal predicament the Free Speech students were in at the time they were tested. Or it may represent a price paid for the greater intellectual and social commitment they demonstrated in contrast to other college students of their generation.

Regardless of the reason for the greater manifestation of anxiety among the Free Speech members, their unusually high scores on the intellectual disposition and autonomy scales indicate their involvement with educational as well as political activism. One last point to be made in all fairness to the national sample, however, is that this group was not so much lacking in intellectual orientation, perhaps, as in the student activists' high degree of intellectualism. When viewed separately they might be regarded as manifesting the average degree of intellectuality one would expect in a college group. However, there is no formula at present which can determine objectively just what the "average degree of intellectuality" is, actually or ideally.

[22] Watts and Whittaker, *op. cit.*

[23] A. W. Bendig, "The Development of a Short Form of the Taylor Manifest Anxiety Scale," *Journal of Consulting Psychology,* 1956, *20,* 384.

There is evidence that a majority of today's students attend college principally to gain professional competence. Keniston has pointed out that what this kind of student prizes above all is "the expertness of the man rather than the man himself" because this is what really counts in the "bureaucratized and organized society" in which he lives.[24] The implication is that most students adhere to this belief regardless of their field of study, but this attitude must be particularly pervasive among that large segment of students who major in applied professional or preprofessional fields, since from the outset they presumably are less intellectually oriented than the more academic students. In the national sample, a majority of the persisters majored in such applied subjects as business, engineering, and education. It was found that most of these students had little deep involvement in intellectual pursuits or concern with social and political reforms and tended to be the most authoritarian and intellectually restricted of all college students observed in the sample.

This finding was first observed in a comparison of the proportion of students at different levels of intellectual dispositions who majored in the liberal arts, education, and technology. For purposes of this comparison, the students' scales on the Omnibus Personality Inventory's Thinking Introversion, Complexity, and Estheticism scales were combined into a single standard scale taken as a comprehensive measure of intellectual disposition. On the basis of the Omnibus Personality Inventory norms, the persisters were then categorized at three levels of intellectual disposition: high—upper 30 per cent of the distribution; middle—middle 40 per cent of the distribution; and low—lower 30 per cent of the distribution.

The representation of the liberal arts majors at the three levels of intellectuality approximates that which would be expected of the normative sample (Table 2). The technical majors (mostly business and engineering) and education majors were consistently lower on all measures of intellectual disposition than the liberal arts majors. Since it is probably fair to say that the low level of intellectual disposition reflects a certain amount of anti-intellectualism, a majority

[24] Kenneth Keniston, "Faces in the Lecture Room," *Yale Alumni Magazine*, April 1966, *35*(7), 20–34.

Table 2

STUDENTS IN THE NATIONAL SAMPLE IN VARIOUS CURRICULA

Major (*percent*)

Level of Intellectual Disposition	Liberal Arts (*N = 1096*)	Education (*N = 572*)	Technology and Business (*N = 899*)
High	28	11	7
Middle	37	34	25
Low	35	55	68
Total	100	100	100

$\chi^2 = 273.96;$ p $< .001$

of the technical and education majors who attended college from 1959–1963 must be described accordingly.

From questionnaire responses it is also known that these students in applied fields were, and very significantly so, the least interested in education for the sake of knowledge, ideas, and creative development; the least interested in such cultural activities as the theater, book-browsing, and artistic activities; and the least concerned about human relations and justice.

In addition, other analyses showed that the technical and education majors were the lowest in autonomy of all the groups under consideration on the three scales of the Omnibus Personality Inventory which purport to measure independence, openness, and flexibility in thinking. For example, on the Autonomy scale, the liberal arts majors obtained a standard mean score of 54.0, compared with with a score of 48.4 obtained by the education majors, and a score of 48.7 obtained by the technology majors. The liberal arts groups differed significantly from the education and technology majors (beyond the 1 per cent level), and this fact generally held true in separate analyses which controlled for level of ability and socio-economic status.

In contrast to these findings, student activists were found to possess a high degree of autonomy and intellectual disposition and to come from the fields of the humanities and especially the social sciences in disproportionately high numbers.[25] As the data above indicate, students in these fields in our sample scored higher in these traits than the students in technical and educational fields. But that is not to say they were all activists. Very few were, and the activists were most likely to be students at a few select liberal arts colleges and universities. Moreover, the liberal arts students in the national sample, considered separately, did not reach nearly the level of autonomy and intellectualism of the activists, as indicated by the Omnibus Personality Inventory scores obtained by the Free Speech members (Table 1). To conclude, then, student activism was associated with curriculum, type of college attended, and a uniquely high level of intellectual disposition and autonomy not shared by the vast majority of students.

ACTIVIST CHARACTERISTICS SINCE 1965

The situation apparently has not changed essentially in the last few years between 1964 and 1969. Baird, referred to earlier, considered the sophomores he studied in the spring of 1965 as activists if they checked three of the following activities: having organized a political group or campaign, having worked actively in an off-campus political organization, having worked actively in a student movement to change institutional policy and practice, or having participated in one or more demonstrations over political or social issues. Although the activists did not score differently on the Dogmatism scale than the other students and did not achieve a signicantly higher grade-point average, they were significantly higher than the other students on such purported self-concept measurements as Leadership, Speaking Ability, Understanding of Others, Sensitivity to the Needs of Others, Originality, Expressiveness, Independence, and Intellectual Self-confidence. On the whole, the activists "conceived themselves as confident, interpersonally capable, sensitive, driving, and talented."[26]

The activists also scored significantly higher on scales having to do with competency and potential in the arts, sciences, leadership, originality, and identification with the intellectual concerns of the faculty. They had a broader range of experiences, had achieved in nonacademic areas, and had participated more in such programs as

[25] Heist, op. cit.; Somers, op. cit.; Watts and Whittaker, op. cit.
[26] Baird, op. cit., p. 11.

honors and independent studies. They were much more likely to be
engaged in social service and leadership activities.

The life goals they checked reflected their significantly greater
desire to be leaders and decision-makers, to be politically involved
and helpful to others, and to receive recognition. They did not, however, give significantly lower ratings to being financially secure, making
their parents proud of them, following a religious code, or being successful in their own business, as might have been expected. Security,
respect, religious codes, and success can be defined broadly; and these
terms may have been interpreted broadly by the activists. Also, had
the left-oriented radical activists been singled out specifically, they
might have shown more rejection of ties to family, religion, success,
and security.

As the matter stands, it cannot be said that all activists reject
all the traditional values of society; but it is evident that Baird's sample
of activists, like those studied previously, are more autonomous, questioning, creative, talented, intellectual, open-minded, and altruistic
than other students.

Comparable secondary analyses of the representative sample
of freshmen in 1966 studied by Astin, Panos, and Creager[27] reflect
most of the findings of previous research. The activists (those who had
demonstrated) were involved in more activities; they were more
aggressive, out-going, and involved in a variety of ways. They were
significantly more likely to perceive themselves as being characterized
by leadership ability, speaking ability, social self-confidence, political
liberalism, and originality. There was a greater proportion of activists
among the students who noted themselves in the top 10 per cent of the
intellectually self-confident. They indicated greater concern with becoming involved in the arts in college, with participating in humanitarian endeavors such as the Peace Corps or Vista, and with becoming a
community leader.

These traits of social awareness and involvement, openness,
esthetic interests, autonomy, and altruism continued to be characteristics of the activistically oriented in 1968 as revealed by the
Fortune survey of October of that year.[28] The *"Fortune*-Yankelovich"
survey consisted of interviews of 718 college and noncollege men and

[27] *Op. cit.*
[28] "What They Believe: A *Fortune* Study," *Fortune.* 1969, 79(1), 70.

women between eighteen and twenty-four years old, a sample taken to be representative as to race, sex, marital status, family income, and geographical region.

Two groups of college students were identified: (1) the "practical-minded," consisting of students who felt that education is "mainly a practical matter," providing money, career, and position in society, and, conversely, (2) the "forerunners," reflecting the attitudes toward career and college that *Fortune* believes will become prevalent in the years ahead and consisting of students who chose the statement that they were less concerned with the practical benefits of college than with the opportunity to "change things rather than make out well within the existing system." The forerunners were not necessarily activists, but presumably activists would come primarily from their ranks, and activists causes would have their sympathy. The third group, of course, consisted of those individuals who had not entered college. The survey report presented the percentage of the three groups who took specified positions on items having to do with current issues, social norms, prominent figures in society, parents, and values and attitudes toward themselves, technology, business, and their careers.

Compared with the "practical-minded" students and their noncollege peers, the "forerunners" exhibited the most independence from family and middle-class norms; the most activistic orientation, autonomy, and esthetic values; the greatest altruistic orientation; and the most individualistic and humanitarian attitudes toward work. More specific consideration of the data is warranted by their currency and the importance of their implications.[29]

Divergence from Family and Societal Norms. None of the three groups manifested an outright rejection of the family, but the forerunners were proportionately least likely to respond that they identified with their family—65 per cent compared with 78 per cent of the practical-minded and 82 per cent of the noncollege group. Rejection of middle-class values was much more apparent among the forerunners, 35 per cent of whom identified with such values, compared with approximately 67 per cent of both other groups. A large generation gap was reported by 69 per cent of the forerunners,

---

[29] The grouping and interpretation of these items are my own.

compared with 56 per cent of the practical students and 48 per cent of the young adults who had not entered college. For many students, therefore, and particularly for the forerunners, the generational conflict theory seems pertinent. But this becomes questionable on the basis of another item: only 24 per cent of the forerunners and an average of 13 per cent of the other young adults felt that there was any great difference between their values and those of their parents. The gap may exist in ways other than beliefs and values. Yet it may also be in great part a myth perpetuated in press, text, and treatise and finally subscribed to as truth by each new generation of college students.

Less than half of any of the three groups felt that they could identify with people of their religion; and, again, this was especially true of the forerunners. Yet, 75 per cent of the noncollege group felt that "living a good Christian life" was important, compared with 54 per cent of the practical-minded and 36 per cent of the forerunners. This is not to say the forerunners lacked idealistic values. As will be seen in subsequent discussion, they were by far the most humanitarian in outlook; and it is in these terms that they may show their "religious" beliefs rather than in the traditional, fundamentalist ethic connotated by the phrase "good Christian life."

In the meantime it is not clear just what the reference group is for the forerunners, a situation which applies to the liberals of the past or present. Eight per cent of the forerunners felt that they could identify with the Old Left; 19 per cent felt they could identify with the New Left, compared with less than 5 per cent of the others. "Doing their own thing" may preclude the label of belonging to any particular social, religious, or political camp.

Tendency Toward Activism. The individualism noted in the last point above does not preclude acceptance of overt activism, however. Sixty-six per cent of the forerunners considered civil disobedience justified, compared with 32 per cent of the practical-minded college students and 18 per cent of their noncollege peers. Sixty-four per cent of the forerunners said that they would welcome more nonviolent protests by black and other minorities, compared with 41 per cent of the practical-minded and 35 per cent of the young adults who did not enter college. Obviously, most of the forerunners were sympathetic to major activist causes.

Autonomy. The forerunners exhibited the greatest degree of autonomy by far in a variety of ways. They were the most open-minded toward themselves and others: in greatest proportion they reported themselves honest with themselves, interested in the different ideas and experiences of the world around them, acceptant of others' peculiarities, and tolerant of others' views. They were least interested in civil regulation in that only a minority of them felt that there should be more emphasis on "law and order" in contrast to most of the other young adults. They showed the greatest need for self-responsibility in that in least proportion could they easily accept having little decision-making power early in their careers. They placed far more stress on independence and individualism: in greatest proportion they felt that there should be more freedom for the individual to do what he wants, that there should be more emphasis on self-expression, and that "doing your own thing" is important; in least proportion could they easily accept outward respect for the sake of career advancement or conformity in clothing and grooming. Generally, a minimum of 15 percentage points distinguished the forerunners from the practical-minded college students on these items; the differences were even greater between the forerunners and those who did not enter college.

Esthetic Values. The forerunners did not express an interest in beauty in any greater proportion than the other young adults. They did, however, welcome more emphasis on the arts in far greater proportion, and they were more predisposed to careers involving the arts. Though beauty in some fashion was important to most of the young adults, the forerunners expressed the greatest interest in the widest variety of esthetic experience.

Altruism. The forerunners' great altruism and social concern were reflected in the fact that a greater proportion of them expressed concern with what is happening in the country, concern with bringing about needed change in society, and the belief that genetic control is not good.

Individualism and Humanitarianism in Work. The greater autonomy and altruism of the forerunners were indicative of their attitude toward work. Again on the basis of considerable percentage differences, the forerunners were decidedly the least likely to feel that hard work always pays off or keeps people from loafing or getting into trouble. They were much more likely to feel that business requires conformity and least likely to feel that it allows for creativity or self-development. In contrast to the others, family and the money to be earned had relatively little influence on the career choices of the forerunners; rather, influencing factors on the forerunners were the opportunity to make meaningful contributions and the ability to express themselves. Their autonomous, humanitarian, even self-actualized values were also reflected in the forerunners' career choices: 64 per cent of these students were predisposed to the teaching arts and helping professions (such as social welfare and psychology), compared with 33 per cent of the "practical-minded" students and 5 per cent of those who did not enter college (and who ordinarily would not be expected to enter these professions).

There are a few scattered exceptions on specific points, but the data obtained on college-aged samples from 1963 through 1968 are for the most part consistent on the differences between the activistically oriented students and the others. Activists, or those most likely to be sympathetic to activism, now, as in the recent past, are marked by traits of leadership, autonomy, intellectual-esthetic interests, social awareness, and involvement with social issues. Other dimensions may be involved in the rising number of protests among minority students, and some protests among blacks and whites alike have led to violence and vandalism. The protests are increasing to the extent that they occurred on thirty-five campuses in April 1969. Some protesters are no doubt dogmatic and little concerned with altruism. But considerable evidence indicates that it is probable that most of the protesters are of the caliber described in the various surveys cited above and that they are protesting for the reasons mentioned at the outset of this paper. Regardless of excesses, the activists may be distinguishing themselves by coming closer than most members of society to realizing the goals of a democratic society.

ROLE OF THE COLLEGE

By now it should be clear that activism involves development of intellectual disposition, autonomy, and social awareness among college students. The implications of the data are that the relatively small but growing number of student activists and their sympathizers are seeking changes in society, beginning with its institutions of higher education, that will reflect and fulfill their ideals and goals. Given the active leadership, dissatisfaction with the status quo, intellectual disposition, autonomy, humanitarianism, and originality found among so many activists, it is evident that the changes that they seek in higher education cannot—and should not—go unheeded by the educational and legislative establishment. Concerted, concerned response from the college is necessary.

The contention here is that student political activism could act as a catalyst and supplement for the kind of educational activism which we view as a crucial part of the learning process. Student activists need not be alienated from the educational establishment but can bring enriched meaning to it. Our further contention is that it is the proper function of the college to activate intellectual and social commitment in its students, rather than resist this function when it is urged by the activists. At least college should make students consciously aware and critical of their own values and beliefs in important areas of concern to themselves and society, even when political activism may not be the final outcome of this increased awareness.

If the function of the college is viewed in this context, its role might then be conceptualized as an activating, facilitating, and mediating agency for students and as a catalytic agency of social change for society. It might activate important learning and personal behavior by stimulating intellectual awareness and growth and an understanding of and concern over social issues. It might facilitate learning and personal development by providing the conditions most conducive to optimum student development. It might mediate between the student and society by providing a moratorium so that students could be free to act in an attempt to draw meaning from and bring meaning to life without fear of reprisals from a more conforming society. In so doing, the college would be providing a catalyst for social change through its graduates. But under present conditions it may have to concentrate all its resources on changing and solving the social problems beyond simply studying them or encouraging its students to deal with them.

That education, and especially higher education, should act as a stimulating and challenging agent for students seems an idea so indisputable that it hardly appears to invite examination. Yet, what is purported in principle often remains unaccomplished in fact. Many graduate from college without ever becoming aware, for example, of the satisfactions that dedicated intellectual endeavor can bring; and, at least on the basis of the data presented in this paper, what is largely missing among current college graduates is the thinking, critical man, deeply aware of his cultural and intellectual heritage, alert to the contemporary problems existing in society, and able to bring historical perspective to present-day difficulties.

Of course, the gaining of such wisdom is a lifelong process, but for that very reason its nurture should begin early, and college should activate and aid, rather than hinder, its development. With our industrial society's emphasis upon narrowly skilled and professional training, however, such an ideal of what college should begin to develop is being lost except by a very few schools and people. Instead, there continues the training of generations of professionals whose major goals are directed primarily to home, job, family, and "getting ahead." Such goals in themselves are not to be criticized, but a danger exists when they are the *only* goals seen as worthwhile. Then people too commonly become egocentric, narrow, and restricted.

In contrast, the minority of student activists seems to be providing a healthy, if sometimes extreme, departure from commonly accepted goals and norms. Whatever point of view one may take about the methods of some of their activities, at least these young people are concerned with the major social issues around them and are earnestly engaged in trying to remedy the ills they see in society. According to the 1968 *Fortune* survey, the majority of students are still the practical-minded, professionally oriented. But the proportion of forerunners most concerned with understanding and improving society is larger than the proportion that would have been expected from our national sample of data obtained five years previously. If the proportion of militant activists has not increased, there is indication of a larger proportion of students sympathetic with many of the activists' concerns. This is important since the influence of the activists is magnified when they rally sympathizers who are anxious to cope with society's problems such as those posed by the activists.

Often coinciding with this concern about social ills is a growing dissatisfaction among students with the type and kind of education they are receiving. There is evidence that the great majority of students are generally satisfied with their education but that a small though growing minority is seriously critical. These critics believe the university has lost its autonomy from the society around it and has become part of the "system." Perhaps the most overt expression of this disenchantment is directed against the new professionalism—a sign of the growing discontent with the trend of higher education in the United States in some of today's more able and valuable students. Speaking for them, Mario Savio, probably the most renowned student leader of the Free Speech Movement, has said, "The futures and careers for which American students now prepare are for the most part intellectual and moral wastelands."[30] Once again, there is Farber, among others, who considers the plight of the student as no better than that of the exploited "nigger."[31]

The important question is what can be done to stimulate both those already highly developed and those so eager to receive a vocational certification in the form of a college degree that they seem impervious to any degree of intellectual stimulation or social awareness. A few answers to this question have come from some of the more able students themselves.

In a 1966 conference sponsored by the National Student Association, the discussion focused on the need to redefine a good education for today's youth. The participating students concluded that any viable definition should embrace at least these three elements: (1) relevance to a world of rapid social change, (2) commitment to the individual as the focus of value in the educational process, and (3) readiness of the educational system to explore diverse and changing needs of the current college population in order to meet the highly diversified developmental opportunities many of these students require. In regard to the last point, it was emphasized

> that at least a significant segment of current student bodies are demanding a voice in the shaping of their own education—not as a right and not because they feel themselves necessarily wiser than their elders, but because they profoundly believe that exercising this responsible privilege is itself educative. A major challenge to many institutions is precisely that of devising the conditions under which students may properly test this condition.[32]

[30] Mario Savio, "An End to History," in H. Draper (Ed.), *The New Student Revolt* (New York: Grove Press, 1965), pp. 179–182.

[31] Farber, *op. cit.*

[32] Edward Joseph Shoben, Jr., *Students, Stress, and the College Ex-*

Other answers are coming from the evaluations, innovations, and educational experimentation proposed or taking place on many campuses.[33] Frequently these innovative efforts involve the collaboration of students, faculty, and administration, as exemplified in the student-organized special courses and the experimental college initiated at San Francisco State College, and now found nationwide. Sometimes these efforts involve collaboration between colleges, at least at the level of sharing ideas and resources, as is the case in the Union of Research and Experimentation in Higher Education. More recently the innovations are beginning to involve collaboration between colleges and their surrounding community as exemplified by urban centers such as those found at the University of Southern California and the proposed urban-centered, urban-oriented college in the Bedford-Stuyvesant area of Brooklyn.[34]

But whatever the nature of the innovation—whether it involves collaboration of colleges, elimination of grades in order to promote learning for the sake of learning, more flexible and widespread use of seminars and field techniques, emphasis upon independent study, student-oriented and student-taught courses, urban-oriented curricula and colleges, the creation of special colleges within a large collegiate complex, or the restructuring of the format of a college—it is hoped that the innovation will activate a new spirit of learning and social awareness among the many students previously not disposed to this kind of educational activism. Such activism might provoke the student professionalist to think more critically from new reference points even if his basic values have not changed. If college should not necessarily liberalize students in this respect, it should at least make them more libertarian.

It is equally important that these kinds of educational experi-

---

perience (Washington, D.C.: Council Press for the United States National Student Association, 1966), p. 19.

[33] See S. Baskin, *Higher Education: Some Newer Developments* (New York: McGraw-Hill, 1965); W. M. Birenbaum, *Overlive: Power, Poverty, and the University* (New York: Delta Books, 1969); Educational Facilities Laboratory, *A College in the City: An Alternative* (New York: Educational Facilities Laboratory, 1969); and B. L. Johnson, *Islands of Innovation Expanding: Changes in the Community College* (Beverly Hills, Calif.: Glencoe Press, 1969).

[34] See Birenbaum, *op. cit.*

mentation should also facilitate personality development and growth for those already predisposed to liberal humanistic learning. Data have shown that colleges do seem to serve this facilitating function much more than does the workaday world.[35] Perhaps if students were given a more innovative college program than many educators have yet envisioned, students might begin to reach that level of development and concern for society that is characteristic of the more able activist students at present. At least, colleges should do their utmost to promote this kind of positive growth and welcome it when it manifests itself on the campus scene.

If the concept of a liberal education were applied to the meaning behind every college degree, then the idea of the college or university as a mediating agency in the society might also be adequately fulfilled. Here, too, then, the student might have an opportunity to develop personally. There are several aspects to the mediating role of the college, but in this sense perhaps its first and most important function is to preserve its autonomy as a way of maintaining academic freedom. In this way the college can serve the spirit of truth and free inquiry—ideals which may often, although not necessarily, clash with the more partisan pressures of the rest of society and even with established elements within the college. In making new discoveries, the college must subsequently act as a mediator between new truths and knowledge and the older established values still dominant in the larger society; it does so by providing a way for society to understand, evaluate, and eventually accept new findings despite the resistance of the status quo.

Another way, then, in which the college or university could serve as a mediating agency in society is by providing its students a moratorium to rethink their values critically and constructively in light of what they learn. Traditionally, college has served the function of a "rite of passage" for young adult entrance into society. For many young people, the period spent in college provides one of the last opportunities to devote all their time to their own intellectual, social, and moral development before the pressures of adult society and responsibilities turn their attention in other directions. This kind of extended moratorium contains several possibilities: it can give students

[35] See Trent and Medsker, *op. cit.*

a chance to insure and expand the ways in which they have developed and to establish more firmly the new identities they are trying to forge; it can provide the opportunity for the opening of proper channels for the free expression of students' ideas about their education and the problems of the society around them, and offer students the opportunity to deal with these ideas and problems; in the process, it can encourage students to assume contributive adult responsibilities; and it can enable many students who are professionally oriented to have a better chance to benefit from a liberal education.

It may well be true, as Kerr maintains,[36] that one of the major functions of college is to prepare people for professional jobs in society, but it is also true that society is frequently in need of revision and change as new knowledge and new ideals arise. Therefore, one of the most important things a student can bring to society is not conformity to its values but rather an open, free, critical, thinking mind, dedicated to truth and human development. If the college can act as mediator for the introduction of the spirit of free inquiry into the community, through both its own values and the values of its students, then society can look forward to seeing an enriched, humanistic perspective brought to it, beyond that which is evident from our survey of recent and previous college graduates.

The college that encourages its students to become involved with social problems inevitably will itself become involved with these problems and with the community burdened by them. But there is another reason why the college must become involved. It seeks to research and understand urban problems and sources of human development in our technocratic urban settings. But it is not sufficient only to analyze these elements in academic, ivory-tower fashion. Society depends upon the knowledge and expertise concentrated in the college in order to become systematically aware of its problems and subsequently to solve them.

To think, as does Barzun,[37] that higher education can be reduced to a glorification of the three R's is controvertible. In fact, the three R's, the development and communication of knowledge, and our

[36] Clark Kerr, *The Uses of the University* (Cambridge: Harvard University Press, 1963).

[37] Jacques Barzun, *The American University: How It Runs, Where It Is Going* (New York: Harper, 1968).

whole cultural heritage might well be best taught and implemented through the innovations proposed. Moreover, there is evidence that colleges following the traditions advocated by Barzun have actually been unsuccessful in realizing these objectives.[38] It is equally controvertible to think, as does John Millett, the Chancellor of Ohio Board of Regents, that the college should remain free from radical criticism or from radically criticizing society on the ground that it is the product of the American affluent majority.[39] The college is not merely a product of society. Its functions are such that it has a key role in delineating and developing society's products. In these complex, changing days when technology frequently leaves large segments of society unprepared for and cut off from technology's benefits, the college cannot magically remain a quiet conscience, as Millett would have it, while remote from and yet subservient to society. Rather, the function of higher education necessitates that it bring its insights, knowledge, and skills to the attention of the community for the sake of the community's own improvement. While maintaining (and improving upon) traditional academic functions, higher education must at the same time be a catalyst and, indeed, a vehicle for social change.

CONDITIONS FOR REFORMATION

Wallerstein sees this expanded role of higher education resulting inevitably in a certain amount of tension not unlike that implied in the above conceptualization of the functions of the college in the face of the many who are resistant to all but the status quo in society. There is agreement here that the tension is essential, particularly given Wallerstein's conclusion that:

> The newer role envisaged for the urban university, one deeply integrated into its immediate environs, subject to a rational societal allocation of priorities, a planning in which the university but also the rest of the community participates, is perhaps less familiar in the traditions of the great universities. Such a role has, of course, been played by many rural state institutions, especially in American history. The research and the curricula of many of the land-grant

[38] Philip E. Jacob, *Changing Values in College* (New York: Harper, 1957).

[39] John Millett, *Reconstruction of the University* (Cincinnati: Institute for Research and Training in Higher Education, University of Cincinnati, 1968).

colleges were long geared to the needs of the agricultural community. Today it is precisely the urban problems of advanced
industrial society that require the urban university to take on new
tasks, and in a new way. Again the demand fits in not only with
the ideals of the left but with the rhetoric of service of many representatives of established values and institutions. To fight for democratic and mutually planned rather than aristocratic and bestowed
service is surely a legitimate objective within the framework of what
are presumably American traditional values.[40]

We would only add that the university so integrated with its
environs would probably be best able to serve all its functions, including—through feedback of knowledge—its function centered primarily on pure research and dissemination of knowledge.

Reform of this kind would offer constructive avenues for the
strengths of the activists and assure attention to their legitimate demands without the necessity of devastating confrontations. Those few
radicals who are as relentlessly close-minded as the most reactionary
within the establishment may never be satisfied without total confrontation regardless of the rapidity and extent of reformation. But
without radical changes in higher education (and society at large)
there will be no possibility of sufficient satisfaction for anyone. The
changes, of course, can occur effectively only under certain conditions.
As we view the situation we would include conditions that may be
summarized under the headings of diversification, innovation, democratization, socialization and reevaluation.

Diversification. For years educators and government officials
have urged universal higher education. Many activists are now insisting that this insistence be more than rhetorical. Yet what is intended
by and what will result from higher education for all is not clear.
Higher education cannot feasibly be all things for all people. Neither
can it extend expectations only to dash them with limited opportunity
and undue curricular and parietal constraints. The nature and needs
of those who seek higher education differ greatly, and the college must
be sufficiently diversified in its programs and modes of education and
service to respond to the needs of the different individuals comprising
its clientele. The diversification must go beyond the current distinction

---

[40] I. Wallerstein, *The University in Turmoil: The Politics of Change*
(New York: Atheneum, 1969), p. 143.

between private and public, select and general, liberal arts and professional, two-year and four-year, or undergraduate and graduate
institutions. There must be diversification across institutions and within
separate institutions in a coordinated, programmatic way that will
make education personally relevant to the creative, to those not attracted to or not ready for college as it now exists, to those who find
it easy to come to college, and to those who are dismayed by it. This
may well mean rethinking the whole notion of college and how it is to
operate. It may also mean putting a college in an educational park,
a tenement house, a factory, or a tent. The important thing is to find
ways to diversify college effectively beyond the traditional stereotypes.

Innovation. The needed diversification of higher education as
we are discussing it implies the necessity for innovation. A perpetual
attempt must be made to improve educational programs by examining
what programs are to be offered and how they may be offered and
evaluated to assure that they are more effective than past programs.
Innovation can easily become a cliché in higher education. The addition of an audio-tutorial laboratory in a college may represent a minimum of innovation if it is handled as electronic gadgetry made to fit in
the long-established curricular mold. The innovation that is needed
involves more than just a new device or even a new idea. There probably are very few really new ideas in education. What is most needed
is a consistently fresh approach to education—an open, flexible search
for superior substance and presentation of that substance. Useful
precedent and tradition should not be ignored, but it is just as important that the educational process not be confined to precedent, the
effectiveness of which has almost never been demonstrated.

Democratization. The innovative search for "relevancy" in
higher education is not possible when it is frustrated by intellectual
dogmatists or other reactionaries who possess inordinate power in the
faculty, administration, or governing board. The paradigm of the
past, such as that described by Woodring,[41] has been the faculty
aligned against the trustees, the administration arbitrating in between,
some students having an occasional say in recent years, and each group
concerned primarily with its own vested, exclusive interests. One of the
most needed innovations in the college is a system of organization that

[41] Paul Woodring, *The Higher Learning in America: A Reassessment*
(New York: McGraw-Hill, 1968).

will promote open communication and flexible responsiveness among these groups in place of their collision. The college may best be governed by congress where there exists an intercommunication and balance of power among the faculty, students, administration, trustees, and, at least in some cases, community representatives. A preconceived notion is that students are too transient and immature to participate in campus governance. In reality, they often are no more transient than the faculty, and they have shown themselves to be quite capable of making momentous decisions affecting their own education and the college in general. As examples, students have been involved in the selection of faculty at Antioch College for some time; at the 1969 annual meeting of the American Personnel and Guidance Association a consistent characteristic of the dozen or so successful college programs for cultural minorities described was that the involved students shared in the decision making of the programs at all levels. In governance, as well as in teaching, students have been a wasted power. A rewarding collaboration between students and the other factors of higher education may be possible; otherwise there likely will result a power struggle even more intense than that so far observed on American campuses.

Socialization. The position here has been that the college is no mere reflection of the affluent majority. It has many roles to fulfill for many publics. As a result, the college must be more concerned than traditionally it has been with socialization in that it must relate more often and more effectively to the different factors of society. As an agent of social change it must be sensitive to the needs of society and must deal personally with its members to achieve collaboration in changes devised to meet the needs. In order to carry out this and other important functions, it is vital that the college surpass what it has done to sensitize its publics to these functions. For instance, the college cannot implement an educational moratorium when student protests are met only by repressive retaliation from both legislators and the immediate community. Citizens and civic leaders alike are in great need of an education whereby they will gain an understanding of the meaning of a college education (including social consciousness and intellectual development apart from professional training) and of the problems and issues this involves currently. This education of the public cannot be accomplished unless large numbers of the college see to it consistently and systematically. The opinions of the established constituency and policy-makers cannot be disregarded or flaunted; instead, they must be opinions that follow from a comprehension of the college.

Re-evaluation. Implied throughout this discussion is the position that the viability and development of higher education is dependent upon proper evaluation. Many studies of the past, such as those contained in *The American College*,[42] are important, but they are not sufficient for the present in design or content. Many of these studies bear replication, but there must be a reevaluation of higher education of yet a different sort. Research must go beyond the assessment of the effectiveness of a particular program or an institution's impact on the personality development of its students. There must be a systematic and comprehensive evaluation of the whole system of higher education. Moreover, to accomplish this purpose, the evaluation itself must be innovative. A thorough explanation of the nature of this type of research and evaluation must be withheld until it can be treated at length. For the moment the essential issue is to note the critical functions of the research. It must delineate the input, process, and outcome variables and the effects of their interactions within and across institutions in reference to discerned criterion variables. It must thereby provide research models that will result in the identification and understanding of the dynamics of higher education from student attitudes to administrative styles, so that decision making and implementation of programs in the college can be made on an informed basis, with a clear notion of the relevant issues, the alternatives available, and what to expect of the different alternatives. It must provide a constant, sweeping monitoring and subsequent evaluation of the system and its different components. In the light either of "the normal" state of affairs or changing situation, there is no other way to respond rapidly to legitimate protest, to deal with problems before they become insurmountable or otherwise to implement adjustments and improvements in the system. We may anticipate evaluative research and research models of this nature from work done at Berkeley's Center for Research and Development in Higher Education; the Carnegie Foundation's national assessment of higher education under Clark Kerr's

[42] Nevitt Sanford (Ed.), *The American College* (New York: Wiley, 1962).

direction; programs under way at the American College Testing Program, American Council of Education, and the Regional Educational Laboratory for the Carolinas and Virginia; and the nationwide evaluation of higher education now under way at the Center for the Study of Evaluation at the University of California at Los Angeles. The actual development of research and evaluation along these lines is a major thrust of the Center for the Study of Evaluation. But it is crucial to have a much broader participation in the evaluation of higher education.

These observations are no doubt obvious to many; they are surely debatable to others. Any debate, however, must consider the alternatives the college has before it. It may maintain its present status, revert to a Barzunian model, and repress resultant criticism and confrontation from student activists. Under the circumstances it will run the risk of being shut down or of becoming ineffectual as it ignores instead of leads the cultural revolution that is evident. Or it may seek additional roles, meanings, and methods that will make its major functions relevant to the needs and natures of its students and other clientele in this period of cultural revolution.

The latter alternative cannot be accomplished easily or immediately. It probably will not satisfy the few activists who are determined on total confrontation with the college, whatever its response. It will, however, probably satisfy most of the activists who will have rendered an incalculable service to higher education by insisting upon being satisfied only through positive changes in the college. In any event, the college and the rest of society must be prepared to absorb and heed a good many activists for some time to come.

The qualities found among student activists suggest that many of them are not merely banner-wavers of the moment who will live out their lives in comfortable suburban homes, forgetting what they were once so excited about on the steps of Berkeley's Sproul Hall or Harvard's yard. Many of them will probably become involved with professional and family life and will doubtless become more mellowed and patient in outlook as they meet their obligations and the kind of responsibilities that come with the attainment of true adult autonomy. But it is probable that the qualities they bring to their meaningful dissent in college will be enduring, positive, and influential and that they will continue to initiate intellectual dissent and social awareness.

They are likely to be heard from, in conversation, in printed word, and in public address. The time is surely right and the need urgent for the college not only to stimulate activism among its students but to provide the circumstances under which it can flourish without negative excesses on the part of the activists or reprisals from society.

Political and Apolitical Students: Facts in Search of Theory

Christian Bay

Why do students active in protest movements tend to do better academically and to be more intelligent and intellectually disposed than more apolitical students? There is a wealth of data to show that this is so, but an astounding absence of efforts to make theoretical sense of it. Moreover, we have known for decades that more liberal or radical students have, statistically speaking, been more intelligent or academically able than more conservative students; and similar relationships have been found with a corresponding regularity in studies, though fewer in number, of adult populations. How can we account for this apparent preponderance of intelligence and intellectual resources on the left side of the political spectrum?

In this paper I hope to contribute toward such a theoretical accounting. Yet, the paucity of theory in an area of so much research activity and general interest is itself an intriguing phenomenon that calls for some explaining. My main task is to try to make theoretical sense of three categories of data: (1) traditional attitude measurement studies, from the 1920s on, mainly administered to students but at other times to adults, which almost invariably have found those who are more liberal doing better on intelligence, educational achievement, and so on, than those who are more conservative; (2) work on authoritarianism and related neurotic tendencies, which again has demonstrated a clear affinity between these tendencies and right-wing views, compared to a much less clear, or more tenuous, affinity with left-wing orientations; and (3) recent work on student political activists, which abundantly shows liberal and leftist militancy to correlate with high academic or intellectual achievement. The attempted theoretical explanation is based on fairly recent work by social psychologists, whose theory of the functions of attitudes is extended toward a theory of individual political rationality as an aspect of human development.

A WEALTH OF DATA

Empirical knowledge about man, or human behavior, has expanded considerably in recent decades, but the lines of advance have as a rule been determined by innovations in research methodology and techniques, and not by either theoretical or practical priorities

61

with respect to felt needs for improved knowledge. Inevitably, it seems, new instruments for gathering facts are quickly being put to use on a large scale, by steadily mounting armies of well-trained social scientists vying with each other for the privilege of feeding the hungry journals. The number of journals, too, and their appetite have been growing, and what they like best are articles crammed with factual data. Theoretical progress has tended to lag far behind advances in techniques of fact-gathering, in the social sciences in general. But there have been other factors operating in the area of special concern here, which happens to be, for one thing, a politically sensitive area.

As we shall see, measurable political attitudes have been studied as facts like any other facts by social psychologists, who in their capacity as empirical researchers have been, obviously, politically neutral. But this neutralism, or value-free orientation, has tended to become more than a wise, indeed a necessary, research strategy; it has tended to become a rigidified, defensive posture, which has discouraged inquiry into the possibility that some political orientations may be "better," in some sense, than others, even when the researchers' own data have kept pressing for inquiry of this kind. These inhibitions have been much less in evidence in the more speculative psychoanalytic literature, and among empirical works to be discussed here the psychoanalytically influenced *The Authoritarian Personality*[1] has most boldly suggested that extreme right-wing political views are likely to be pathological. The authors were quickly charged with left-wing bias, or at least with partisanship, by other social scientists who firmly believe, it appears, that all "extremism" is pathological.

But this line of criticism expresses another bias, or ideology, which is less visible only because it is so thoroughly and so widely accepted in the Western world among social scientists and among the general public: that political moderation and a firm commitment to the processes of democracy are requirements of sound common sense, or perhaps that extremism or lack of firm commitment to democracy—in a word, radicalism, right or left—indicates a probability of neurosis of some kind. Within this ideology, a position which frequently flatters itself with a claim of being beyond ideologies, marking "the end of ideol-

---

[1] T. W. Adorno, E. Frenkel-Brunswick, D. J. Levinson, and N. Sanford, *The Authoritarian Personality* (New York: Harper, 1950).

ogy,"[2] all moderately liberal and conservative ideas are deemed equally "healthy," while outside the fold of conventional moderation, it is assumed, cool rationality has given way to neurosis, or at least to unreasoning passion.

In this way the very acceptance of democracy's formal processes has been an obstacle to open-minded theorizing about possible psychological differences associated with more conservative versus more liberal or radical views. While there is no ideological obstacle to theorizing about the neurotic nature of extremist views, provided one writes either about both extremes or about leftist extremism only,[3] it appears generally assumed that within democracy's fold "one idea is as good as another," at least in psychological terms.

I have developed elsewhere the profoundly conservative implications of this unqualified commitment to the forms of democracy, and I have shown how it has encouraged and been encouraged by the massive research investments in the sociology of politics only, to the virtual exclusion of work in the psychology or especially the psychodynamics of politics.[4] In our pluralist order it has become an apparent axiom that political priorities are to be determined by the outcomes of apparently (but in fact not so very) democratic processes. In our unequal social order, as in every other, there are immensely strong vested interests marshalled against questioning the existent, stable processes of political control; and our kind of democracy has become almost perfected as an instrument to prevent political or socioeconomic changes of any magnitude.[5] The "end-of-ideology" ideology has tended

[2] See Joseph LaPalombara, "Decline of Ideology: A Dissent and an Interpretation," *American Political Science Review,* 1966, *60,* 5–16; and works cited therein. Also see my "The End of Politics," *Journal of Conflict Resolution,* 1961, *5,* 326–335.

[3] In contrast to the authors of *The Authoritarian Personality,* Harold D. Lasswell in his pathbreaking *Psychopathology and Politics* (Chicago: University of Chicago Press, 1930) assumed that left-wing radicalism indicated psychopathology, and I have not seen him taken to task for political bias on this account.

[4] See my "Politics and Pseudopolitics," *American Political Science Review,* 1965, *59,* 39–51; "Behavioral Research and the Theory of Democracy," unpublished paper, 1965; and "Beyond Pluralism: The Problem of Evaluating Political Institutions in Terms of Human Needs," unpublished paper, 1966.

[5] For example, Gabriel Kolko demonstrates that there has been *no* redistribution of income in America between 1910 and 1960; the maldistribution

to extend among social scientists, too, an almost unqualified commitment to our status quo preserving processes of democracy, although *our* kind of vested interests have been different.

In addition, I would like for the sake of brevity to mention in passing four additional intellectual tendencies among contemporary social scientists, each of which may have its bearing on our usual reluctance to theorize about the reams of available data on the psychology of liberalism or conservatism: (1) by and large we tend to be liberals, at least in the sense that we want to be tolerant, at least, of all "democratic" ideas; one aspect or consequence of our desire to be tolerant is that we usually lean over backwards to avoid any position that would, even by implication, make scientific claims for our own political views; (2) freedom of speech and inquiry, so vital to our functioning, seems so generally associated with democratic forms of government that we may be reluctant to inquire into the drawbacks of our political system; (3) an unqualified commitment to democratic processes enables us to avoid the difficult research problems pertaining to the study of man's "real" needs, so that we may study wants (that is, perceived or felt needs) and demands and other manifest behavior instead—an area in which we are well equipped with research methods and techniques. Finally (4), and this is a point closely related to the previous one, theorizing about social and political systems and their maintenance permits much neater input-output models, which are also handier for research purposes, if we avoid the distracting and exceedingly complex task of relating the system-variables to psychodynamic needs as distinct from manifest wants.[6]

In fact, the intellectual vested interest among social scientists in avoiding serious study of psychodynamic need priorities, as distinct

---

remains enormous. See his *Wealth and Power in America* (New York: Praeger, 1964 [1962]).

[6] In addition, increasing knowledge of how to maintain existing social systems must be more attractive to the powers that be, including the fund-granting powers, than increasing knowledge of human needs that are left unfulfilled by existing institutions. However, while there surely are long-run system maintenance factors operating to support existing trends in social science on this basis, I believe that few social scientists would be so motivated; we may be politically and psychologically naive but few of us are illiberal in the sense of deliberately downgrading human needs in relation to the maintenance requirements of existing institutional systems.

from hierarchies of expressed wants and manifest preferences, may well have been the single most crucial factor to account for four decades of pregnant data on psychological factors in liberalism and conservatism left theoretically adrift. How can we begin to understand the etiology of fundamental differences in political attitudes until we are willing to begin formulating and testing, as best we can, propositions about man's fundamental nature and needs, in addition to his manifest behavior tendencies?

TRADITIONAL ATTITUDE STUDIES

The invention and subsequently the continued improvement of techniques for the measurement of attitudes, together with increasingly sophisticated techniques of correlational analysis and the related knacks of applied statistics, have stimulated an enormous number of studies of attitudes and relationships between attitudes, beginning around 1920. A large category of attitude studies dealt with political orientations. Among the latter studies there must have been hundreds reported in the journals of the twenties and thirties which either focused on or paid attention to characteristics of radical versus conservative attitudes and their respective correlates.[7]

There is one difference in particular between students with more radical or liberal views and students with more conservative views[8] that shows up in study after study: more radical students kept scoring higher either on intelligence tests or by way of academic grades,

---

[7] "An attitude is a mental and neural state of readiness, organized through experience, exerting a directing and dynamic influence upon the individual's response to all objects and situations with which it is related." This is Gordon W. Allport's definition of 1935, which in 1950 still seemed useful to him and in 1966 still seems useful to me. See his *The Nature of Personality: Selected Papers* (Cambridge, Mass.: Addison-Wesley, 1950), p. 13. However, I shall use the term with less precision, and terms like *belief, opinion, views,* and *orientation* somewhat indiscriminately in this paper, because my interest is in the whole pattern of political orientations rather than their analytical components. Compare Lester W. Milbrath's definition: "Political attitudes are cognitions about and positive or negative feelings toward political objects." *Political Participation* (Chicago: Rand McNally, 1965), p. 50.

[8] The large majority of attitude studies in the twenties and thirties were limited to college students. Apart from voting and public opinion studies, the same is true of the majority of attitude studies today.

compared to more conservative students. There were exceptions, but there is no gainsaying the general tendency.[9]

Beginning around 1930, there also have been a good number of studies of attitude change, especially during the college years, and more are being published today. In Newcomb's classic study of Bennington students during the late thirties, published in 1943, the fact that most students left college considerably more liberal or radical than they entered as freshmen is accounted for mainly in terms of peer-group influence.[10] The more strongly peer-group acceptance is desired, the more proneness to adhere to the fashionable political views; "nonconservative attitudes are developed at Bennington primarily by those who are both capable and desirous of cordial relations with their fellow community members."[11]

But why was Bennington a breeding ground for radicals and liberals in the 1930s? Newcomb's explanation is plausible but atheoretical: Bennington College was founded in 1932, the year FDR took office, and many faculty members were interested in and sympathetic to the New Deal, as were many other American intellectuals at the time. But is there nothing about the educational process itself that should lead us to expect, in the best colleges, a liberal rather than a conservative climate? To this question Newcomb's otherwise excellent study does not address itself.

Let me conclude this part of my discussion by relating a few of the most pertinent facts from Samuel A. Stouffer's valuable 1955 volume, *Communism, Conformity, and Civil Liberties*—a study which in a sense marks the culmination, though by no means the conclusion, of the long tradition of increasingly sophisticated political attitude surveys.[12] Stouffer's data were harvested by 537 skilled interviewers,

---

[9] Speaking of the literature reporting research on conservative attitudes on American campuses, Newcomb reports an almost unanimous finding: "Whatever the context of the term 'conservatism,' those who show it least on any given campus tend to make higher scores on intelligence tests, or to make better scholastic records, or both, than those who show it most." Theodore M. Newcomb, *Personality and Social Change* (New York: Holt, 1943), p. 171. See also his "Determinants of Opinion," *Public Opinion Quarterly*, 1937, *1*, 71–78.

[10] Newcomb, *Personality and Social Change, op. cit.*, pp. 148–49.

[11] *Ibid.*

[12] New York: Wiley, 1966 (1955).

employed by two leading national opinion research organizations, who interviewed 7,933 Americans, representative of the whole adult population, during May–July 1954; and an additional 1,500 community leaders, independently sampled.

One finding of significance is that community leaders invariably are more tolerant of the freedom of dissent, compared to the bulk of the population. For example, 84 per cent of the leaders would allow a socialist to speak, compared to 58 per cent of the general population. For the atheist's right to speak, the corresponding figures are 64 per cent compared to 37 per cent; for the communist's, 51 per cent compared to 27 per cent.[13]

Stouffer then constructed a scale of tolerance of nonconformists, based on composites of replies to all his tolerance questions. On this scale, distributions compared as follows:

Community leaders: $5 + 29 + 66 = 100\%$ $(N = 1500)$
National cross section: $19 + 50 + 31 = 100\%$ $(N = 4933)$

where the three figures represent, respectively, "less tolerant," "in between" and "more tolerant."[14]

For present purposes I am interested only in the question, Who are Stouffer's "more tolerant" respondents? In one important sense of "liberal," these can be considered the more liberal Americans, at least as of May–July, 1954. First, they are younger: 47 per cent of those in their twenties, compared to 18 per cent in their sixties, are "more tolerant"—and there is a linear relationship for the in-between age groups. Second, the more liberal respondents are better educated: 66 per cent of the college graduates, compared to 16 per cent of those with grade schools only, and again a clear linear relationship. Further breakdowns indicated, too, that the better educated are more liberal also for matching age levels, while the younger are more liberal also

[13] *Ibid.,* pp. 29, 33, and 11. This generalization holds for leaders of very conservative organizations, too, compared to *their* memberships, according to Stouffer; although McClosky has reported data which suggest that the Republican Party might be an exception. See Herbert J. McClosky, "Issue Conflict and Consensus among Party Leaders and Followers," *American Political Science Review,* 1960, *54,* 406–427.

[14] Stouffer, *op. cit.,* p. 51. Stouffer's figures reflect the research instruments and have no value, of course, apart from the significant difference they show between tolerance levels of leaders and cross-section.

at matching levels of education. Stouffer also found that optimism concerning one's personal future—generally higher for younger than for older people—correlates highly with liberalism (or, in his terms, tolerance).[15]

In addition, Stouffer found a clear relationship between urbanization and liberalism, both nationally and for each region of the United States: West, East, Middle West, South. And degree of liberalism is also related to region, with descending degrees from West to South in the order just listed; respectively, 46 per cent, 40 per cent, 31 per cent, and 14 per cent "more tolerant" were reported by one of the two survey organizations, and by the other, 40 per cent, 39 per cent, 33 per cent, and 18 per cent. The corresponding breakdowns for the urban-rural factor were, respectively, for Metropolitan Areas, Other Cities, Small Towns, Farms: 39 per cent, 28 per cent, 26 per cent, and 16 per cent; and 40 per cent, 32 per cent, 23 per cent, and 19 per cent.[16]

By way of explanation of these and related findings Stouffer suggests that a factor essential to tolerance may be "contact with people with disturbing and unpopular ideas." Schooling *"puts a person in touch with people whose ideas and values are different from one's own."* So does urban living. And so, probably, does living in the West, where a higher proportion than elsewhere has lived in other regions before.[17]

But why is it that the younger people, regardless of levels of education, tend to be more liberal than the older people? The only hypothesis Stouffer suggests is that it is easier for the young to be optimistic about their personal future; and degrees of optimism ("my life will be better") are significantly related to youth and also to tolerance, as his data bear out. But why should optimists tend to be tolerant of nonconformists? Stouffer here merely states that "there

15 *Ibid.*, Chapter 4.
16 *Ibid.*, Chapter 5.
17 *Ibid.*, pp. 125–128 (Stouffer's italics). The cities of the Far West, "which have grown at such an astonishing rate by recruiting from all parts of this country, are the highest of all in our scale of tolerance," writes Stouffer (pp. 127–128). One puzzle emerges here: why does Northern California and especially the San Francisco Bay Area in so many surveys come out as more liberal than Southern California, where the rate of population growth has been much higher?

is substantial psychological theory which would predict a relationship between optimism about personal affairs and tolerance toward non-conformists"; he elaborates only to the extent of suggesting the need for scapegoats for individuals who are very troubled and the availability of Communists and other nonconformists as "obvious targets for blame, directly for the world's troubles and indirectly, if sometimes unconsciously, for one's personal troubles."[18] Is this all there is to the relationship he demonstrated between youth and liberalism?

AUTHORITARIANISM

In *The Authoritarian Personality*[19] a number of factors were found to be related to neurotic authoritarianism as measured by the F scale. Among these were Political-Economic Conservatism, measured by the PEC scale in its several forms, all of which gave a high score to respondents indicating a high degree of "support of the status quo and particularly of business; support of conservative values; desire to maintain a balance of power in which business is dominant, labor subordinant, and the economic functions of government minimized; and resistance to social change."[20]

There are serious methodological shortcomings in this work, as is often the case with pioneering ventures. Scales for the measurement of authoritarianism or conservatism are useful devices for distinguishing high scorers from low scorers, but from the moment we start to intercorrelate scores from different scales we run into the problem that the composition of each scale is, in a sense, arbitrary: it could plausibly have been composed of any number of alternate items instead. For this reason data indicating that a given group of respondents score higher on one scale (say, the PEC scale) than on another (say, the E scale, or Ethnocentrism scale) are spurious.[21] While it makes no sense to say that a group of respondents (there were no

---

[18] *Ibid.*, p. 100.

[19] Adorno *et al., op. cit.*

[20] *Ibid.*, p. 157. Examples of "conservative values" suggested by the authors are the admiration of private ambition, success in financial terms, competitiveness (pp. 154–155).

[21] This is overlooked, for example, on pp. 164–165. The best general critiques of methodological shortcomings in this study are found in Richard Christie and Marie Jahoda, *Studies in the Scope and Method of "The Authoritarian Personality"* (Glencoe: The Free Press, 1954).

population samples from which to generalize) is more conservative than ethnocentric, it can make good sense to demonstrate that those who come out high on authoritarianism tend to come out high on conservatism as well, and vice versa—as was indeed found $(r = 0.5)$, although it is only of marginal significance.[22]

However, even this kind of finding may be challenged by the charge that the affinity may have been built into the research instruments. One of the major critics of *The Authoritarian Personality,* Milton Rokeach, makes this charge, and his own subsequent work toward developing a politically neutral Dogmatism scale has added emphasis to his critique and made a strong case for its validity.

While Edward Shils earlier had charged the authors of *The Authoritarian Personality* with a kind of ideological blindness to the phenomenon of authoritarianism on the left, a charge based on political assumptions of his own rather than substantive evidence,[23] Rokeach's charge was specific: There was something wrong with the F scale; it was politically slanted and could tap only right-wing dogmatism. To demonstrate that he could remedy this defect he not only developed a Dogmatism scale which claimed to be politically neutral along major conventional right-left dimensions; he also proceeded to substantiate this claim by developing two Opinionation scales, one measuring vehement intolerance of leftist views and the other doing the same for rightist views. Having achieved a reasonably high reliability for both Opinionation scales in several samples, Rokeach proceeded to demonstrate that his Dogmatism scale, *unlike* the F scale, the E scale, and, of course, the PEC scale, correlated positively not only with his Right Opinionation scale but with his Left Opinionation scale as well.[24]

Now, strictly speaking there probably is no such thing as a politically neutral scale, unless it be devoid of all social content; what

[22] Adorno *et al., op. cit.,* p. 207 and Chapter Five.

[23] See his "Authoritarianism: 'Right' and 'Left,'" in Christie and Jahoda, *op. cit.,* pp. 24–29; and my own counter-critique in Bay, *Structure of Freedom* (New York: Atheneum, 1965 [1958]), pp. 209–10. My book reviews *The Authoritarian Personality* and major criticisms of the study at some length in its Chapter Four.

[24] See Rokeach, "Political and Religious Dogmatism: An Alternative to the Authoritarian Personality," *Psychological Monographs,* 1956, 70(18), 1–43; and his *The Open and Closed Mind* (New York: Basic Books, 1960), especially Part Two.

Rokeach showed is that the F scale does not while his own Dogmatism scale does correlate with the degrees of vehemence (which presumably were symptomatic of the closed-mindedness) with which leftist as well as rightist opinions are held, at least in certain populations. As a matter of fact, Rokeach notes that both his Dogmatism scale and his combined Opinionation scale show a weak but consistently positive relationship to conservatism, and also that dogmatism in all his samples shows somewhat closer affinity to right than to left opinionation. He raises but dismisses perhaps too lightly the possibility that his scales are less neutral than intended; his principal explanation is that Communism, unlike fascism, is humanitarian in its ideology (or *content,* as he puts it), at least; and that the same to a more modest extent may be true of liberal versus conservative ideology.[25] In support of his belief that the psychological functions of Communist beliefs may differ from those of fascist beliefs he cites the phenomenon of *disillusionment* which, he believes, occurs far more often among former Communists than among former Nazis or fascists, indicating a sudden awareness of contradictions within the Communist creed which may not exist within fascist creeds, whose anti-humanism pertains to ends as well as means, or content as well as structure. He also refers to Robert Lindner's theory that Communists more often have neurotic problems, often guilt-related, while fascists more often are psychopaths, or people with an underdeveloped conscience.[26]

Another, more massive study comparing conservatives to liberals is reported by Herbert McClosky, whose more than 2,000 respondents were drawn from Minnesota population samples. These are his principal findings of relevance here: (1) "By every measure available to us, conservative beliefs are found most frequently among the uninformed, the poorly educated and so far as we can determine, the less intelligent"; (2) "Conservatism, in our society at least, appears to be far more characteristic of social isolates, of people who think poorly of themselves . . . who are submissive, timid, and wanting in con-

<hr />

[25] See his "Political and Religion Dogmatism," *op. cit.,* pp. 38–39, and *The Open and Closed Mind, op. cit.,* pp. 126–127.

[26] See Lindner, "Political Creed and Character," *Psychoanalysis,* 1953, 2, 10–33. On disillusionment among former Communists, see Gabriel A. Almond, *The Appeals of Communism* (Princeton, N.J.: Princeton University Press, 1954).

fidence"; and (3) "In the four liberal-conservative classifications, the extreme conservatives are easily the most hostile and suspicious, the most rigid and compulsive, the quickest to condemn others for their imperfections and weaknesses, the most intolerant, the most inflexible and unyielding in their perceptions and judgments. Although aggressively critical of the shortcomings of others, they are unusually defensive and armored in the protection of their own ego needs. Poorly integrated psychologically, anxious, often perceiving themselves as inadequate, and subject to excessive feelings of guilt, they seem inclined to project onto others the traits they most dislike in themselves."[27]

McClosky divided his respondents into four categories: "liberals," "moderate liberals," "moderate conservatives," and "extreme conservatives"; these labels suggest that he felt he had more "extreme" conservatives than liberals in his main samples. The three tables he presented are astoundingly consistent in yielding entirely linear correlations from "liberal" to "extreme conservative," without a single exception; "moderate liberals," for example, are found to be higher on hostility, lower on education and intellectuality, and so on, than "liberals"; and McClosky claims that his data "could be buttressed by numerous other related findings in our studies, and the relationships so briefly presented here could be elaborated in dozens of ways."[28]

McClosky's analysis of these striking findings is couched more in descriptive than in developmental terms. For example: "From whatever direction we approach him, the prototypic conservative seems far more impelled to contain, to reject, and to take precautions against, his fellow creatures."[29] But why? McClosky is cautious indeed on this score. The closest thing to a suggestion of a casual relationship is his statement that "education is likely to lead to liberal rather than conservative tendencies."[30] Among his concluding cautionary remarks, he says that conservative doctrines "appear, in some measure, to arise from personality needs, but it is conceivable at least, that both are

[27] See Herbert McClosky, "Conservatism and Personality," *American Political Science Review*, 1958, *52*, 35–38 and 27–45.

[28] *Ibid.*, p. 38. It would be most interesting to see the data on McClosky's two special samples of extreme right-wing and left-wing believers, which are left unreported on this occasion. Which of the unilinear correlations will pertain to the extremes of the spectrum, too? *Ibid.*, p. 34.

[29] *Ibid.*, p. 42.

[30] *Ibid.*, p. 41.

the product of some third set of factors." Conservatism and a host of undesirable personality traits clearly, in these Minnesota samples, "go together. *How* they go together, and which is antecedent to which, is a more difficult and more elusive problem."[31]

There has been a remarkable lack of follow-up of this striking demonstration of affinity between degrees of conservatism and widely disvalued personality and social characteristics. If *The Authoritarian Personality*'s findings of affinity between conservatism and neurotic authoritarianism can be questioned on methodological grounds, and if Rokeach's data only mildly suggested a similar affinity, McClosky's tables appear methodologically solid and of great theoretical import.

RECENT STUDIES

I attempt no exhaustive survey of all available data on student activism or student leftism generally. The sources on which I draw are almost wholly concerned with University of California and especially Berkeley students, but the patterns of data to be presented are not specific to California students. They are entirely in line, as we shall see, with the data reviewed above, demonstrating high positive relationships between degrees of radicalism or militant liberalism and factors like scholarly or intellectual achievement.

Hanan C. Selvin and Warren O. Hagstrom, in December 1957, while things were still fairly quiet on that University of California campus, did a study of the views on civil liberties in a sample of 894 Berkeley students. Wisely anticipating that abstract statements favoring the Bill of Rights would sooner indicate conformism than liberalism, these investigators elicited responses to specific civil liberties issues involving conflicts with other values. On the basis of these responses they constructed a Libertarianism Index, with which they divided their sample in three groups: highly libertarian, 34 per cent (302); moderately libertarian, 46 per cent (409); slightly libertarian, 20 per cent (183).[32]

The "highly libertarian" group is a category delimited by the

[31] *Ibid.*, p. 44.
[32] Selvin and Hagstrom, "Determinants of Support for Civil Liberties," in Seymour Martin Lipset and Sheldon S. Wolin (Eds.), *The Berkeley Student Revolt* (New York: Anchor, 1965), p. 499 and pp. 494–518. Originally published in *British Journal of Sociology*, 1960, 2, 51–73.

research instruments used and, like Stouffer's "more tolerant" group, it is useful only for comparisons within the same study. However, by way of comparing responses to certain specific questions identical with or closely resembling questions asked by Stouffer, Selvin and Hagstrom were able to show that Berkeley students in 1957, even as freshmen, were considerably more libertarian than were Stouffer's national cross-section *or* his national sample of community leaders three years before.[33]

But of greater interest here are the data comparing the highly libertarian students with the Berkeley student body in general. In a linear relationship, again, the proportions of highly libertarian students on the Berkeley campus ascends from freshman to senior and graduate level: 21 per cent, 29 per cent, 34 per cent, 40 per cent, and 54 per cent. The relationship between libertarianism and grades is inconclusive in the lower division but crystal clear in the upper division: among A to $B+$ students 54 per cent are "highly libertarian," compared to 37 per cent among B to $C+$ students and 25 per cent among students at C level or below.[34]

Children of blue-collar workers among Berkeley students are libertarians more often, by a wide margin, than are children of parents better able to support their offspring financially through college; this is true in spite of the fact that blue-collar parents average lower educational attainments than other parents and are likely to be relatively nonlibertarian themselves. "Greater economic independence, in the sense of self-support," conclude Selvin and Hagstrom, "is strongly associated with having more libertarian attitudes than one's parents."[35]

Among male students the social science and humanities majors were by a wide margin found more libertarian than the rest, with engineering and education (a field that has recruited low achievers in Berkeley) and business administration at the bottom. Among female

[33] *Ibid.*, p. 501. Compared to Paul F. Lazarsfeld and Wagner Thielens, Jr.'s sample of social science teachers, however, Selvin and Hagstrom's comparison is inconclusive. See Lazarsfeld and Thielens, *The Academic Mind* (Glencoe, Ill.: Free Press, 1958).

[34] Selvin and Hagstrom, *op. cit.*, 503 and 511. Students tend to work harder in the upper division, with a clearer sense of purpose and perhaps of identity; and grades there presumably reflect relative academic ability (though not necessarily intellectual ability) better than in the lower division.

[35] *Ibid.*, p. 504.

students, social welfare majors were most libertarian, while life science majors shared the next level of libertarianism with social science and humanities majors, and with education majors once again at the bottom.[36] And, finally, fraternity and especially sorority students— who are least likely to get to know well people with unorthodox ideas —are least likely to be libertarians, compared to students with other living arrangements.[37]

In November 1964, when the student rebellion at Berkeley was under way, Robert H. Somers interviewed a carefully drawn sample of 285 Berkeley students. He found 63 per cent to favor the goals of the Free Speech Movement, while about 34 per cent approved of the FSM's tactics; clearly favoring goals as well as tactics were 30 per cent, and Somers calls this group the *militants,* while the *moderates,* again 30 per cent, clearly supported FSM's goals but not the means used, and 22 per cent, *conservatives,* were opposed to the ends sought as well as the tactics used.[38]

For my purposes the crucial findings of this study are summarized as follows by Somers: "it is hard to overlook the fact that in our sample there is a strong relation between academic achievement and support for the demonstrators. Among those who reported to our interviewers a grade-point average of *B+* or better, nearly half (45 per cent) are militants, and only a tenth are conservatives. At the other end, over a third of those with an average of *B−* or less are conservatives, and only 15 per cent are militants." If the FSM represented a minority of students, Somers concluded, it would be "a minority vital to the excellence of this university."[39]

[36] *Ibid.,* p. 512. There has been a considerable upgrading of the field of education on the Berkeley campus in the last ten years, since this study was made.

[37] *Op. cit.,* p. 514.

[38] See his "The Mainsprings of the Rebellion: A Survey of Berkeley students in November, 1964," in Lipset and Wolin, *op. cit.,* pp. 537–540 and pp. 530–557. The remaining 18 per cent could not be clearly categorized in either of the three groups.

[39] *Ibid.,* p. 544. Somers also reports, in a footnote, that "the 800 students arrested in the Sproul Hall sit-in of December" tended to be high-achieving students, according to a survey conducted by graduate students of political science. The correct number of students arrested, if one can trust police records, is not 800 but 773. See William A. Watts and David N. E. Whittaker. "Some Socio-Psychological Differences Between Highly Committed Members

Early in 1965, Paul Heist did a study of a sample drawn from a list of more than 800 persons said to have been arrested in the Sproul Hall sit-in (but see above, note 39); on advice of their legal counsel, about 50 per cent of the 33 per cent sample refused to return the questionnaire but the rest cooperated, 128 in all, and an additional sixty FSM activists were recruited subsequently as subjects for the study. In addition, a sample of ninety-two 1964–65 seniors were given the same two questionnaires. Also, Heist had access to the same attitude inventory data from 340 1962–63 seniors, and from "2500+" entering freshmen, all at Berkeley.

One of the two questionnaires elicited biographical information, while the other was an attitude inventory seeking measures of variables such as *Autonomy* (nonauthoritarian thinking), *Thinking Introversion* (a liking for reflective abstract thought), *Theoretical Orientation* (degree of interest in using scientific methods in thinking), *Impulse Expression,* and *Lack of Anxiety.*[40]

Most of Heist's data have not yet been analyzed, but in a preliminary paper he reports that FSM respondents scored significantly higher than his other respondents on Autonomy and on Impulse Expression. "These integrated results, especially when interpreted in light of the scores on several other scales, indicate a higher level of cultural sophistication, a greater release from the institutional influences of the past, and a greater openness and readiness to explore the world of knowledge and ideas."[41]

Heist developed an Intellectual Disposition Index on the basis of six of the twelve scales in his attitude inventory, and with this instrument divided his FSM sample and his three general student samples according to eight "degrees," from low to high Intellectual Disposition. Here is what he found: "For the total FSM group we find almost 70 per cent in the top three categories and none in the bottom three, and it is to be remembered that a large proportion, in

---

of the Free Speech Movement and the Student Population at Berkeley," *Journal of Applied Behavioral Science,* 1966, 2, 41–62. Watts and Whittaker dispute the finding referred to at the beginning of this note.

[40] There were twelve scales in Heist's personality inventory, and they are briefly described in an appendix to his paper, *Intellect and Commitment: The Faces of Discontent* (Berkeley: Center for the Study of Higher Education, 1965), mimeographed.

[41] *Ibid.,* p. 20.

fact, the majority, of the FSM persons were freshmen, sophomores, and juniors. The number of persons in these upper categories in the senior sample amounts to 25 and 31 per cent. The Free Speech Movement drew extraordinarily larger proportions of students with strong intellectual orientations, at all levels (freshmen through graduate)."[42]

If it is granted that the FSM political activists were academically more proficient and also (more importantly, in my view) more gifted with intellect, or more developed intellectually, than most other Berkeley students at the time, it may nevertheless be argued that the FSM'ers may have been more neurotically rigid or dogmatic than their peers. Did they tend to be "true believers" in Eric Hoffer's sense— young lunatics, eager to sacrifice themselves for extremist causes because they were attempting to flee from their own selves, seeking to escape unresolved neurotic problems?[43] In America it has been fashionable, as we have seen, even among social scientists, to associate political extremism with unresolved psychological problems.

William A. Watts and David N. E. Whittaker's study of FSM activists compared to Berkeley students generally started with the opposite hypothesis, however: "We expected that FSM members would be more flexible as defined and measured by personality tests of flexibility-rigidity . . . than their counterparts who were less committed, neutral, or even opposed to the Movement."[44]

Their study was based on questionnaires administered to a chance sample of 172 participants among the 1,000–1,200 students who "sat-in" at Sproul Hall in the afternoon of December 2, 1964 (and who were on this occasion not arrested, or not yet, except for the two-thirds who stayed on all night). In addition, the same questionnaire was given to a random sample of 182 Berkeley students at about the same time; 146 of these cooperated. The instrument included a twenty-seven-item rigidity-flexibility scale, which need not be described here. The most important result of this study, for present purposes, is its indication of "strong support for the prediction of greater flexibility among the FSM members." The authors conclude: "This latter finding is of particular interest considering the purported rigidity of the FSM members in negotiations with the University

[42] *Ibid.*, pp. 21–22a.
[43] Eric Hoffer, *The True Believer* (New York: Harper, 1951).
[44] *Op. cit.*, p. 2.

administration, and suggests the necessity of distinguishing between a trait of rigidity as psychologically defined and commitment."[45]

The other findings of the study by Watts and Whittaker should be noted in passing. First, with additional samples drawn for this purpose[46] they failed to establish greater academic achievement on the part of the FSM'ers compared to other students, and concluded that these activists were quite typical or average with respect to grade-point averages.[47] While Watts and Whittaker's objective check is more trustworthy than the data on grade-point averages reported in the Somers study, which were based on respondents' information, I am inclined to discount, until substantiated by further research, this particular finding by Watts and Whittaker, because it appears to run counter to so many other findings. It may well be valid for the 773 who were arrested, though I would like to see a replication of the study, which can easily be done; if it is valid for this group, I would still doubt that it is valid for FSM activists generally. It is possible, for example, that the most *academically* as distinct from *intellectually* oriented students[48] among FSM activists felt greater anxiety than the rest about their academic credits, and were more likely to shrink from taking the most extreme risks.

Secondly, the FSM students were far more likely to have parents with advanced academic degrees, compared to the cross-section sample: "approximately 26 per cent of the fathers and 16 per cent of the mothers of the FSM sample possess either Ph.D. or M.A. degrees compared to 11 per cent and 4 per cent respectively in the cross-section."[49] This finding does not contradict Somers' finding that student militants were more likely than the rest to have blue-collar fathers. Among several factors that could be taken into account here I would emphasize the difference between having militant attitudes and being prepared to jeopardize academic achievements; the

[45] *Ibid.,* pp. 16–18.

[46] One hundred eighty-one students' names were drawn from the district attorney's arrest list for December 3, while 174 names were drawn, again at random, from the student directory. *Op. cit.,* p. 10.

[47] *Ibid.,* p. 46.

[48] I discuss this distinction in "A Social Theory of Intellectual Development" in Nevitt Sanford (Ed.), *The American College* (New York: Wiley, 1962), pp. 984–985 and 991–994.

[49] *Ibid.,* p. 11 and Table 4.

value of academic credits may well look somewhat larger to the self-supporting student from a working class background, than they do to students from families in which academic proficiency or intellectual gifts or future financial safety tends to be taken for granted. The latter category among the militants may be more likely to risk jail and expulsion for their beliefs.

I have confined this brief inquiry to activists on the left, who are far more significant than those on the right, both by their numbers (at least in the better universities), and by their tendency to persist in political activities disturbing to the university "image" desired by most administrators and trustees. Insofar as rightist student groups, the most important one among them at the moment being Young Americans for Freedom, have staged demonstrations, they have usually been ad hoc counter-demonstrations, directed against issue-oriented protests by liberal or leftist student activists; there have been no protracted campaigns or even articulate political programs; and while student leftists have tended to be fiercely independent of older leftists, or of the "generation over thirty" generally, there has been no evidence of a corresponding intellectual independence among organized rightist students.

INDIVIDUAL POLITICAL RATIONALITY

The most promising approach to theorizing about the psychological nature of liberal and radical versus conservative political attitudes, I believe, is to consider what kind of functions political opinions may serve for those who hold them, in terms of their personality and social needs. It is quickly apparent that the function of serving a rational, realistic understanding of the political world is one but only one possible function of a person's "politics."

The overall function of any political or other social opinion, write M. Brewster Smith, Jerome S. Bruner, and Robert W. White, is to strike a "compromise between reality demands, social demands, and inner psychological demands."[50] Daniel Katz distinguishes between rationality (or reality-testing) motives, value-expressive motives, social acceptance motives, and ego defense motives.[51] These are sug-

[50] See their *Opinions and Personality* (New York: Wiley, 1960 [1956]), p. 275.

[51] See his "The Functional Approach to the Study of Attitudes,"

gested analytical categories; specific opinions usually serve a mixture of needs or motives. The relative weight of each type of motive varies from person to person, from attitude to attitude and from time to time; few of us, if any, are free of neurotic ego defensiveness, and none of us are free of social acceptance needs, or desires for consistency and for realistic understanding of the world in which we live.

In their 1954 paper, Irving Sarnoff and Daniel Katz applied their three[52] categories of motives in a discussion of a clearly *undesirable* type of attitude, namely anti-Negro prejudice; and one of their main concerns was to show how a better understanding of the motives of attitudes could facilitate processes of attitude change. Thus, to the extent that prejudice is rationally founded—on the basis, say, of the limited knowledge available to many a Southern American white boy or girl—it presumably can be influenced by new knowledge. To the extent, however, that prejudice is based on social acceptance motives, it will take evidence of an entirely different kind of influence or do away with it—namely evidence that such a change of opinion would not reduce a person's acceptance in whatever groups he wants to be or become part of. To the extent, finally, that ego defensive motives determine the prejudice, it may take psychotherapy to reduce it.[53]

All political and social attitudes may be analyzed in much the same psychodynamic terms; whether the attitude in question be deemed desirable or undesirable by the observer is an issue entirely independent of what processes may have shaped it. But if it is permissible to consider a certain type of attitude, like anti-Negro prejudice, undesirable, and a reasonable object of efforts toward attitude change, then surely it may also be permissible to make a normative judgment of the relative desirability of each type of motive on which political attitudes may be based.

Actually, what Sarnoff and Katz have done is not so much to argue that prejudice should be reduced, as it is to theorize about how

---

Public Opinion Quarterly, 1960, *24,* 163–204, and Irving Sarnoff and Daniel Katz, "The Motivational Bases of Attitude Change," *Journal of Abnormal and Social Psychology,* 1954, *49,* 115–124.

[52] Katz added a fourth, "value-expressive" type of motive in his 1960 paper (see note 51).

[53] If value-expressive motives are at work, to that extent the individual presumably would require assistance in restructuring his self-image without drastic loss of self-confidence.

it can be reduced, by way of first achieving a better understanding of its motivational bases. Similarly, all I wish to do for the moment is to theorize about how a more enlightened citizenship and a more "real" democracy can be achieved, by way of a better understanding of psychological obstacles to task-oriented intelligence and rationality in political opinion formation.

There is evidence, wrote Gardner Murphy more than twenty years ago, "that functional intelligence can be enormously enhanced, first by the systematic study and removal of individual and socially shared autisms, second, by the cultivation of curiosity, and third, by the art of withdrawal from the pressures of immediate external tasks, to let the mind work at its own pace and in its own congenial way."[54]

The most fundamental obstacle, of course, to the "freeing of intelligence" is the active presence of ego defensive motives. Severely repressed anxieties about one's worth as a human being, which may well be the result of a childhood starved of affection, may predestine a person to become a "true believer" in Eric Hoffer's sense—a person who seeks a new collective identity because he cannot live with his own self.[55] Such anxieties, if unresolved, may predestine a person to become an authoritarian or an anti-authoritarian[56] personality, a bigot, a right-winger, or, more rarely, a left-winger. This type of person is not psychologically free; his views may keep his anxieties and fears manageable but contribute no realistic understanding of the external political world.

Some of the data discussed above can be understood in this light; Adorno *et al.,* Rokeach, and McClosky all found right-wing

[54] See his "The Freeing of Intelligence," *Psychological Bulletin,* 1945, *42,* 16 and 1–19.

[55] See his *The True Believer, op. cit.* I do not accept the other side of his argument, however, asserting that all "fanatics" are fleeing from themselves, in this sense. This argument is profoundly conservative in the sense of being indiscriminately anti-extremist; cf. my argument above. A member of the French or Algerian *maquis,* or of the Viet Cong, surely may be a fanatic for other than personality-deficiency reasons; and so may an American, if, for example, he feels strongly about issues pertaining to justice or the use of violence. One does not have to be a neurotic to abhor the American warfare in Vietnam. Perhaps, on the contrary, one has to be in less than full control of one's rational faculties, whether due to paranoid anxieties or to the pragmatic intellectual constraints of political office or other social role, or aspiration, in order to support it.

[56] See my *Structure of Freedom, op. cit.,* pp. 207–217.

views statistically associated with indices of neurosis of one kind or another. But what of McClosky's finding that, for example, "liberals" appeared less hostile than "moderate liberals," and what of the data discussed in the preceding sections?

To account for such data we need to consider the prevalence of social acceptance motives, too, as obstacles to the freeing of political intelligence.[57] To the extent that a person is deeply worried about his popularity, his career prospects, his financial future, his reputation, and so on, he will utilize his political opinions not for achieving realistic insight but for impressing his reference groups and his reference persons favorably. These processes of obfuscation may be conscious or, more likely, subconscious, but they are above all pervasive in our society, and in every other society, too—above all in highly competitive and socially mobile societies, in which the difference between success and lack of it may make for vast differences in prospects for the satisfaction of physical and self-esteem needs, and perhaps for many other kinds of needs as well. Social-acceptance-motivated political beliefs serve the individual's desired image, status and career, and so on, but contribute little toward a realistic understanding of his political world—at least insofar as it extends beyond his immediate reference groups and persons.

Social-acceptance-motivated opinions may well tend to be liberal in some university faculties, as charged by some conservative writers, including conservative students wishing to explain why liberalism increases with amount of education.[58] But by and large, in every stable social order, they tend to be conservative, or at most mildly liberal, firmly within the established framework of constitutional objectives and processes. In every stable society there are rich and poor, strong and weak, privileged and underprivileged; and not only political power and influence but social status and respectability are associated with seeing political problems through the eyes of the former rather than the latter, in each paired category.

Statistically speaking, therefore, *more conservative views,*

[57] To simplify and to keep from prolonging the argument, I shall omit Katz's fourth type of motive, the value-expressive one, from further discussion here.

[58] For example, see Robert W. Naylor, "Why Intellectuals are Liberal," *Western Politics,* 1966, *1,* 33–37.

among students or adults generally, are likely to be less rationally, less independently motivated, than more radical-liberal views. I am by no means arguing, of course, that liberal and radical views cannot be neurotically motivated. The point is a more modest one: the frequency of neurotic motivations—now including not only deeply repressed anxieties about the individual's own worth but also milder ego deficiences such as constant worry about popularity or career prospects —is probably higher the further away the politically active person is from the left side of the political spectrum (I did not say left *end*).

The statistical data surveyed make good sense if viewed in this perspective. With reference to the Berkeley data, surely one should expect ego defensiveness to be manifested by a fear of anarchy and equality and lead the individual to detest both the style and the objectives of FSM-type movements. And the more intensely or neurotically one is preoccupied with career worries, the less one would be disposed to mingle with the student rebels; these students, more typically, appear to have decided that certain values are more dear to them than conventional career prospects. As rebels they are more likely to have made a choice and to have marshalled the intellectual and emotional resources, at some point, to stick to it, also in situations of severe stress. Obviously, some will for spurious or chance reasons pursue neurotic social acceptance needs with FSM-type groups as their reference systems; but this happens in almost every group, and is likely to occur with less frequency in a rebellious political action group than in less demanding and socially more homogeneous groups like, for example, fraternities and sororities.

As Albert Camus saw, only rebellion, on some level, can expand consciousness; "with rebellion, awareness is born." Awareness of being human, of being more than an aspiring carpenter, merchant, lawyer, educator, or military officer. Or dutiful son or daughter. "In our daily trials rebellion plays the same role as does the *'cogito'* in the realm of thought: it is the first piece of evidence. But this evidence lures the individual from his solitude. It founds its first value on the whole human race. I rebel—therefore we exist."[59]

Camus' portrait of the rebel presents a normative ideal in persuasive terms: to become fully human, a constant tendency to be

[59] See Camus, *The Rebel* (New York: Vintage, 1958 [1956]), pp. 15 and 22.

revolted by and to rebel against oppression and injustice is required. While I admit to sharing this normative position, my present argument is empirical, though speculative: I submit that it will help make sense of all the data reviewed in this paper if we consider Camus' rebel a developmental model—a probable type of person to develop to the extent that not only ego defensive but more mildly neurotic social acceptance anxieties are resolved or successfully faced up to.

This kind of theory is bound to be speculative if only because such social anxieties are so pervasive. Yet it is possible to argue that the various data associating leftism with academic competence, intelligence, psychological and socioeconomic security, and so on, may be seen as tending to support this theory. Further research in this area is desirable and feasible, and can be usefully focused by this kind of theory, as I argue in my conclusion.

The more secure and sheltered a person's infancy and childhood, and the more freedom that educational and other social processes have given him to develop according to his inner needs and potentialities, the more likely that a capacity for political rationality and independence will develop, simply because the likelihood of severe anxieties is relatively low. In addition, again converting Camus' ideal into empirical-theoretical currency, the better the individual has been able to resolve his own anxieties, the more likely that he will empathize with others less fortunate than himself. A sense of justice as well as a capacity for rationality is, according to this theory, a likely development in relatively secure individuals, whose politics, if any, will therefore tend toward the left—toward supporting the champions of the underdog, not the defenders of established, always unjust, institutions. And young people, with the proverbial impetuousness of youth, are likely to seek extremes of social justice, or militant means, simply because their emotions, and more particularly their sense of elementary morality and justice, have not yet been dulled by daily compromises and defeats to the extent that most older persons' emotions have been.

Now there are some older persons, too, who for all the toll of many years of practical experience, seem to have remained able to share the basic moral and political outlook (if not the views on tactics) of militant student activists. As I read some of Erik H. Erikson's recent work, he appears to conclude that man's sense of social responsibility and his degree of social sensitivity depend on his maturation beyond the Freudian psychosocial stage of genitality; he calls this hypothetically higher developmental stage *generativity:* "I refer to man's *love for his works and ideas as well as for his children,* and the necessary self-verification which adult man's ego receives, and must receive, from his labor's challenge. As adult man needs to be needed, so—for the strength of his ego and for that of his community—he requires the challenge emanating from what he has generated and from what now must be 'brought up,' guarded, preserved—and eventually transcended." Erikson describes parenthood as "the first, and for many, the prime generative encounter," but argues that those who approach or reach the generative stage of psychosocial development to that extent *need* to teach, to instruct and influence, and in other ways actively work for the good not only of their own children but of their community and their society, or mankind, as well.[60]

Let me sharpen my own position as follows: Every new human being is potentially a liberal animal and a rebel; yet every social organization he will be up against, from the family to the state, is likely to seek to "socialize" him into a conveniently pliant conformist.

Many parents and some schools are child-oriented, it is true, to the extent of trying to give children the security and freedom to develop according to their own inner needs and potentialities. With a good start of this kind, such children may, when they approach adulthood, be able to resist the socializing of privilege-defending states, universities and other established institutional pillars of the status quo; if so, they become the student rebels, the civil rights workers, or the peace activists. A small minority, but perhaps a growing one, at least in terms of influence among young people.

CONCLUSION

I have theorized about man's potentially liberal nature and about every society's and every social organization's tendency to defend established interests at the expense of the quest for justice and rationality that anxiety-free, radical liberalism would pursue. In our great universities this struggle between youthful radicalism and establishment conservatism, fortified by authority, full-time staffers, ample funds

---

[60] See Erik H. Erikson, *Insight and Responsibility* (New York: Norton, 1964), especially pp. 130–32. Also see his "Youth: Fidelity and Diversity," *Daedalus,* Winter 1962, *91,* 5–27.

and plenty of alumni and mass media support, is fascinating to watch because nowhere else do we find as gifted and spirited fighters, on both sides of the fence. Also, the composition of the student leadership changes from year to year, making it hard to predict from one year to the next where the lines of battle will be drawn.

While I have left no doubt where my sympathies are in this battle, my purpose in this paper is not to cheer for student political activism but to explain the nature of this phenomenon in line with existing empirical data. Having attempted to outline at least a direction for useful theorizing in this area, let me conclude by suggesting a few lines for continuing research.

First, however, may I admit to a charge that is likely to be fired against this paper: I agree that this paper, whatever else it may accomplish, does seek to dignify my own left-inclined views or prejudices with a garb of scientific respectability; I certainly do claim that leftist views, statistically speaking mind you, are associated with better education, fewer neurotic tendencies, and so on, than rightist views— or even than moderate, "centrist" views.

My defense is that a vast array of research data seems to me to support this contention and that there consequently is a case for saying it out loud, even if one is bound to provoke angry rebuttals. But these rebuttals ought to be fortified by data, too, if they are to be given weight. *Ad hominem* speculations about the possible motives of an individual author will hardly be of interest to many and will not contribute to a better empirical theory to account for the data reviewed.

How can we most fruitfully push for firmer and more extensive knowledge of the psychological determinants of political orientations?

1. Children's moral and political concepts, as they develop, must be much more studied. One Polish study by Hannah E. Malewska, for example, ought to be followed up: she found that children's notions of moral norms become more responsible (less formal and superficial) the less severely disciplinarian their parents and the more urbanized their surroundings.[61] Work on children's politics is on the increase, but often restricts itself unduly to cognitive aspects.[62]

[61] See H. E. Malewska, "Religious Ritualism, Rigid Ethics, and Severity in Upbringing," *Polish Sociological Bulletin*, 1961, *1*, 71–78.
[62] An exception is Fred J. Greenstein, *Children and Politics* (New Haven: Yale University Press, 1965).

2. Work on political socialization, especially on a comparative basis, involving similar as well as different socioeconomic orders, can do much to widen our understanding of the eternal tension between individual needs and socializing institutions.

3. Studies of student politics should be expanded, and be supplemented by studies, preferably simultaneous, of faculty and university administration politics—without assuming in advance that student politics should be the principal target of controls, or present the main "problem."

4. Patricia Richmond and I a few years ago found that among liberals in a pacifistically oriented organization, the more "extreme" supporters of rights of specific unpopular minorities tended to be somewhat less dogmatic, in Rokeach's sense, than the more moderate supporters of such rights.[63] More work is needed to improve on instruments like Rokeach's Dogmatism scale, and to develop additional instruments to measure neurotic obstacles to rationality in the general population, so that we might discover how widely and in what types of contexts it is true that resolution of anxieties and reduction of other psychological burdens stimulate tendencies toward rationality, political activism, leftism, and related phenomena.

5. The list could be prolonged, but let me in conclusion mention the valuable, still small but apparently growing literature that seeks in-depth understanding of the political views and their motivations in particular individuals, whether prominent or humble, and whether dead or still living. Harold D. Lasswell's *Psychopathology and Politics,* pathbreaking but dated, has been referred to above. A masterly political biographical study in psychological terms is *Woodrow Wilson and Colonel House* by Alexander and Juliette George.[64] Justly famous is Erik H. Erikson's *Young Man Luther*[65] Arnold A. Rogow's *James T. Forrestal* is particularly valuable for its searching analysis of the issues associated with possible mental disorder in high office.[66]

Among psychological studies of the politics of humbler individuals, who are left anonymous, reference has been made to Smith *et al., Opinions and Personality,* a study limiting its scope to attitudes

[63] Christian Bay and Patricia Richmond, "Some Varieties of Liberal Experience," unpublished paper, 1960.
[64] New York: John Day, 1956.
[65] New York: Norton, 1958.
[66] New York: Macmillan, 1964.

toward the Soviet Union.[67] Three other very useful works are Robert
E. Lane's *Political Ideology,* a study of fifteen "average" New Eng-
landers, mostly working men;[68] David Riesman's *Faces in the Crowd,*
dealing with "average" Los Angelese;[69] and an excellent Australian
study of five more or less politically active individuals, *Private Politics,*
by Alan F. Davies.[70]

The task of making psychological sense of the political views,
or their absence, in individuals, as much as in categories of individuals,
offers boundless opportunities for meaningful research.

---

[67] Smith *et al., op. cit.*
[68] New York: Free Press, 1962.
[69] New Haven: Yale University Press, 1952.
[70] Melbourne: Melbourne University Press, 1966.

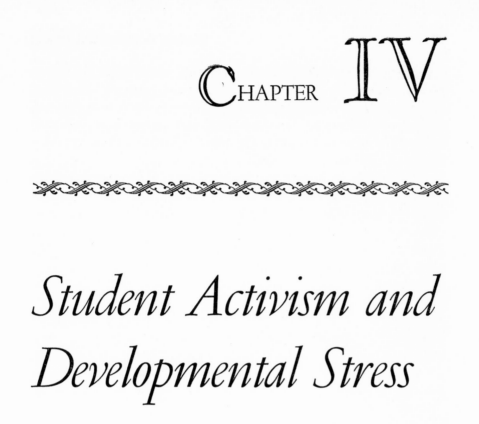

Chapter IV

Student Activism and Developmental Stress

Donald R. Brown

The American university suddenly finds itself catapulted out of the age of student apathy into a period characterized by activism often accompanied by violent disruptions of the university. Already the forces of reaction are mobilized to pressure administrators, particularly in public institutions, to get tough. The passion of the forces of law and order and the general public reflect the utter disappointment and lack of comprehension of a society that sees its most privileged sector seemingly rejecting the basic tenets of the American ethos. Indeed, the alarm has spread to the liberal Establishment as personified in the most distinguished person of George F. Kennan. As one reads his *Democracy and the Student Left,*[1] one cannot avoid the pathos of the confrontation of those who should be in agreement but who have fallen out over questions of means, of faith, and, most of all, of style—that is, civility, rationalism, and even physical appearance.

How can we explain the unquestioned fact that perhaps not more than 2 per cent of the total of American students can often command such wide support among their fellows about such issues as American foreign policy, the poor, civil rights, ROTC, defense research on campus, blacks on campus, and increasingly the curricular requirements and quality of teaching itself?

Most of the answers that have been provided tend to emphasize the crisis nature of the American campus scene in which youth have lost faith in the normal processes of government and its ability to right obvious wrongs. Mayor John Lindsay of New York expressed this view very succinctly in a speech at Yale reported in the *New York Times:*

> If you wonder why so many students seem to take the radicals seriously, why they seem to listen to clearly unacceptable proposals and tactics, ask yourself what other source in the past has won for itself the confidence of young people. Is it the government, telling us that victory in Vietnam was around the corner, or that we fought for a democratic ally that shuts down newspapers and jails the opposition? Is it the military, explaining Bemtre that "it became necessary to destroy the town in order to save it"? Is it the moralizer, warning of the illegality of marijuana smoking as he remembers

[1] Boston: Bantam Books, 1968.

90

fondly the good old days of illegal speakeasies and illegal bathtub gin? Is it the television commercial, promising an afternoon of erotic bliss in Eden if you only smoke a cigarette which is a known killer? Is the university, which calls itself a special institution, divorced from worldly pursuits, while it engages in real estate speculation and helps plan and evaluate projects for the military in Vietnam?[2]

The points made by Mayor Lindsay are not disputable—there is an increasing moral outrage on the campuses. Should this outrage be allowed to excuse the young from individual responsibility for their actions and from the need to approach solutions in the light of pragmatic reason rather than intuitive romanticism? It is over this difference of style that the forces are joined.

The matter of life-style may be a normal reaction to our current high degree of economic affluence. This difference has taken a tremendous amount of pragmatic pressure which used to work as an important force for controlling the young. We were unprepared as a society for this change but will presumably learn to live with it. Then one could argue that, if the war in Vietnam were resolved, if blacks were to make significant gains, if poverty were eliminated in America, and if the next President were a folk hero of the intelligentsia, then student activism would lose its appeal and all would return to normal on our campuses albeit with greatly increased student power as a result of current gains.

It is my thesis that, while the more violent outbursts may decrease, the basic sources of student unrest are only inflamed by these crucial social and political issues but not totally caused by them. The current issues provide the rallying point. Robert Frost is reported to have replied to a group of television reporters who wanted him to say that this is the worst or most dangerous or most difficult time man has ever lived through. After the poet was finally able to make himself heard above their persistent attempts to make him say what they wanted to hear: "Yes, yes, yes, it's a terribly difficult time for a man to try to save his soul—about as difficult as it always has been."[3]

There are student stress and unrest. To some extent there have

[2] *New York Times,* May 4, 1969.
[3] Spencer Brown, "We Can't Appease the Younger Generation," *The New York Times Magazine,* November, 27, 1966, p. 57.

always been unrest and considerable stress among university students. The upset follows from the nature of growth during late adolescence; it is exaggerated today, as it has been in other historical periods, by unusual and pressing social concerns. The real question is not whether student discontent is new but rather what accounts for it as a natural phenomenon of growth, and what *new* features of the present educational scene in America can account for its current manifestations, directions, and visibility.

Most discussions of this topic in recent months have concentrated on the very visible student outbursts, and as a result the student activist has captured the public concern. Such an image is unfortunate for a real understanding of what seems to me to be happening, both because it tends to dull us to the continuing and more subtle questions of the problems inherent in student development and because it emphasizes, contrary to Frost's warning, the crisis nature of the events only. This view, in turn, leads to seeking the sources of the problem solely in the external and institutional features of our society rather than, at least in part, in the developmental process itself. Also such explanations have the unfortunate tendency of excusing the individual from responsibility for his actions—a condition that would be very disruptive of our way of life if it were to increase even further among the young. Let me suggest rather that we look at student development as a process, an attempt to find the broader sources of unrest that support the increasingly frequent and very active outbursts.

First, however, consider the following statements, which seem to me to account for the greater visibility and activity of students on the national scene.

1. The college student population has grown astronomically since 1946. The more students, the greater the visibility and, more important, the greater the pressures which arise on campus from overcrowding and depersonalization.

2. College attendance is increasingly seen as a necessity in an ever-increasing technological and affluent society such as present-day America. Student population has increased far faster than the general population growth. However, the pragmatic relevance of college has decreased as affluence allows students to seek the social sciences and humanities versus the more directly applied areas of knowledge.

3. Students come from a wider range of the population on all

demographic dimensions than they previously did and, consequently, present new challenges to the colleges as socialization agencies. Here one need hardly make the obvious reference to the increasing presence of black students on the campus as a prime illustration of the changing sources of student population.

4. The post-Sputnik emphasis on the meritocracy and the sellers' market consequent to the increased numbers has put students under great competitive stress for admission even to the less prestigious institutions.

5. In terms purely of visibility, the news-hungry media tend to fan the sparks of unrest by massive and immediate publicity which has no trouble in finding among our campus population its own performers. The instantaneity of our current culture is frightening to behold. Students are exposed, through television, to a range of events occurring throughout the world almost as direct personal experience—events that were never experienced in a lifetime by the preceding generation. There is bound to be a generalization and spread of effect from campus to campus.

6. The sophistication of students about their individual rights in respect to the university and to the society and about the insensitivity of faculties and administrators within the institutions of higher education to the crying need for immediate and meaningful reform has increased considerably.

7. The better academic preparation in the secondary schools following the massive curricular reform movements which started in the middle 1950s has resulted, in part, in students who have tasted good teaching and want more of it.

8. Students are painfully aware of the contradictions of a society in which affluence and freedom exist side by side, for all to see, with poverty and the enslavement of ignorance, discrimination, and hopelessness. The hope is for peace but the harsh reality is war. The hope is for meaning but the immature can see only the hypocritical glitter of Madison Avenue materialism.

9. Emphasis on the existential view of self-determination, responsibility, and deep meaningful and personal communication on the essence of one's self-identity and existence is gradually replacing the older emphasis on pragmatism in action and privacy in personal matters as the mass ethic of the younger intelligentsia. This new em-

phasis is part of the conflict of style and faith so evident in the appearance and rhetoric of today's student leaders. It is also reflected in many art forms—for example, in two movies, *The Graduate* and *Joanna,* to single out a couple of popular examples.

10. The inherent loneliness of youth as it seeks self-definition and clarity has been increased by the rise of anonymity accompanying the moral blandness of a society in which guilt is hard to define and therefore impossible to expiate.

11. The student generation has a phobia of the increasingly technological mechanization of the societal means of dealing with large numbers, as personified in the IBM card, which threatens the less stouthearted with an overwhelming crisis of depersonalization. This phobia is coupled with a rather naive view that technology has advanced to the point where personal effort and work are no longer required except on the part of a few specially recruited and trained technicians.

12. The changing image of college life from the social to the intellectual has caused increasing numbers of entering students to have unrealistically high expectations of the curriculum, the faculty, their peers, and of the intellectual life which are unfortunately rarely fulfilled.

13. Physical maturation has been taking place at a lower and lower chronological age for the last several decades. While this speeding up of physical maturity has been going on, we have been systematically delaying psychological, social, and economic maturity in our student population by increasing the length of years devoted to study in preparation for assuming one's life roles. This kind of delay results in greater and greater delay of the independence and gratification that come with striking out on one's own—which traditionally took place at ages seventeen to twenty in previous generations.

In an attempt to explain the current manifestations of student unrest in contrast to its ultimate causes, it has been popular in sociological circles to emphasize the influence of peer groups for both educationally beneficial as well as intellectually pampering effects. Friedenberg states this view very cogently in his *The Vanishing Adolescent:*

In the adolescent peer group, youngsters not only teach one another;

they learn from one another. They learn to feel about others and about themselves and in some cases to love. Respect for real competence . . . is the trustworthy foundation on which real love must be built . . . and response to the hard-core of actuality in the person loved; it must be a response to the person-in-operation as a person, so to speak.[4]

Indeed, the partial surrender of autonomy to the peer group, be it a group that emphasizes conventional social responses, militant activistic responses, or Friedenberg's existential search for unity with one's fellows, at first blush seems to offer solace to the loneliness inherent in the adolescent situation, when much of one's energy is directed toward the question, What am I and where do I fit meaningfully into society? The trouble starts when the blush fades, and at some later point in life the inherent direction of becoming is stifled in the borrowed values of the groups.

I find it instructive to take a frankly individual developmental view of students. This is not to say that the social-cultural environment of the university does not play a very important role in the structuring of student life, but rather to point out that, regardless of the power of the group in influencing and directing the behavior of the individual —whether in a university or any other area of life—in the final analysis, the group operates as a subculture which provides a characteristic range of stimulation, goals, and rewards. For these stimuli, goals, and rewards to be effective, they must be perceived, internalized, and appreciated by the student. In the last analysis it is through the individual student that all group effects are mediated.

The reason for this disclaimer is to permit me to direct your attention to an approach to the understanding of the unrest of the students in institutions of higher education through a model which starts with a developmental theory of the individual in a complex social environment such as a university. I would argue that, if a student is thwarted and frustrated in this normative developmental sequence, he will, if he is to survive, often be forced to turn to readily available groups for his goals and rewards. At the present time, certain peer cultures categorized by social activism and protest are highly visible and, because of the lack of ideological commitment presently

[4] Edgar Z. Friedenberg, *The Vanishing Adolescent* (Boston: Beacon Press, 1959), pp. 65–66.

required for membership (in contrast to the movements of the 1930s and 1940s) all can easily gain entrance. These groups are especially attractive because they offer excellent opportunity for the expression of the moral outrage so present in many of our sophisticated and sensitive youth, and provide a sense of social accomplishment in a seemingly very complex and frustrating society.

This anchoring in a theory of individual development has many advantages when we are forced to operate, as we are, in a highly pluralistic educational structure such as ours. Let me try to make this point and some of my previously listed statements clear by referring to descriptions of students and their approach to education in different historical eras. It is helpful before one views the present situation with alarm to look back with Robert Frost and try to understand the alarming situations of the past.

George Stern has called my attention to a statement by one of the great Eton masters written in the 1860s—a period when education of any sort was reserved for a social, cultural, and economic elite.

> You go to school at the age of twelve or thirteen; and for the next four or five years you are not engaged so much in acquiring knowledge as in making mental efforts under criticism. A certain amount of knowledge you can indeed with average faculties acquire so as to retain; nor need you regret the hours that you have spent on much that is forgotten, for the shadow of lost knowledge at least protects you from any delusions. You go to a great school, not for knowledge as much as for arts and habits; for the habit of attention, for the art of expression, for the art of assuming at a moment's notice a new intellectual posture, for the art of entering quickly into another person's thoughts, for the habit of submitting to censure and refutation, for the art of indicating assent or dissent in graduated terms, for the habit of regarding minute points of accuracy, for the habit of working out what is possible in a given time, for taste, for discrimination, for mental courage and mental soberness. Above all, you go to a great school for self-knowledge.[5]

As one ponders Cory's statement, one cannot but be reminded of the old warning that the metaphysics of yesterday is the common sense of today and the nonsense of tomorrow. That is to say, that while

[5] William Cory, "Eton Reform," quoted by G. Adan, "William Cory," *The Cornhill Magazine*, 1938, p. 208.

what Cory described as the goals of a liberal arts education still hold today as they did in the 1860s in upper-class England, nonetheless the sociological derivations of our students in the university and college of the 1960s differ considerably, and twenty-five years from now will differ even more. For many years our students came from much the same class as those that Cory was describing; but sometime shortly after World War One, the proportion of Americans attending high school increased astronomically and this desire for education burst into the college scene about the time of World War Two. It has been increasing ever since so that today we find it necessary to think at least twenty-five years ahead in order to be prepared for the ever-increasing onslaught of students. This trend is bound to have far-reaching consequences on the nature of education and the needs that students bring to our institutions of higher learning. How has this manifested itself since World War Two?

Consider the bulging enrollments immediately following the war, when the veterans were flocking to our campuses. These were young men and women of above average college age who had been brought up during the Great Depression and then found themselves deeply involved in World War Two. Their values and goals were clear. They knew who the great enemies were. First, there were the problems of economic inequity and irresponsibility, which could be defeated by the "new economics," and later there were the evils of totalitarianism and fascism, over which they had waged a long and bitter struggle ending in total victory—or so it seemed. Now they retreated to the nurturing security of alma mater, with the help of a benevolent GI Bill, to prepare themselves for the fruits of a better life for which they had made so many sacrifices. Today, of course, this is the generation over thirty. They knew what they were doing in college and their devotion to their studies and pragmatic approach to the curriculum had profound effects on the university. Practically overnight the Hollywood rah-rah culture of the campuses was dealt its death blow and was ultimately finished off by the rise of the meritocracy following the launching of Sputnik. They had seen society marshal its resources and solve, at least for the time, economic and political problems of life-or-death proportions. Faith in an ordered and continued use of intelligence and sustained effort within the social mechanism was the lesson which they brought out of their experience. The present generation suffers from having the benefits of affluence, which has insulated them from the opportunity, delusional as it may seem, to see society solve problems at first hand.

Immediately following this group on the campus there came the children of the new affluent society now coming to college in larger numbers than ever before and consequently from much more diverse educational and cultural backgrounds. Our attention was called quite forcibly to their appearance and to the disparity from the good old days at "City College," when, as memory had it, no one but first-class intellects with real commitment and social concern manifested on every side populated the campuses. Philip Jacob, in his study on value change in college students, summarizes the orientations of the group as: (1) an absorbing self-interestedness, directed essentially toward satisfying the desires for material well-being, privacy within one's own male-oriented family domain and relief from boredom; (2) group dependence, which causes students to bring personal conduct and standards into line with the expectations of groups to whom they turn for a sense of belongingness, or look upon as vehicles to self-advancement; (3) social and political indifference and irresponsibility; and (4) an instrumental approach to reason and morality, which pulls them into the service of pre-set personal goals.[6]

Jacob was, of course, describing what we all came to think of as the age of student apathy—in many ways a most comforting age during which to be a member of the Establishment. Contrast this with a quote from an article which appeared in the University of Michigan student newspaper. "The American student is breaking out of his cocoon" is the lead.

> The eruption started in the late 50's when students (whose older brothers and sisters had thought the smooth move was to mind one's own business) were stirred by the civil rights movement and began to emerge from their study carrels and fraternity houses to make their dent on the world. They were a new generation bred in prosperity. These students did not remember the war. To seek material reward—the house in Scarsdale, the pretty wife, and the steady job —was not enough because it was so obtainable. To be satisfied with

[6] Philip Jacob, "Social Change and Student Values," in D. R. Brown (Ed.), "Social Changes and the College Student: A Symposium," *Educational Record,* 1960, *41*(4), 338–341.

the return to normalcy was not enough because normalcy was already the way of life. They took their tactics from Gandhi, their idealism from philosophy class, their money from Daddy. They worked hand in hand with civil rights groups such as CORE, NAACP, SNCC, and SCLC. The results of the movement were civil rights acts, the voting rights bill, and the emergence of the American student. Realizing that they had the power to influence events, students broadened their involvement so that it ranged from criticizing foreign policy to organizing the poor. Thus, the idealism of the civil rights movement led to an alienation from the multi-university and the hope for an idealistic "community of scholars" as the way for the future. The democratic nature of the movement led students to hope that they could have a meaningful voice in governing their own affairs at their universities; and the success of the movement made students realize that they could implement their goals.[7]

This passage makes it appear that the vast majority of students were caught up in the rising activism of the civil rights movement and ultimately in the concern about the nature of the university. We know from the work of Katz and Sanford that at most only about 15 per cent of the students on an extremely active campus are so involved.[8] Granted that these descriptions, which are applicable to historical periods over the last hundred years, refer not to the modal situation but rather to the salient situation. They do tend to represent the highly visible peaks of student behavior in the mass rather than individual students on the one hand or the majority of students on the other. These are the dominant images that characterize the periods, not necessarily the dominant behavior. They do represent, however, a powerful force.

If we take a demographic view of the matter and attempt to understand these seeming changes in the value orientation of the university students as reflections of the population from which they are recruited, we must admit that college attendance has not only increased numerically but has increasingly attracted segments of our population with different life expectancies from those to which the more traditional liberal arts curriculum was originally attuned. We are dealing here with what Joshua Fishman referred to as a population

[7] *Michigan Daily,* February 20, 1966.
[8] Joseph Katz and Nevitt Sanford, "Courses of the Student Revolution," *Saturday Review,* December 18, 1965, pp. 64–67.

change rather than a value change.[9] For example, the increasing numbers of veterans attending college on the GI Bill and its various revisions since World War Two, working class children attending on government loans or state scholarship programs, the meritorious attending on National Merit Scholarships and similar competitive awards for students with outstanding high school attainment, Negro youth attending on the various new grants directed toward their recruitment —all of these groups bring new value constellations to our colleges, and the realities of their post-college lives will undoubtedly be different from those of the classical liberal arts college student, who could postpone his vocational plans until graduate school and even, sometimes, forever. It is interesting to speculate on the differences in the atmosphere of universities which follow from the obvious fact that not only have the sources of students changed, as the well-established universities have increasingly culled the cream of admissions, but also at the same time the recruitment of faculty has been very much influenced by these previous population shifts in college attendance. It is not idle speculation to propose that a large proportion of faculty just now entering into senior positions, not to mention junior faculty, come from the GI Bill crop which flooded graduate schools with the sort of Ph.D. material that rarely aspired to such educational heights in an earlier era. As I look back on my own college experience, I am struck by how much more similar in socioeconomic background current faculties are to their students than were my faculty, who tended to represent a kind of upper-class, traditional, scholarly gentlemen with considerable family wealth. All this is bound to make for profound changes in our universities.

Let me now try to analyze this diverse population and present some theoretical assumptions about the nature of development in students. For the sake of argument I will maintain that at the moment students come to us holding, to varying degrees, one of the following often mutually exclusive stereotypes or images of the purpose of higher education.

Our current research shows that students tend to preselect themselves not only into differing universities but even into different programs within the same university in a manner which is highly

---

[9] Joshua Fishman, in D. R. Brown, *op. cit.,* pp. 342–345.

correlated with which of these images they hold as measured by self-nomination on the Clark-Trow types.

The first of these images is that of the development of the intellect and the growth of the personality. Here the emphasis is on the broadening of the intellectual horizons of the students along with consequent maturing and stabilization of the personality. The liberal arts curriculum as classically defined is accepted as the golden road to these goals and the product is hopefully "cultured." The stress in this type of education is on being rather than on doing. The image is best represented by the statement that I quoted from the Eton schoolmaster, Cory. Friedenberg, in his *Coming of Age in America,* puts it in more modern terms:

> The highest function of education I would maintain is to help people understand the meaning of their lives, and become more sensitive to the meaning of other people's lives and relate to them more fully. Education increases the range and complexity of relationships that make sense to us, to which we contribute, and on which we can bring to bear ethical and practical judgment.[10]

This image is increasing today but with a certain anti-intellectual insistence on "relevance" and direct experiential emphasis so well illustrated by the increasing popularity of sensitivity groups and non-content-oriented experiential courses.

Second, there is the still widely held image of college as a place to acquire occupational training. As a society becomes both affluent and technologically advanced, the demand for highly trained personnel increases. The colleges rush in to fill the demands of the market, albeit sometimes with reluctance. The university, particularly the public university, experiences great pressure from its constituents to fulfill this type of demand. This pressure, at the same time, increases the demand for a college degree as it cheapens it as a symbol of professionalization. The degree comes to cover a multiple of sins committed in the name of education. All sorts of occupational groups join in and demand college programs in their fields. One often has the feeling that in such programs fake pearls are being cast before real swine. The emphasis in this kind of education is on doing and on

[10] Edgar Z. Friedenberg, *Coming of Age in America* (New York: Random House, 1965), p. 75.

being able to do rather than on being. These students have resolved the question of identity prematurely, perhaps. They tend not to be attracted by movements espousing social change, since their purpose is to join the mainstream at a step up the ladder.

The third dominant image relates to the collegiate fun culture, which is the one most often portrayed in the mass media image of college, particularly before the rise of the meritocracy. However, the idea of college as a never-ending series of increasingly romantic social events leading to blissful union to be punctuated by glorious home-comings is still a real image for adolescent girls in particular. Here the emphasis is on learning the sex role as popularly conceived. Per-haps this image never did exist to the extent that Hollywood and college fiction would have it.

The students, coming as they do from the larger society, bring with them one or another of these three views of higher education. Therefore, they start their college experience with views that are to varying degrees incongruent with the generally held values of the faculty and the high-sounding official ideology of the institution. The faculty see themselves as seekers of knowledge in specialized areas and privileged critics of the society. Indeed, they demand special privileges of tenure and academic freedom in order to permit the un-hampered pursuit of these goals. In recent years, because of the nature of the market, they have indeed demanded almost complete freedom even from teaching. At the same time they are asked to educate a semi-captive audience which holds values often widely discrepant from their own and often widely variant within any given classroom. Here certainly are the seeds of conflict and the resolution of this conflict is often stressful. The students are not without resources of their own for avoiding the issues of this conflict and the educational benefits which can fall from its rational resolution. They can create a "peer culture" that either largely perpetuates the general societal values held outside the college and turn to this new subculture for their goals and their rewards, or openly challenges the state of society and provides a comfortable way to engage in social and individual revolt. It is the latter peer-group identification which is becoming more and more frequent and which achieves the highest visibility on campuses today.

The challenge for the university is to become aware of the groupings and subcultures that exist among students so that they can rationally plan to enlist the very powerful forces inherent in these groups to influence the openness of their members to educational experiences. At this point, we see the mediation between the individual view and the social group approach.

As we have seen, the society and, indeed often, the university are not completely clear about the goals of higher education. Therefore, it is not surprising that the students, unable to face the multiplicity of challenges to their self-image, find themselves forced to seek clarity in group identifications which reinforce the old and familiar or set new and often rebellious goals. In the case of male students, with their ever-increasing commitments to an occupational role, the ability to fuse the contrasting value orientations is often rather painless and usually proceeds with considerable social support in the service of occupational preparation. Such an effort can, however, result in considerable stress due to unrealistic aspirations and consequent fear of failure or to insensitive and arbitrary parental pressure for one role over another. The situation is not so painless for women, and, indeed, with the increasing intolerance for idiosyncratic roles such as that of feminism, the situation is becoming more confusing rather than less. In the case of women, the whole question of the nature of sex identity and its relation to the intellectual life casts a very disturbing complexity over the whole issue.

Having described the general area of conflict inherent in society and in higher education, let me now turn to the entering freshmen. If we think of the stage of late adolescent development that precedes young adulthood, we can assume that the entering college student is somewhere in this stage on his way to goals of higher integration and more precise differentiation of the personality. The striking fact of this stage is the ascendancy of the cognitive and rational controlling mechanisms over the impulses which previously dominated the determinants of behavior. These controls are not yet mature; they tend to be rigid, overdetermined, and impulse seems capable of bursting through at any point. This is true to some extent of all of our students.

Sanford, in *The American College,* has put it well when he describes the freshman as follows:

The freshman tends to be like a convert to adulthood, an enthusiastic supporter and imitator of adult ways who knows what it is to backslide—which he sometimes does. The achievement of flexible control, the arrangement in which there is genuine freedom of impulses because there is little danger of their getting out of hand lies ahead; nevertheless impulses are now inhibited or contained with sufficient effectiveness so that the young person can turn his attention to other matters. He is now ready to concentrate upon his relations with the external world—to improve his understanding of that world and to find a place within it.[11]

This state of affairs offers both an opportunity and a danger to the development of a system of adult values. After all, one of the main functions of the university is to develop resources within the individual where that particularly human function—the ability to evaluate and act on the basis of one's evaluational decision—is fostered. Turned as they are to the outside world, freshmen are sensitive to and capable of identifying with a whole new range of adult models and institutions on which can be based an often new and broader sense of values. However, also as a consequence of increased awareness and greater cognitive sensitivity, the freshman becomes aware, often for the first time, of the corruption, hypocrisy, and cynicism to be found in many corners of a complex society such as ours. Freshmen are brought together in new groupings with new temptations and challenging, exciting activities and intellectual patterns. We have recently seen some of the results of this awareness where it would appear that a significant minority of the students have suddenly taken the first image of higher education that I presented very seriously indeed only to discover that the institution, or "Establishment" as they refer to it, was no longer as committed to this intellectual image as they had been led to believe. Indeed, a lot of the recent conflict on the campuses centers about the students' discovery that the university is not devoted solely to their immediate and personal educational development. To many of them this seems like a betrayal, but, of course, on more mature reflection they come to realize that the multiplicity of the university is but a mirror of the multiplicity of the society which it serves. Perhaps institutions of higher education ought to have re-

[11] Nevitt Sanford (Ed.), *The American College* (New York: Wiley, 1962), p. 260.

mained more aloof from the pressures of the society that support and create them. This is a large issue in itself.

Upon the freshman's arrival at college, to some extent the immediate support of family and community are withdrawn or at least become more distant, often as contact is made with a new set of values. On today's educational scene, the student faces considerable sources of threat and consequent distress from the homogeneity resulting from selective admissions which tend to cast doubts on the academic competence of the student, from the relative lack of structure and externally imposed schedule that he had in high school, from his generally increased workload, from his doubts of social confidence in the new—seemingly sophisticated—environment, from the rapidly apparent discrepancy between expectations and reality, and finally, from the often great distance maintained by the faculty.

The freshman understandably seeks new sources of support in the face of all these assaults. The easier choice is the readily available support of peers who can minimize the threat by offering subcultures in which the student can more readily determine his own stake by his choice of an appropriate subculture from among those available. Of course the choice itself is stressful—but infinitely less so than going it alone. If this total identification with the peer culture which can exist within and on the periphery of an institution persists for four years in an unaltered form, education is likely to be a failure. It will fail either because the student keeps a value structure which developed before college and which will remain untested against the broader horizons of the university, or because, in his anxiety to avoid rejection by the valued group, he will adopt a set of values by simple imitation. Values acquired in this manner, whether from faculty or through the influence of student culture, are not internalized but are merely borrowed for the occasion. For values to become internalized they must be reflected on and made the object of the individual's best efforts at judgment and decision making.

Closely related to the internalization of value is the development of self-esteem, which also is at first very sensitive to the appraisal of peers and of faculty. The development of self-esteem will ultimately lead to a sense of identity and mastery, but this goal may take all of college and longer to reach. One of the most convincing defenses of the intensive major in a curricular structure is the kind of mastery, and its implications for the development of the individual, that can be achieved by study of a subject in depth. It is important that the institution provide an open channel for its students to switch identities often during their college careers, to avoid both too narrow a range of choices and too early a commitment which will hamstring the individual for life. For example, a young woman who flees into marriage in the sophomore year has chosen sides too soon to maximize her development.

It remains, then, a challenge to higher education to guide the student through this crisis in values toward the ability to evaluate and judge what is perceived in a way that permits change and development, and, indeed, nurturance, but does not lead to complete alienation from parents, community, and society. What is desired is an internalized sense of values based on a strongly developed sense of dignity and pride in self.

What can the college do to foster growth during these years? In general there are three main dimensions along which students can be expected to grow; they are very much influenced by the curriculum, the available peer cultures, and the nature of the residential structure of the institutions. They are:

1. Freeing of impulse through the opportunity to learn and manipulate the symbols of human experience in imagination through contact with literature, philosophy, and the arts while not directly committing oneself. Let us not underestimate the value of empathy through imagination in the overall educational process.

2. Enlightenment of conscience to the point where the individual believes in what he ought to do because he has arrived at a moral code by reasoned judgment. Contact with diversity, training in disciplined analysis of thought, and a tolerant but committed faculty who make their own values explicit to the student are invaluable here, along with sound liberal arts coverage of content.

3. Differentiation and integration of the ego such that the student increases his scope while becoming at the same time more of a unity. That is, perceptions and thought become more and more differentiated and personal responses more and more discriminating and interrelated. Then a young woman, for example, could see herself as being feminine and educated.

I would suggest that the problem that faces the university of today, and one which will increase in the future, is how to bring together in the common pursuit of these intellectual and personal goals an increasingly diverse supply of students, who are drawn more and more widely from all areas of the population as the economic wherewithal for education becomes more available. It seems obvious that in order to accomplish this challenging task, the university must bring student groups into the service of student development. In order to do this, colleges must operate on several levels at once. For example, it has long been assumed by the better residential colleges that students largely educate one another, even in the most rigorous academic disciplines. While this may still be true in the small residential colleges, unfortunately with the rapid expansion and increasing specialization of knowledge coupled with the increasing cafeteria-like offerings of our universities, it is rare in the larger universities that two students come together outside of class who have a common academic experience to share. Given the inherent shyness of young people, coupled with their great need to communicate with one another, a situation which throws them together in a university but provides little shared intellectual experience will quite naturally lead them to seek ways of interacting that are not necessarily congruent with the purposes of the university and indeed are often openly anti-intellectual. Therefore, the university should consider new ways of grouping students in the curriculum, in the residential arrangements and in scheduling such that larger numbers will have some common shared intellectual life which will serve as a foundation for intellectual and social interaction. Very often students are forced in their noncurricular groupings into nonintellective areas of concern by the denial of easily integrated experiences which stem from the academic content of their institutional endeavor.

Two projects at the University of Michigan are relevant here. The first project is the Pilot Program. It was conceived as a way of reducing the stresses inherent in the divorcement between intellectual values and the residential life of a large campus. This was most manifest in the lack of intellectual life in the residence halls at the university. The Pilot Program, then, is a community in revolt against the forces of anonymity and alienation which threaten to undermine the educational objectives of a large university. The program consists of approximately 600 volunteer entering freshmen of both sexes in the literary college. They are assigned to the dormitories, known as the Pilot Residence. These students are permitted to register for sections of regular introductory freshman courses which are reserved for members of the Pilot Program only. Thus the student might conceivably find himself in as many as three of his freshman courses along with his immediate dormitory mates. There is no infringement in any way on the right of the student to choose his curriculum within the structure of the college rules. In addition, the instructors of these sections are made aware of the nature of the Pilot Program and are encouraged to have meals in the Pilot Houses with their students and, indeed, if at all possible, to schedule class meetings within the dormitory as well. A further aspect of the Pilot Program involves the selection of specially selected resident fellows who act as counselors and tutors to the students. These fellows are selected from among the graduate students on the basis of their intellectual commitment and ability to serve as intellectual mentors rather than as disciplinarians in the dormitories and are expected to offer a problem center course which may be elected by Pilot students.

The program is the responsibility of a committee of faculty from the College of Literature, Science, and the Arts, and of representatives from the residence halls personnel of the university. This committee is somewhat unusual in that it attempts to institute policies in almost every area of undergraduate education, including staffing of residence halls, design of undergraduate courses, academic counseling, as well as registration and classification procedures. The committee reports directly to the dean of the college.

So far the program does not sound startlingly different from what has been occurring at other institutions in recent years. The program, however, does have some unique features, and I shall limit myself to mentioning two of them. The first is that it is considered frankly experimental and therefore is being continuously evaluated from a variety of points of view. The point of view that interests us most is the perspective on the development of students and the implications for student stress and unrest. A study of Pilot students with comparison students in the Literary College as a control shows that the Pilot students tend to self-select themselves into the program on the basis of a greater need for contact with faculty. This need for contact with faculty seems to be based upon their recognition of a greater sense of dependency and requirement of intimacy on their part. They tend more often to come from smaller high schools and small towns than from large urban centers. They recognize before coming to the university the threat of size and consequent anonymity. The Pilot Program students at the end of the year express far greater satisfaction with the nature of residential life at the university and, in particular, with the quality of the residential staff. They are more critical and demanding of faculty and faculty performance but are also more satisfied with the progress they have made in the freshman year and the overall quality of the university.

One of the most striking conclusions from the evaluation of the Pilot Program so far is the amazing amount that can be accomplished in reducing student stress and loneliness while increasing student dignity and competence (as measured by standardized instruments such as the Student Activities Index[12] and College Characteristics Index[13]) by such relatively simple and inexpensive devices as the grouping and scheduling of students. Perhaps the major implication is the obvious working of a Hawthorne effect. If so, then along with Nevitt Sanford, I would say that we should maximize the new and the exciting in our educational arrangements, in order to increase this kind of involvement on the part of the faculty and students.

One reason for emphasizing techniques such as these for reducing stress can be found in the data we have collected on three successive cohorts of entering freshmen. In the course of a large number of paper-and-pencil questionnaires and inventories, the students were asked to complete the College and University Environment Scales.[14] Our students filled out the CUES battery before they arrived at the university and were asked to complete the inventory as a description of the university as they expected and hoped it would be. The students under these instructions described their expectations about the uni-

[12] George Stern, "Student Activity Index," Psychological Research Center, Syracuse University, 1958.

[13] George Stern and C. Robert Pace, "College Characteristics Index," Psychological Research Center, Syracuse University, 1958.

[14] C. Robert Pace, *College and University Environment Scales* (Princeton, N.J.: Educational Testing Service, 1963).

versity on the five scales which Pace has developed from the instrument as follows:

They do not see the university as a place where practicality will be greatly emphasized. The Practicality scale consists of a "combination of items which suggests a practical, instrumental emphasis on the college environment. Procedures, personal status, and practical benefits are important. Status is gained by knowing the right people, being in the right groups and doing what is expected. Order and supervision are characteristic of the administration and of classwork. Good fun, school spirit, and student leadership in campus social activities are evident."[15] Interestingly enough, those items which the students do choose in the scaled direction refer with great agreement to good fun, school spirit, and student leadership in campus social activities. Other data from upperclassmen would indicate that this part of the entering student's perception of the university is quite unrealistic in terms of present student life.

Similarly, the students score much higher than one would expect on the Community scale, which consists of items portraying "a friendly, cohesive group-oriented campus. The environment is supportive and sympathetic. There is a feeling of group welfare and group loyalty which encompasses the college as a whole. The campus is a community. It has a congenial atmosphere."[16] While it is true that there is a sense of community to be found on a campus like Ann Arbor, it is almost a caricature to describe it in the above terms. Any student who seriously expects to find this kind of small college and small town atmosphere is bound to have to make some serious readjustments in his expectations, with consequent distress and unrest.

Pace's Awareness scale is practically a description of my three dimensions of student growth discussed above. The items included reflect "a concern and emphasis upon three sorts of meaning—personal, poetic, and political. An emphasis upon self-understanding, reflectiveness, and identity suggest the search for personal meaning. A wide range of opportunities for creative and appreciative relationships to painting, music, drama, poetry, sculpture, architecture, etc., suggest the search for poetic meaning. A concern about events around the

[15] *Ibid.*, p. 24.
[16] *Ibid.*

world, the welfare of mankind, and the present and future condition of man suggests the search for political meaning and idealistic commitment. What seems to be evident in this sort of environment is a stress on awareness, an awareness of self, of society, and of esthetic stimuli."[17]

On this scale the entering students see the university as being an environment totally of this sort. Of the thirty items on the scale, these pre-freshmen see their prospective campus in this light at least 70 per cent of the time on each item. Since the instructions ask the students to describe the university as they hoped and expected to find it, one can assume that the students are committed to the notion of self-development and intellectual growth, albeit perhaps unrealistically or even romantically. While it is true that the university strives to be this sort of place and, as a function of the self-selection of students who share these expectations, is to a large extent such an environment, it falls far short of the hopes and aspirations of these entering students. Take, for example, the item which is agreed to by 99.7 per cent of the sample, "tutorial and honors programs available to qualified," or the near unanimous agreement with the expectation that "a noted philosopher-theologian would always draw a capacity crowd at a lecture." It seems unlikely that a student who shared the expectations on this scale would not find some disappointment and consequent unrest before the end of the freshman year.

On the other hand, the students do seem to be aware of the general lack of propriety on such a campus, which has often been the complaint of the administration and some faculty since they score extremely low on this scale measuring "an environment that is polite and considerate."

And finally, on Pace's Scholarship scale the entering students again score extremely high, agreeing over 75 per cent of the time with twenty-six out of the thirty items. These items are descriptive of the state of scholarship they expect on the campus. They "describe an academic scholarly environment. The emphasis is on competitively high academic achievement and a serious interest in scholarship. The pursuit of knowledge and theories, scientific or philosophical, is carried

[17] *Ibid.*, p. 23.

out rigorously and vigorously. Intellectual speculation and interest in ideas as ideas, knowledge for its own sake, and intellectual discipline— all these are characteristic of the environment."[18]

Here again one cannot help wondering whether the 80 per cent of the students who expect most professors to be thorough teachers who will probe fundamentals, or the 97 per cent who expect that lectures by famous scientists will always be very well attended, or the 80 per cent who hope that class discussion will typically be vigorous and intense, will find their hopes realized. One cannot help being impressed by the source of stress which may well arise in students holding these expectations for their education, if not for themselves, at least for their peers, when they come up against the realities of academic life on a large, albeit good and exciting, campus. Indeed, one wonders if any faculty could live up to the image that these students see as their hope for the next four years.

It is even more incumbent for the institution which projects such an image to the high schools to find ways of maximizing its realization of this image for the students. The Pilot Program described above is one such attempt. Another at the University of Michigan is the Residential College for 1,200 students in the liberal arts. Here a faculty committee has had the opportunity to plan during a leisurely period of three years a total college, complete with its own physical plant. The unique features of this college, as compared to any other existing small residential college, are that this college is an integral part of a large university with all of the resources of a large university at its service. To maximize these resources, this college does not have a separate faculty but draws upon the regular faculty of the university for its staff on a part-time basis. In addition, this plan is unique in that the living arrangements and their relationship to the intellectual environment of the college were designed by faculty in complete coordination with the structure of the curriculum before the college started. Furthermore, there was the opportunity to pretest certain of the new core courses in the Pilot Program described above. Finally, its uniqueness stems from a concerted effort to apply the knowledge of student development and evaluational techniques directly to the continuing evolution of this institution.

[18] *Ibid.,* p. 25.

To evaluate the effects of the Residential College on its students a carefully controlled study has been designed with the cooperation of five other universities conducting somewhat similar experimental in- novations for undergraduates. They are the University of California at San Diego, the University of California at Santa Cruz, Florida State University, the University of Kansas, and the University of the Pacific. At each of these schools, representative samples of entering students have been studied on a variety of instruments, self-reports, intensive interviews, and participant observation by a team of technographic observers. I shall limit myself to a few comments about the findings from the Michigan study only. In this instance all students entering the Residential College in two successive years were asked to partici- pate in the study with data being collected before entrance, at the end of the first year, and at the end of the second year. The pro- cedure was repeated on a second cohort now about to enter their second year. In addition, the observers also studied a control group of students who had requested admission to the Residential College but for whom there was not space available, but who are attending the larger liberal arts unit in the university and are matched to those who are in the Residential College, as well as a further control group of the individuals in the larger college who had not expressed interest in the Residential College.

I will refer only to findings that are statistically significant and that relate to our concern with student stress and possible disruptive action. First of all, on entrance the students who volunteer for the college describe themselves as more intellectual and academic in their orientation than do students not interested in the Residential College experience; they are matched on all other entrance criteria. Following a year in the college, these students express phenomenally greater satisfaction with faculty than their controls at the University of Michigan, greater satisfaction with their peers, and moderately more satisfaction with the administration. The above result holds in spite of a very high change in all measures of liberalism and anti-authoritar- ianism among these students, even though all the groups entering the university are reasonably high on measure of liberalism and anti- authoritarianism upon entrance. On each of the measures which relate to the dimensions of growth to be expected within the model I pre- sented during college attendance, the Residential College students show greater change over the period studied than the control groups.

On measures of how one spends one's daily time in the academic setting, the Residential College students have far more time spent in the company of faculty, actual academic classroom peers, college administrative officials, and resident fellows. They report a greater proportion of time spent in academic pursuits such as studying and intellectual activities in open discussion as well as greater participation in esthetic and cultural activities available at the university than either of the control groups. They report far greater involvement and feeling of participation and control in the daily life of the college and of their own academic career.

One might expect a paradox in the increase in liberalism along with the greater sense of satisfaction. However, this is explainable in terms of the possibility of complete community government which can take place in a unit of the size of the Residential College, which currently consists of approximately 500 students but will ultimately include 1,200 students. There have been several occasions over the last two years when very significant issues have been raised by the students in the direction of reform of the quite rigorous core curriculum required of these students. In each instance, the students found that open confrontation tactics seemed simply out of place in the governmental structure and the possibilities for change which were open to them. As a result of rational discussion and constitutional procedures, in two instances going all the way to hearings with the board of regents, changes have been made which have satisfied the vast majority of the students in the college as well as the faculty and administration. It is interesting to note that during the very year when the undergraduates of the larger liberal arts college of the university carried on an intensive campaign to abolish the foreign language requirement for the Bachelor of Arts degree almost to the point of disrupting the university, the students in the Residential College voted to retain the much-more rigorous language requirement which is included in their curriculum after prolonged discussion of the merit of the issue and the value of language instruction as well as the type of language instruction which is most productive. In the larger college, no such dialogue seemed capable of emerging and the issue was fought on a power basis only.

Perhaps the best indication of our effectiveness in respect to providing an academic environment in which the students can express their concern and effect responsible action is the reaction of the local SDS, which admits that the Residential College provides an unproductive source of recruits because we have "co-opted" their militant stance into the service of the "new Establishment." One should not conclude that the students in the college are lacking in political involvement. Quite the contrary. The college had the largest per capita involvement in a sit-in staged at the local county building in support of aid to dependent mothers and raised the largest per capita amount to provide bail money for those members arrested. During the 1968 presidential campaign, the students of the Residential College were far more active than a comparable sample of students in the larger university. On every measure of involvement in national and local issues, the students show a higher level of concern. At the same time, they are far more involved directly in the local political and academic issues in running their college.

As the results of the studies reported here only very sketchily become available, it is assumed that changes will be fed back, not only into the Residential College and Pilot Program but into the life of the university itself. It may well be that the only feasible way for a large university to organize its governmental structure would be to break the students into academically relevant groupings such that student government representatives could speak for some real constituency to whom they were responsible and in contact with, rather than to continue the current practice of campus-wide elections.

The implication of these educational experiments for student unrest is quite clear. The assumption is that a large part of student stress and unrest is due not only to conditions beyond the campus—although these conditions have become more determining than in the past—but to the discrepancy between students' expectations and preparations for college today and the reality of our institutions and the rate of growth that has taken place with consequent changes in the socialization problems which face the university. Hopes for intimate contact with faculty and peers, the expectation of a sense of community, the existential hope for deep interpersonal and intrapersonal communication, and the need for true intellectual stimulation can make for an exciting student body, but it can also make for a restless college if the institution is not ready and structured in such a fashion that it can meet these hopes for any but a small segment of the student body.

It is interesting that in an earlier study[19] in which the perception of the ideal student by a faculty was probed, it was found that what the current students seem to expect in terms of the nature of their university experience and of their own development at the university was precisely what faculty responded to in their nominations of ideal students during the senior year at Vassar. If we could arrange the mechanisms inherent in large complex environments such as ours so that these two sets of expectations and desires could be better matched, perhaps a very important source of student stress could be eliminated. It is my hunch that only a variety of academic formats, of which I have referred to only two possibilities, will decrease the sense of anonymity and powerlessness which today's students find so frustrating and depersonalizing. Such restructuring could provide the opportunity for the kind of growth and increased humanness that we all hoped a higher education in a free society would provide. The experience that students can gain in the creation and change of such colleges, where the opportunity exists for their direct participation in these changes, could bode well for future creative change in the larger society to which they will bring their skills and enthusiasm as well as the faith that they will have acquired in their ability to effect constructive social change.

[19] Donald R. Brown, "Non-intellective Qualities and the Perception of the Ideal Student by College Faculty," *Journal of Educational Sociology,* 1960, *33*(6), 269–278.

CHAPTER V

Social and Cultural Meanings of Student Revolt

Richard Flacks

117

The phenomenon of student rebellion has, in the past year, come to appear international in scope. During the past few months student demonstrations and strikes have paralyzed universities and shaken the political systems in societies as far apart, culturally and geographically, as Japan and France, Mexico and West Germany, Czechoslovakia, Italy, and Brazil. The simultaneity of these outbursts and the similarities in style and tactics of many of the student movements have led many observers to assume that there is a worldwide revolt of the youth, which is new historically, and which derives from a single set of causes. It is obvious, however, that student movements, acting in opposition to established authority, are not at all new. For example, student revolutionary activity was a constant feature of Russian life during the nineteenth century. It played a major role in the revolutions of 1848 in Central Europe. The Communist movements in China and Vietnam grew out of militant student movements in those countries. In Latin America, student movements have been politically crucial since the early part of this century. Youth and student movements were a dramatic feature of life in pre-World War One Germany; the Zionist movement among European Jews had its roots in the German youth movement. Since World War Two, student movements have helped bring down regimes in Asia and Latin America. It is clear that the events of recent months are in certain respects merely further expressions of a long tradition of student rebelliousness.

But just as it would be a mistake to think that the student revolts are historically new, it would also be an error to uphold the conventional wisdom which asserts that youth are "naturally" rebellious, or idealistic. There are, of course, good reasons for believing that some segments of the youth are likely to be particularly disposed to revolt, particularly attracted to new ideas, particularly prepared to take direct action in behalf of their ideals. But it is by no means true that rebellious, experimental, or idealistic behavior is a general characteristic of young people—indeed, it is probably the case that in any historical period the majority of the young, as Bennett Berger has remarked, are not "youthful." Moreover, it is even less true that youthful impulses in support of radical change inevitably take the form of distinct, autonomous political movements against the established political system. For instance, such movements have been quite rare in the United States and other advanced Western countries until the present decade. Although significant minorities of students and other young people have been active participants in movements for social change in the United States, Britain, France, and the smaller capitalist democracies, these societies have not had movements created by and for youth, independent of adult organizations, containing a strong element of rebellion, not only against injustice, but against the authority of the older generation. The feeling that there is something new about generational revolt is not accurate in global terms; but it is substantially correct for societies like our own.

There is a need for a theoretical framework to account for the emergence of oppositional movements among youth—a framework which can embrace the fact that such movements have become a feature, not only of developing preindustrial societies, but of apparently stable advanced industrial nations as well. In searching for such a framework, two classical theoretical perspectives might be expected to provide some help. One, obviously, would be Marxian theory, which, after all, was created in an effort to account for the rise of revolutionary movements in contemporary society. But Marxism, since it emphasizes the role of classes as revolutionary agencies, has a difficult time assimilating student revolutionary action. First, students do not themselves constitute a class. Second, students do occupy class positions, but these are very typically privileged ones. Indeed, one fact about the American student movement is that participation in it tends to be associated with high family status and income,[1] and the same pattern may be found in other countries as well. Thus, a problem for Marxian theory of revolution would be to account for the mass defection of students from their families' class, and for the tendency of privileged youth to identify with the plight of the dispossessed in their society. This is particularly problematical in the advanced industrial societies: here we have a situation in which at the present time organized political and cultural opposition to capitalism appears to be more extensive and militant among students than among workers. There

[1] D. Westby and R. G. Braungart, "Class and Politics in the Family Backgrounds of Student Political Activists," *American Social Review*, 1966, *31*, 690–692.

is no straightforward way to derive this fact from the body of Marxian theory.

A second theoretical perspective which one might find useful is that of Parsons. Indeed, one of the few theories about the conditions giving rise to generational conflict is that of Eisenstadt,[2] whose perspective flows directly from Parsons. This perspective focuses less on the revolutionary thrust of student and youth movements than on their functional character. What is most salient to Parsons and Eisenstadt is the formation of distinctive groups or movements among persons at the same stage in the life-cycle. The appearance of such groupings among youth is seen as a consequence of the differentiation of the family from the occupational structure, resulting in a sharp discontinuity between the values and role expectations operative within the family and those prevailing in the larger society. As youth move out of the family and experience such discontinuities, major problems of socialization are created by the necessity for youth to successfully orient toward occupational roles. Such problems are not manageable within the family, nor within institutions of formal schooling. What is needed are institutions which can combine some of the features of family life with those of the occupational structure. Youth groups, youth cultures, and youth movements serve this function of aiding the transition to adulthood by combining relations of diffuse solidarity with universalistic values.

This perspective predicts that the sharper the disjunction between family values and those in the larger society, the more distinctive and oppositional will be the youth culture. In particular, one would expect that students in societies undergoing a rapid breakdown of traditional authority, and in which new bases of legitimation had not yet been established, would most acutely experience problems of achieving adult status, and would be most likely to form autonomous, oppositional movements. By the same token, young people in the advanced, stable, industrial, democratic societies, although experiencing marked discontinuity between familial and occupational roles, would not experience the same intense cultural dislocation found in develop-

[2] S. N. Eisenstadt, *From Generation to Generation* (Glencoe, Ill.: Free Press, 1956); and Talcott Parsons, "Youth in the Context of American Society," *Daedalus,* 1962, *91,* 97–123.

ing countries. For, although familial and occupational roles are dis-
junctive in advanced industrial countries, families in these societies
tend to be congruent in their values and expectations with other institutions. Thus the industrialized societies would exhibit distinctive
youth cultures, but these implicitly support other socializing agencies
in identity formation and orientation toward adulthood. In short, the
Parsons-Eisenstadt perspective leads us to expect student movements
in societies where traditional authority is disintegrating under the impact of industrialization, Western ideas, and modernizing trends, and
where families continue to adhere to traditional culture. Depicting
industrial societies as ones in which both parental and political authority support modernity and change, this perspective leads us to expect
a distinctive, but integrated, youth culture, but not an alienated,
oppositional, revolutionary one in societies like our own.

As I have suggested, this perspective was a viable one—until
this decade. Now each passing year makes it less and less easy to assume the stability of the developed Western societies, less and less
safe to adopt the view that the United States represents some culmination point in cultural development, or that there is a fundamental
congruence among socializing, political, and economic institutions and
the values which prevail within them in our society.

A comparative perspective on student movements and generational revolt leads us to seek a theoretical framework which transcends
the Marxian view of the sources of revolutionary impulse in capitalist
society, and the Parsonian view that such impulses are not characteristic of advanced industrial society. If such a framework existed
it would undoubtedly constitute a synthesis of Eisenstadt's insight that
student movements are a symptom of cultural disintegration and the
Marxian insight that capitalism and its culture are themselves unstable
and capable of being negated.

If recent events lead us to discard the view that student movements are characteristic only of societies in which traditional culture
and authority are breaking down, we nevertheless ought to be able to
specify why such movements have been endemic under such conditions.
The Parsons-Eisenstadt hypothesis provides us with at least a partial
answer: the university student in an agrarian society is someone who
is compelled to abandon the values with which he was raised, who is
exposed to a set of new cultural influences, but who is becoming an

adult in a historical period in which the new values have not been
clarified, new roles have not been created, new authority has not been
established or legitimated. The student movement, with its diffuse,
fraternal interpersonal life, its identification with the masses or the
people, its disdain for privilege and authority—combined with a commitment to rationalism, democracy, nationalism, and other "modern"
values—enables them to develop the political skills and motives which
may be necessary to challenge the established elites, enables them to
undergo the personal transition which is an aspect of the historical
transition through which the whole society is going.

In addition to this hypothesis, which locates the sources of
"strain" in the cultural and psychological consequences of modernization, there are at work in such societies other equally powerful factors
which make such movements extremely likely.[3] There is, for example,
the widely remarked fact that typically in developing countries there
is an "overproduction" of educated youth—the available jobs for
university graduates often are not commensurate with the training or
aspirations they have as a result of their educational attainment. Prospective or actual unemployment, and the frustration of aspiration, is
presumably a politicizing experience for many educated youth in such
societies.

Another politicizing and radicalizing feature of these societies
is, of course, the backwardness and authoritarianism of political authority. Political authority in these societies plays a paradoxical role for
students; on the one hand, it sponsors the formation and expansion
of a university system in order to promote technical progress, while
simultaneously it resists the political, social, and cultural transformations which such progress requires. In this situation, students inevitably
come into conflict with the state and other established elite institutions.
Obviously, the more intransigent the established elites are with respect
to nationalist, democratic, and modernizing aspirations, the more likely
it is that the student movement becomes the breeding ground for a
"counter-elite," and the spearhead of revolutionary politics.[4]

[3] Seymour Martin Lipset, "Students and Politics in Comparative Perspective," *Daedalus*, 1968, *97*, 1–28; P. Altbach, "Students and Politics,"
Comparative Education Review, 1966, *10*, 175–187.
[4] J. Ben-David and R. Collins, "A Comparative Study of Academic

Still another factor likely to generate discontent is the quality of life in the universities of these societies. Living and working conditions are likely to be extremely impoverished. The schools are likely to be overflowing, the quality of instruction and facilities for study are likely to be totally inadequate, and material poverty among students is likely to be substantial.

If cultural disintegration, overproduction of the educated, reactionary regimes, and university conditions generate discontent leading to politicization and radicalism, additional factors promote the emergence and growth of autonomous student movements in developing nations. For example, the autonomous character of student movements in these countries is facilitated by the absence of other oppositional forces. To the extent that peasants, workers, and other strata are poorly organized or passive or suppressed, students, with their high degree of interaction and their sophistication, may become the only group in a society capable of initiating oppositional activity. Moreover, students may have a degree of freedom for political action which is not available to other opposition forces. This freedom may in part be due to the fact that many student activists are the offspring of elite or upper status families, in part because of the recognition of the fact that students are indispensable to the future of the society, in part because of an established tradition of university autonomy which makes it illegitimate for police power to invade the campus. Given the relative leniency toward students, and the ambivalence of authorities toward them, instances of repressive action taken against students are likely to be especially discrediting to the regime. Thus, the weakness of other oppositional forces, the wide opportunities for intensive interaction available to students, the large numbers of students likely to be concentrated in particular locales, and the special freedom for political expression which they are likely to have all combine to foster the growth of a student movement as an independent oppositional movement.

The conditions we have been describing may be regarded as the classic pattern presaging the emergence of students as a revolutionary force. Put another way, these conditions help us understand

Freedom and Student Politics," in Seymour Martin Lipset (Ed.), *Student Politics* (New York: Basic Books, 1967), pp. 148–195.

why student oppositional movements have been a regular feature of developing societies.

Our analysis has suggested that the classical student movement is a symptom of marked cultural incoherence, of political stagnation, and of severe problems of identity for educated youth in the face of the social and technological changes associated with the process of modernization. Because this analysis emphasizes that student movements are an aspect of the modernization process, it appears to be quite inadequate for accounting for the rise of student movements in societies like our own, which are not agrarian, which are not dominated by traditional culture and authority, which are not struggling to achieve national identity and independence, where democratic, rationalistic, and egalitarian values prevail, where families orient their offspring toward active achievement in a technological society, where the freedom to organize political opposition is available and used. At least at first glance one would be led to believe that the advanced industrial capitalist societies of the West would provide the least hospitable soil for a revolt of educated youth.

Yet a student movement has grown up over the past decade in American society. Over these years, it has become increasingly radicalized, and indeed now includes an avowedly revolutionary wing. Like the classical movements, it contains a strong component of generational revolt—that is, of implicit and explicit hostility to the authority of older generations, and an emphasis on the moral superiority of the young as such and on their capacity to be an agency of social transformation. Like the classical movements, the student movements of the West are intensely anti-authoritarian, egalitarian, and populist. They also resemble the classical type in being completely independent of other, "adult" political groups.

Are there any ways to comprehend the appearance of such a movement in American society that will account for its comparability with classical student movements?

The most parsimonious hypothesis, perhaps, would focus on possible similarities between the immediate situation of the student in the advanced industrial societies and in the developing countries. For example, it seems plausible that the rapid expansion of higher education, with its great influx of young people to the universities, has led to a devolution in the quality of educational institutions and of student life in the United States and Western Europe. It is also plausible that the rapid growth in the numbers of educated youth has produced the same kind of sectional unemployment of the educated which is present in the developing nations.

There may be considerable validity to these hypotheses; indeed, much of the commentary on the French student revolt has emphasized these factors as crucial ones. But it is much harder to see how they can be applied to the American case. For instance, data on the distribution of student protest on American campuses quite clearly show that the student movement had its origins at the highest quality state universities and prestigious private universities and colleges, that the movement continues to have its widest following on such campuses, and that it has only recently spread to schools of lower prestige and quality.[5] There is, in short, a negative correlation between the quality of an institution and the proportion of its student body which is activist, and between the selectivity of an institution and the radicalism of its student body.

It is equally hard to make a case that the student movement in the United States originates in overproduction of educated youth. In the first place, there is no dearth of opportunity for college graduates. Still, one might hypothesize that students who are attracted to the movement experience "relative deprivation"—for example, they may be students who cannot hold their own in academic competition. The data on student protesters indicate otherwise, however; there is, in fact, a tendency for activists to have above average academic records in high school and college, and most of the several studies on student protesters indicate they include a disproportionate underrepresentation of students with poor academic records.[6] Student protesters come from families with high income and occupational status; they tend to be most prevalent at the top schools; they have above average aptitude for academic work, and perform at above average levels. If there is an overproduction of educated youth in this society at this time it is hard

[5] Richard E. Peterson, *The Scope of Organized Student Protest in 1964–65* (Princeton, N.J.: Educational Testing Service, 1966).

[6] Richard Flacks, "The Liberated Generation: An Exploration of the Roots of Student Protest," *Journal of Social Issues*, 1967, *23*, 52–75.

to see how this would affect the structure of opportunities available to the academic elite from which activists tend to be recruited.

It seems clear that any effort to explain the rise of a student movement in the United States must take account of the fact that the movement originated among highly advantaged students, that it did not begin as a revolt against the university, and that its active core contains many students whose aptitudes, interests, values, and origins suggest a strong orientation to intellectual and academic life.

Indeed, one of the most striking findings about American activists has to do with their intellectualism. I refer here not only to the variety of studies which find activists exhibiting intellectual interests and achievements superior to those of the student body as a whole; more persuasive and more sociologically relevant are findings concerning the socioeconomic backgrounds of participants in protest activity. These findings may be briefly summarized as follows:[7] activists are disproportionately the sons and daughters of highly educated parents; in a large proportion of cases, their parents have advanced graduate and professional degrees; a very high percentage of activists' mothers are college graduates; the parents tend to be in occupations for which higher education is a central prerequisite: professions, education, social service, public service, the arts; both businessmen and blue- and white-collar workers tend to be underrepresented among the parents of activists; family interests—as they are expressed in recreation, or in dinner-table conversation, or in formal interviews—tend to be intellectual and cultural and relatively highbrow; these are families in which books were read, discussed, and taken seriously, in which family outings involved museums and concert halls rather than ball parks and movies. They were families in which values were taken seriously—conventional religion and morality were treated with considerable skepticism, while at the same time strong emphasis was placed on leading a principled, socially useful, morally consistent life. They were, finally, families in which education was regarded with considerable reverence and valued for its own sake, rather than in utilitarian terms.

In short, the student movement originated among those young people who came out of what might be called the intellectual or

[7] *Ibid.*

humanist subculture of the middle class. In the last two years, it has become considerably more heterogeneous, but it was created almost exclusively by offspring of that particular stratum.

At first glance, it would seem that nothing could be more incomparable than the situation of these middle-class American youth and the situation of educated youth in underdeveloped countries. The former, as we have said, can look forward to an array of high status occupational opportunities. Their lives as students are well subsidized, comfortable, and intellectually rich. Their parents are highly "modern" people, playing central cultural roles, well informed about and sympathetic with the latest cultural developments. All of this is especially true in comparison with the position of educated youth in developing countries, whose futures are extremely uncertain, whose lives as students are likely to be meager and oppressive, whose families are likely to be locked into traditional ways and attitudes and stand as positive hindrances to the emancipation of their children.

These contrasts are striking, but they may be quite superficial. What I want to do is to restate some of the major factors which we have seen to be central in accounting for the appearance of classical student movements—and try to determine whether comparable factors are at work in American society, especially in relation to the situation of students who come out of the educated middle class.

We have said, after Eisenstadt, that a central determinant of the appearance of youth and student movements is sharp discontinuity between values embodied in the family and those emerging in other institutional contexts. From this perspective, as we have suggested, the student movement serves as a secondary institution—a way of reestablishing family-like solidarity to ease the achievement of independent adult identities and role-orientations. For youth in developing countries, discontinuity arises because of the fundamental conflict between the traditional orientation of the family and the modernizing orientations encountered in the university and the cosmopolitan community associated with it. This kind of discontinuity could not be one experienced by the offspring of the educated middle class in America—if anything, students from this stratum are likely to experience less disjunction between familial and university values than any other group of students. But there are grounds for feeling that humanist youth in America do experience a kind of discontinuity between family and

larger society that may have comparable implications for the establishment of identity.

Our studies of the parents of student activists show that these
parents differ from others in the middle class in the following respects:

First, as mentioned above, there is a strong commitment to
intellectuality and culture, and a considerable disdain for mass culture
and mass leisure. Their children were expected to be intellectually
aware and serious, artistically creative or at least appreciative, serious
about education and self-development.

Second, these parents were unusual in their political awareness
and their political liberalism. Although they were not necessarily
politically active, they tended to stress to their children the necessity
for social responsibility and service, and active citizenship, and encouraged their children to support racial equality, civil liberties, and
other liberal political goals. In this respect, these families were likely
to see themselves, correctly, as different from the vast majority of
politically passive or conservative families in their community.

Third, these parents were overtly skeptical about conventional
middle-class values, life-styles, and religious orientations. Most of these
parents were explicitly secular; those who were actively religious
tending to belong to particularly liberal religious denominations, or to
have a strong social gospel kind of religious commitment. Many of
these parents were articulate critics of conventional middle-class mores
—by which, in particular, they had in mind sexual repressiveness,
materialism, status-striving, and strict methods of rearing children.
Many were quite explicit in hoping that their children would be more
successful than they had been in leading self-fulfilling, socially responsible lives rather than participating in the "rat race," the "suburban
way of life," the "commercial world."

Finally, these parents tended to express these values implicitly
through the structure of the family and the styles of child rearing which
they adopted. These were parents who encouraged self-expressive and
independent behavior in their children, who interacted with each
other and with their children in relatively democratic ways, who refused to impose conventional stereotypes of masculine and feminine
conduct on their children (for example, they tended to foster esthetic
and intellectual interests in their boys, and assertive behavior on the
part of their girls). It was not that these parents were unusually "per-

missive" or overindulgent—for instance, their very explicit expectations about intellectuality and social responsibility indicate that they did not adopt a laissez-faire attitude toward their children. But they rather consciously organized family life to support anti-authoritarian and self-assertive impulses on the part of their children, and rather clearly instructed them in attitudes favoring skepticism toward authority, egalitarianism, and personal autonomy.

Now what happens when these intellectual, anti-authoritarian, socially conscious, somewhat unconventional children move on to school and street and peer group? I think it is clear that they are likely to experience a considerable discontinuity between the values they encounter in these settings and the values with which they were raised. They are likely to find authority in school to be petty, arbitrary, repressive. They are likely to feel considerable isolation from the conventional culture of their peers. They are likely to be particularly sensitive to the hypocrisies, rigidities and injustices of particular institutions and of the society as a whole as they experience it.

Most American youth experience some dislocation as they move from their families into the larger society, if for no other reason than that the rapidity of social change prevents any family from adequately preparing its offspring for the world as it actually is developing, and because proper, moral behavior for children in the American family is inescapably different from proper, moral behavior in the competitive, impersonal society beyond. The existing primary and secondary institutions—school and youth culture—which Parsons and others have expected to be serviceable in easing the transition to adulthood, have failed to incorporate humanist youth, who were in fact raised to question many of the fundamental premises of these institutions. As more and more such youth have entered upon the scene, they have tended to find each other, and to create a kind of counter-culture, much as black urban youth, similarly unincorporated, have created theirs. This new humanist youth culture embodies norms concerning sex-role behavior, worthwhile activity, and personal style which are quite opposed to those which prevail in conventional adolescent society; it expresses values which seem quite subversive of conventional middle-class aspirations, and an attitude toward adult authority which is quite clearly defiant. The American student movement is an expression of that new youth culture, although by no means the only one.

In a peculiar sense, then, the appearance of a student movement and a rebellious youth culture in American society in recent years supports the Eisenstadt hypothesis that such phenomena are rooted in sharp discontinuities between family values and values in the larger society. It is a peculiar kind of support for that hypothesis because, unlike the classical case, the discontinuities we refer to do not have to do with incongruence between a traditional family and a modernizing culture. If anything, the reverse may be the case.

As we have suggested, a second major factor contributing to the rise of classical student movements has been the overproduction of educated youth—a factor which appears to be largely absent in the American situation. Nevertheless there are severe problems for humanist youth with respect to vocation. These problems have to do not with the scarcity of opportunity but with the irrelevance of the opportunities which do exist. One of the most characteristic attributes of students in the movement (and an attribute which they share with a large number of apolitical students) is their inability to decide on a career or a vocation. This indecision is less the result of the wide range of choices available, than of the unsatisfactory quality of those choices. What is repellent about the existing opportunities is not that they are incompatible with the status or financial aspirations of these youth, but that they are incompatible with their ideals. Business careers are rejected outright as acquisitive, self-seeking, and directly linked to that which is defined as most corrupting in American society. Careers in government or conventional politics are regarded as either self-deluding or selling out. Professional careers—particularly such established professions as law and medicine—are attractive to some, but only if one can become a doctor or lawyer outside of the conventional career lines; otherwise such careers are regarded as just as acquisitive as business. Teachers and social workers are seen as agents of social control; a few are attracted to scholarship or science, but with profound anxiety. To take an ordinary job is to give up any chance for leading a free life. In general, embarking on a career within the established occupational structure is regarded as morally compromising either because it leads to complicity with established interests or because it requires abandoning personal autonomy or because it draws one away from full commitment to radicalism or because it signifies acceptance of the norms and standards of bourgeois society or because it means risking corruption because of material comfort and security.

Although some of these attitudes are undoubtedly the result of participation in the movement rather than a determinant of such participation, it is clear that an underlying revulsion with conventional adult roles and established, institutionalized careers pre-dates movement involvement for many students. One reason for believing that it does is the fact that such revulsion is observable among young people who do not become political activists; indeed, a widespread restlessness about becoming committed to conventional careers and life-styles is evident on the American campus. This has been particularly surprising for those of us who remember the decade of the fifties and the prevailing feeling of that era—namely, that affluence was producing a generation which would be particularly conformist, complacent, status-conscious, and bourgeois.

It now appears that the opposite may be equally true. Although people with high status and material security may typically be motivated to maintain their position, it is also the case that being born into affluence can foster impulses to be experimental, risk-taking, open to immediate experience, unrepressed. For some, at least, growing up with economic security in families of secure status can mean a weakening of the normal incentives of the system and can render one relatively immune to the established means of social control, especially if one's parents rather explicitly express skepticism about the moral worth of material success. Postwar affluence in our society has had the effect of liberating a considerable number of young people from anxieties about social mobility and security, and enabled them to take seriously the quest for other values and experiences. To such youth, established careers and adult roles are bound to be unsatisfying. What is the sense, after all, of binding oneself to a large organization, of submitting to the rituals, routines, and disciplines of careerism, of postponing or foregoing a wide range of possible experience—when there is little chance of surpassing one's father, when the major outcome of such efforts is to acquire goods which one has already had one's fill of, when such efforts mean that one must compromise one's most cherished ideals?

In newly industrializing societies, students become revolutionaries, or bohemians, or free intellectuals and artists, because established careers commensurate with their education had not been created. In our society, large numbers of students do the same, not because opportunities for conventional achievement are absent but because they are personally meaningless and morally repugnant. We began with the proposition that a blockage of economic opportunity for the educated is a determinant of student movements. Our comparative analysis leads us to a reformulation of this proposition: any condition which leads to a weakening of motivation for upward mobility increases the likelihood of student rebellion. Such conditions can include either blocked opportunity or high levels of material security. In short, when numbers of youth find occupational decisions extremely difficult to make, their propensity for collective rebellion is likely to increase.

What we have so far been discussing may be described as a kind of cultural crisis—the emergence of a sector of the youth population which finds its fundamental values, aspirations, and character structure in sharp conflict with the values and practices which prevail in the larger society. We have said that, in certain respects, this conflict is similar to that experienced by youth in societies undergoing rapid transition from traditional to modern culture—and in both cases, we find these youth responding to their crisis by banding together in movements of opposition to the older generations and attempting to generate what amounts to a counter-culture.

In some ways, this kind of crisis is not new in American society. For more than a century, at least, small groups of intellectuals have expressed their revulsion with industrial capitalism, and the commercialism, philistinism, and acquisitiveness they saw as its outcome. By the turn of the century, what had largely been an expression of genteel criticism was supplanted by a more vigorous and intense revolt by some educated youth—expressed through bohemianism and through a variety of political and social reform movements. Indeed, opposition to Victorian morality and business culture has been characteristic of American intellectuals in this century,[8] and the emergence of large numbers of humanist youth out of relatively intellectual families is an indication of the impact this opposition has had on the society. What was once the protest of tiny pockets of intellectuals and artists has

[8] Richard Hofstadter, *Anti-intellectualism in American Life* (New York: Vintage, 1966).

become a mass phenomenon, in part because the ideas of these earlier critics and reformers were taken up in the universities and became part of the world-view of many members of the educated middle class. These ideas influenced not only sentiments regarding commercialism, material success, and intellectuality, they also had a direct bearing on the treatment of women and the raising of children, since an important element of anti-bourgeois thinking had to do with the emancipation of women and the liberation of the child from repressive and stultifying disciplines.

What is new in this decade is, first of all, the degree to which this cultural alienation has become a mass phenomenon—an extensive, rooted subculture on the campus and in major cities, with a wide and steadily growing following. Equally important, the present movement is new in the degree to which it has expressed itself through political opposition—an opposition which has become increasingly revolutionary, in the sense that it has increasingly come to reject the legitimacy of established authority and of the political system itself.

As we have previously pointed out, political rebellion by students in other countries has largely been a response to authoritarian, reactionary regimes—regimes which were incapable of or unwilling to adapt to pressures for modernization, and which tended to meet such pressures by attempting to repress them. Thus, classical student movements tend to arise out of the cultural crisis created by the processes of modernization, and tend to go into active political opposition when the political system stands against those processes.

It is perhaps hard for American social scientists to understand why American students should undergo a similar reaction to the American political system. After all, many of them have spent years demonstrating that the system was pluralist, democratic, egalitarian, and highly flexible; thus, while it may be rational for Russian, Chinese, or Latin-American students to have become revolutionary in the face of tsars, warlords, and dictators, it is, for them, irrational for students in the United States and other Western countries to adopt revolutionary stances against liberal, democratic regimes.[9]

To understand why the cultural alienation of intellectual youth in America has become politicized and radicalized requires a historical

---

[9] Nathan Glazer, "Student Power at Berkeley," *The Public Interest,* Fall 1968, 3–21.

analysis, the details of which are beyond the scope of this paper. Without attempting such an analysis we can, I think, at least point to some of the most relevant factors.

The first point would be that culturally alienated intellectuals in America have not historically been revolutionary. They have, instead, either been antipolitical or have placed their hopes in a variety of progressive reform movements. In part they have been sustained by the view that the national political system, whatever its flaws, had progressive potential because of its democratic character. They have also been sustained by comparisons between the American system and the rest of the world.

During the New Deal and World War Two period, a kind of culmination was reached in the formulation of an ideological perspective for the educated class in America. At the heart of this perspective was the view that inequality, injustice, and business culture could be controlled and offset by effective political and social action through the federal government. The rise of labor as a political force, the passage of social legislation, and the subsidization of reform by the government would create the conditions for a just and humane society. Not incidentally, the expansion of the public sector would also create vast new vocational opportunities for educated people with humanitarian concerns—in education, in social service, in public health, and mental health, and child care, and public planning, and all the rest. Thus the creation of the welfare state and an American version of social democracy was crucial for the expanded intelligentsia, not only because it provided a solution to the social ills that contributed to their alienation, but also because it offered a way to realize themselves vocationally outside of the business economy and in terms of their values. It was in this ideological milieu that the parents of the present generation reached maturity.

In the past twenty years, however, two things have been happening simultaneously: on the one hand, the ranks of the educated middle class have greatly expanded, owing in considerable degree to government support of higher education and of public sector types of occupations which required advanced education; on the other hand, the social benefits anticipated from this development have not been forthcoming—that is, liberal politics have not eradicated gross social inequality, have not improved the quality of public life, and perhaps above all have not created a pacific, internationalist global posture on the part of the American government. Instead, the educated middle-class person is likely to see his society as increasingly chaotic and deteriorating, to feel that enormous waste of material and human resources is taking place, and to believe that his nation is not a liberalizing force internationally, but perhaps the reverse.

The offspring of this stratum, as they began to throng the nation's universities in the early sixties, entered political involvement at just the point where their parents had begun to experience disillusionment with progressive ideology. But the early phase of the student movement tended to continue traditional middle-class faith in the democratic process. The New Left, in its beginnings, rejected all received ideology—for fairly obvious reasons, it found neither social democracy nor Marxism-Leninism nor liberalism at all adequate foundations for renewing radical politics. Indeed, in an early age, many New Leftists would not have attempted to create a youth-based radicalism at all, they would instead have found their way into one or another established radical or reform movement. It is important to realize that the exhaustion of existing ideologies in postwar Europe and America meant that young people with radical impulses had to start afresh. The starting point in the United States was to take democratic ideals seriously; to try to make the system work, by participating in and catalyzing grass-roots protest against glaring injustice—particularly against segregation and the threat of nuclear holocaust. Such an outlook included a fairly explicit expectation that the creation of protest and ferment from below would provide an impetus for major change at the top—on the part of the federal government (in behalf of the constitutional rights of Negroes, for example) and on the part of established agencies of reform such as the churches, the universities, the labor movement. Until about 1964, this political model seemed to be working to a considerable extent—civil rights laws were passed, the Kennedy Administration was moving toward detente with the Soviet Union, a war on poverty was declared, and a spirit of social renovation seemed to be taking hold in the society. In this situation, the SDS and other student radicals retained a considerable willingness to operate within the conventional political system; it is well to remember, for example, that in the election campaign of 1964, SDS adopted the slogan, "Part of the Way with LBJ."

The escalation of the war in Vietnam marked a turning point for radical students—it began a process of progressive disillusionment with the political system, a process which, for many, has culminated in a total rejection of its legitimacy. I cannot here recount in any adequate way the series of events which contributed to this process; but it is clear that the war itself was crucial to it, as was the use of the draft to prosecute that war and to "channel" young men educationally and occupationally, as was the failure of the war on poverty (a failure directly experienced by many young activists as they tried to work in poverty areas), as was the transformation of the black movement from a struggle for integration to a far more radical struggle for liberation and economic equality, as was the revelation that many universities actively contributed to the war effort and military research, as was the increasing use of the police to suppress protest demonstrations in the streets and on the campuses, as was the failure of the political parties to recognize their liberal, doveish constituencies. In short, for young people who identified with the cause of racial equality, who despised war and militarism, and who had hoped to construct lives based on humane, intellectual, and democratic ideals, by 1968 American society did seem largely reactionary, authoritarian, and repressive.

This perception is heightened and reinforced by other, more fundamental beliefs. For example, it is very difficult to accept the amount of squalor, inequality and misery in this society if one is aware of the fact that the society has the material resources to guarantee a decent private and public life to the whole population. It is very difficult to accept war and the arms race and the expansion of militarism when one is convinced that these institutions have the capacity to destroy the human race. And, finally, it is very difficult to maintain a calm long-run perspective, if one believes that the society has the capacity—in its technology, in its large-scale organizational structure, and in the character structure of millions of its members—to obliterate personal autonomy, individuality, and free expression. Many radical students, in other words, have a profound pessimism about the chances for democracy, personal freedom, and peace; this pessimism, however, leads toward activism rather than withdrawal because many are convinced that the probable future is not a necessary one. The events of the past four or five years have overwhelmingly confirmed their sense of the main social drift, but what has sustained the impulse to act has been the rapid growth of resistance among many in their generation.

Briefly, then, our argument to this point has been something like the following: the expansion of higher education in our society has produced a social stratum which tends to rear its children with values and character structures which are at some variance with the dominant culture. Affluence and secure status further weaken the potency of conventional incentives and undermine motivations for upward mobility. The outcome of these processes is a new social type or subculture among American youth—humanist youth. Such youth are especially sensitized to injustice and authoritarianism, are repelled by acquisitive, militaristic, and nationalistic values, and strive for a vocational situation in which autonomy and self-expression can be maximized. They have been politicized and radicalized by their experiences in relation to the racial and international crises, and by the failure of established agencies of renewal and reform, including the universities, to alleviate these crises. They also sense the possibility that opportunities for autonomy and individuality may be drying up in advanced technological societies. One of the reasons that their political expression has taken generational form is that older ideologies of opposition to capitalism and authoritarianism have failed in practice.

We have also been saying that, although it is clear that the situation of these youth is enormously different from the situation of educated youth in underdeveloped countries, there are important analogies between the two. Both groups of youth confront the problem of discontinuity between family tradition and the values of the larger society. Both confront major problems of vocation and adult identity. Both confront political systems which are stagnated and repressive, and find few resources and allies external to themselves as they attempt to change that system.

There is a final issue in the comparative analysis of student movements that I want to raise. In our discussion of the classical movements, we suggested that the appearance of such movements was a clear sign that processes of fundamental social and cultural change were at work, and that these movements were not simply the result of certain pressures operating on a particular group of young people in a society but more importantly they were indications that traditional, agrarian society was being transformed by processes of industrialization and modernization. It is clearly important to ask whether the appearance of student movements in advanced industrial societies are similarly signs that a new social and cultural era is struggling to emerge.

There are those who believe that the current crop of student revolutionaries is not the vanguard of a new social order, but rather, in the words of Daniel Bell, "the guttering last gasps of a romanticism soured by rancor and impotence."[10] In this view, student unrest in industrial societies is regarded as analogous to the protests of the first waves of industrial workers, who resisted their uprooting by the machine. Now, it is argued, high status intellectually and artistically inclined youth resist their incorporation into large-scale organizations —an incorporation which, nevertheless, is as inevitable as was the imposition of the factory on the rural lower classes.

Such a view does implicitly recognize that a major social transformation may be in the making. What I find objectionable in it is the implication that the new radicalism of the young is irrelevant to the nature of that transformation. An alternative view would emphasize the possibility that large-scale social, political, and cultural changes are occurring, that these are reflected in the social origins and focal concerns of student rebels, and that the existence of student rebellion may be a determining feature of this process of change.

First, at the cultural level, the student movement and the new alienated youth culture appear to reflect the erosion, if not the collapse, of what might be called the culture of capitalism—that cluster of values which Max Weber labeled the Protestant Ethic—a value system which was appropriate for the development of capitalism and the entrepreneurial spirit, but which has lost its vitality under the impact of the bureaucratic organization of the economy, the decline of entrepreneurships, and the spread of affluence. The erosion of this culture is reflected in the transformation of family structure and child-rearing practices, in the changing relations between the sexes, in the replacement of thrift with consumership as a virtue. As Joseph Schumpeter predicted many years ago, bourgeois culture could not survive the

[10] Daniel Bell, "Columbia and the New Left," *The Public Interest*, Fall 1968, 61–101.

abundance it would generate.[11] Thus, the cultural crisis experienced very sharply and personally by humanist youth really impinges on the whole society. It is a crisis because no coherent value system has emerged to replace what has deteriorated; but it is hard not to believe that the anti-authoritarian, experimental, unrepressed, and romantic style of the youth revolt does in fact represent the beginnings of the effort to create a workable new culture, rather than the last gasps of the old. Such a view gains support when one observes the degree to which the youth revolt has affected popular culture and attracted the interest, if not the total involvement, of large numbers of young people in this country and abroad.

A second major social change which underlies the student movement is the rise of mass higher education. If the student movement is any indication of the possible effects of higher education, then one might have the following expectations about the coming period. First, the number of people in the middle class with critical attitudes toward the dominant culture will rapidly rise. In my view, critical feelings about capitalist culture—particularly negative attitudes toward symbols and ideology which support competitive striving, acquisitiveness, narrow nationalism, and repressive moral codes—are enhanced by exposure to higher education. Such feelings are further reinforced by entrance into occupations which are structurally not bound into the private, corporate economy—for example, occupations associated with education, social service, social planning, and other intellectual or human service work. These occupations embody values which tend to be critical of the culture and of the going system, and tend to have an ethic which emphasizes collective welfare rather than private gain. It is important to recognize that the current student activists were born into the social stratum defined by these occupations, and many students with activist sympathies end up in these occupations. Data collected by Samuel Lubell[12] show a general tendency for students oriented toward such occupations to move toward the left, politically. In a certain sense, then, the student movement may be seen as an outgrowth of a new

[11] Joseph Schumpeter, *Capitalism, Socialism, and Democracy* (New York: Harper, 1950).
[12] Samuel Lubell, "That 'Generation Gap,'" *The Public Interest*, Fall 1968, 52–60.

level of occupational differentiation—that is, the development of a distinct stratum organized around these occupations. This stratum is one of the most rapidly growing occupational sectors, and its political impact can already be seen, not only on the campus, but in such developments as the new politics movement during the recent elections. I am not arguing that this new middle class of intellectuals, professionals, upper white-collar workers, technical workers, public employees, and the like is politically homogeneous, or class-conscious, or radical. Indeed, it contains many antagonisms, and its participants are hardly ready for massive collective action, let alone the barricades. But it does seem to me that the student movement, with its opposition to nationalism and militarism, its identification with egalitarian ideals, and particularly its opposition to bureaucratic and rigid authority in the university represents a militant version of the kinds of attitudes which are increasingly likely to prevail in the stratum I am referring to. It seems particularly likely that the spread of mass higher education will mean increasing pressure against bureaucratic forms of authority, and for "participatory democracy" within the institutions in which the newly educated work. The political trajectory of the educated class will, in large measure, be a function of the responsiveness of the political and economic system to their demands for more rational domestic and international policies, more personal autonomy and participation in decision-making, and a more authentic and humane cultural and public life. More Vietnams, more racial turmoil, more squalor in the cities, more political stagnation, more debasement of popular culture—in short, more of the status quo is likely to increase the availability of members of this stratum for radical politics.

One may continue at great length to enumerate other cultural and social changes which seem to be implied by the appearance of a student movement in our society. For example, it clearly signifies a process of change in the position of youth in the society—a change which involves protest against the subordination of youth to rigid and arbitrary forms of authority in the school system and in the general legal system, and which also may involve an extension of youth as a stage of life beyond adolescence.[13] The student movement may also

---

[13] Kenneth Keniston, *Youth as a Stage of Life* (New Haven: Yale University, 1968), mimeographed.

signify a general decline in the legitimacy of military authority and nationalist ideology—a decline associated with rising education levels, with changing character structure, and with the impact of mass communications.

My point in mentioning all of these potential cultural and social transformations is not to stake a claim as a prophet, but rather to urge that we take seriously the possibility that the appearance of student movements in advanced industrial societies really does signify that a new social and cultural stage is in the process of formation. A comparative perspective leads us to that hypothesis, because the classical student movements were, as we have suggested, just such signs. If we were to take the student movement in our own country seriously in this sense, then we would, I believe, be less likely to assume the stability of our social and political order and the cultural system sustaining it, less likely to dismiss campus unrest as a momentary perturbation or a romantic last gasp, less likely to focus on particular tactics and bizarre outcroppings of the youth revolt. Instead, we would open up the intellectual possibility that our kind of society can undergo major transformation, that it can generate, as Marx anticipated, its own "internal contradictions" and "negations," and that the future need not be like the present only more so.

Chapter VI

Psychology of a Strike

Mervin B. Freedman, Paul Kanzer

During the academic year 1968–69 student strikes occurred on the campuses of San Francisco State College and the University of California at Berkeley. Increases in enrollment for blacks and Third World students and autonomy for black and Third World studies were the prime demands of the strikers. On both campuses appreciable numbers of white students actively supported the strike. At Berkeley, faculty support was negligible except for teaching assistants. At San Francisco State a significant body of faculty members, chiefly members of the American Federation of Teachers, joined the striking students. By the end of the academic year the strikes had ended. Few concessions had been wrung from "the Establishment." The strikers were frustrated and bitter. The citizens of the state of California were outraged. Their duly elected lawmakers in Sacramento were tripping over one another in their haste to enact legislation that would punish rebellious students and faculty members and the institutions that "shield" them. This paper analyzes certain elements of the social psychology of these strikes and of the character and personality of the individuals involved.

Psychoanalysts describe complex human behavior as "overdetermined." All the forces that combine to produce the behavior cannot be identified, nor can their relative influence be categorized. One need but look at the card file on "Hamlet" in any library to recognize the accuracy of the concept of overdetermination. No matter how brilliant and penetrating the analyses of the character and motivation of Hamlet, there is always room for more. So it is with any complex social event like a strike. Its roots are historical, economic, and political, to name but a few of the disciplines that must be called upon to explain events of such great complexity.

FROM SIT-IN TO STRIKE

At Berkeley in 1964 a unique event occurred: the emergence of activism on campus with the campus as target. Between 1958 and 1964, a great expansion in student activism took place—for example, civil rights marches, sit-ins in public places and business establishments to protest racial discrimination, and demonstrations against the House Un-American Activities Committee. In 1964, the Free Speech Movement at Berkeley turned its attention, for the first time in the student

143

activist movement, to the processes of education itself, requesting sweeping changes in the administration of the university, in the curriculum, and in teaching methods. The movement was almost entirely nonviolent. Brushes with the police were peripheral, involving such actions as blocking a police car. The primary unlawful act was an orderly sit-in in the administration building of the university. After the fashion of the nonviolent civil rights demonstrations of the times, the students when they were arrested offered no resistance to the police.

For some time the Berkeley demonstrations were followed by comparable nonviolent and disciplined actions—for example, the teach-ins concerned with mobilizing opposition to the war in Vietnam. Gradually, however, campus demonstrations became less disciplined and more violent, culminating in the events at Columbia, San Francisco State, Berkeley, Cornell, and other campuses. Although the guerilla warfare at the Democratic Convention in Chicago in 1968 took place in the streets rather than on the campus, the actions may be regarded in many ways as an offshoot of campus protest.

Obviously the orderly sit-ins and demonstrations of several years ago and the more disorderly and violent demonstrations and strikes of the past year have many similarities. The goals, for example, are much the same—an end to racism in society and on the campus, greater student autonomy, opposition to ROTC and the military, and the like. But certain differences are well worth noting. The Free Speech Movement at Berkeley enjoyed wide support—from faculty members, from students, from the liberal press, from liberal public opinion, from the families of the strikers, and so on. The strikers at Berkeley and San Francisco State enjoyed no comparable support. Although they condemned police brutality, the traditional liberals of California were "turned off" by the intimidatory tactics of the striking students. It is difficult to imagine a radical cause in the San Francisco Bay area that does not receive substantial support from the affluent intellectuals who reside in the Berkeley hills. But these strikes were such. Except for the striking faculty at San Francisco State, faculty support was minimal. And as we shall discuss below, family support was often not forthcoming.

Intimidation of people and damage to property were the primary reasons for the failure of the strikers to mobilize much support on the campus, or in other communities, or among at least the educated public. One may argue that the Establishment pays little or no attention to peaceable protest, that the violence accompanying the Berkeley and San Francisco State strikes was minimal and hardly compares with the violence that accompanied social protest movements of the past—for example, the labor movement in the 1930s.[1] Violence and intimidation were nevertheless important factors in alienating potential supporters from the strikers' cause. Intimidation of people and damage to property were prominent among the reasons why faculty members on California state college campuses other than San Francisco State who belonged to the American Federation of Teachers did not support the strike in appreciable numbers. Peaceable protest may stir but little interest. Violence, on the other hand, divests a cause of moral suasion.

Differences in atmosphere or ethos between a sit-in, as exemplified by the Free Speech Movement, and a strike command attention. The morale of participants in a sit-in is likely to be high and the feeling of shared community strong. One of the sharpest images of the participants in the Free Speech Movement that lingers in the mind is the singing of Christmas carols. At Stanford during the academic year 1968–69 a number of demonstrations, including several sit-ins directed mainly at the Stanford Research Institute, occurred. Although some of the Stanford protests involved property damage, the actions were orderly in the main. And spirit was high. At one of the sit-ins a wedding took place—complete with minister and candlelight wedding supper. The sense of community that often enters into the sit-ins is an important element. Sometimes participants in a sit-in stay "too long," because they do not wish to lose the secondary enjoyment that accrues from the sense of shared community. This is a trenchant comment on the absence of opportunity for cooperation and shared experiences that characterizes most campuses these days.[2]

Given the competition of contemporary academic life, a student rarely has the opportunity to cooperate with other people in a venture that has meaning for all participants. Team sports are lightly

---

[1] See Richard Axen, "Faculty Response to Student Dissent," in G. Kerry Smith (Ed.), *Stress and Campus Response: Current Issues in Higher Education 1968* (San Francisco: Jossey-Bass, 1968), pp. 106–112.

[2] Nevitt Sanford, *Where Colleges Fail* (San Francisco: Jossey-Bass, 1967).

regarded by guardians of academic integrity, but team sports provide
a student with a rare opportunity to work with others toward a common end. "Old-fashioned" sit-ins similarly serve the function of coun-
tering the atmosphere of competitiveness and isolation that has pre-
vailed on most campuses for the last two decades. Often a sit-in is by
no means a matter of simple rebellion.

The atmosphere of a strike, as exemplified by the situation at
San Francisco State and Berkeley, is something else again. A strike is a
grim situation. Action takes place on many fronts, in buildings and out
of buildings. Property damage and personal injury are likely to occur.
Police often assault strikers, and strikers often assault police. Leadership is fragmented, and various groups of strikers "do their own thing."
Perhaps among the minority groups involved—for example, the blacks
or Chicanos—a sense of community develops out of shared experiences,
comparable to the Free Speech Movement; among the whites the
sense of community is fragmentary and transitory.

Impulse and Control in Dissident Students. If the student
rebellion scene has changed from controlled sit-in to less disciplined
strike over the course of the past few years, the question arises as to
whether the kinds of students who are involved have changed. The
students involved in the Free Speech Movement at Berkeley, particularly those arrested during the sit-in at Sproul Hall, have been studied
by several researchers.[3] Student activists and demonstrators at Chicago
have been studied by Flacks (Chapter Five, this volume) and at
Pennsylvania State by Westby and Braungart.[4]

[3] J. N. Block, N. Haan, and M. B. Smith, "Activism and Apathy in
Contemporary Adolescents," in J. F. Adams (Ed.), *Contributions to the Under-
standing of Adolescents* (Boston: Allyn and Bacon, 1967); Paul Heist, "Intellect
and Commitment: The Faces of Discontent," in O. Knorr and W. J. Minter
(Eds.), *Order and Freedom on the Campus* (Boulder, Colo.: Western Interstate
Commission for Higher Education, 1965); Joseph Katz and Associates, *No Time
for Youth* (San Francisco: Jossey-Bass, 1968); G. Lyonns, "The Police Car
Demonstration: A Survey of Participants," in Seymour Martin Lipset and
Sheldon S. Wolin (Eds.), *The Berkeley Student Revolt* (New York: Anchor,
1965); R. H. Somers, "The Mainsprings of Rebellion: A Survey of Berkeley
Students in November, 1964," in Lipset and Wolin, *op. cit.;* and William Watts
and David Whittaker, "Free Speech Advocates at Berkeley," *Journal of Applied
Behavioral Science,* 1966, *2,* 41–62.

[4] D. Westby and R. Braungart, "Class and Politics in the Family Backgrounds of Student Political Activists," *American Sociological Review,* 1966,
31, 690–692.

These studies were carried out independently by researchers from several disciplines. Their findings converge, however. The parents of activist students of several years ago were higher in income, occupational status, and education than the parents of nonactivist students. These parents were politically more liberal. Their child-rearing practices were more permissive, and they had closer relationships with their children than parents of nonactivists. Disagreement was also expressed more openly in the homes of activist students. Such findings "put into question the 'conflict between generations' thesis that has been advanced as one explanation of the activist protest. Many activists seem to be acting in conformity with their parents' values, but they want to express these values in a purer, less compromising, and energetic way than they think their parents do. Moreover, they seem to be using the freedom of dissent and the affection they have experienced at home as a yardstick by which to measure the behavior and attitudes of the authorities in school and in society at large."[5]

All but one of these researches report that the grade-point averages of activists were higher than those of nonactivists. Their verbal SAT scores were higher as well. The activists scored higher on scales measuring theoretical orientation, liking for reflective thought, diversity of interests, and estheticism. Based on their high academic aptitude, interest, and achievement, Somers described the activists as "a minority vital to the excellence of [the] university."[6]

These psychological measures indicate that activists have a rich and complex inner life. "They display pronounced sensitivity and responsiveness to the needs of other people and strong humanitarian and idealistic tendencies. One might think of them as psychologically complex people who smart under institutional conditions that restrict their opportunity for personal experience and communication with other people. At the same time, their psychological capacities for autonomy and initiative do not make for the withdrawal form of protest that characterizes the alienated person. The activist expresses his impulses and feelings, instead of denying them and consigning them to partial atrophy."[7] A psychiatric observer of these activists of several years

[5] Joseph Axelrod, Mervin B. Freedman, Winslow Hatch, Joseph Katz, and Nevitt Sanford, *Search for Relevance* (San Francisco: Jossey-Bass, 1969).

[6] Somers, *op. cit.*

[7] Axelrod *et al., op. cit.*

ago asserted, "Activism is, presently, a generally healthy aspect of the process of maturation."[8] Keniston arrived at similar conclusions, when he studied young people who were protesting against the war in Vietnam.[9]

Studies of activist students of the last year or year and a half are complicated by the presence and prominence among them of students of minority background, particularly blacks. Except for issues of civil rights and racial discrimination, the protesters of several years ago on college campuses were almost entirely white and mostly middle class in origin. Concerning the white protesters of the last year or year and a half—as for example, in the San Francisco State and Berkeley strikes—it cannot be assumed that the results of studies of activist students of several years ago hold true for them. The relevance and accuracy of much social research are rendered increasingly dubious by the swift pace of change of social events. Complex social research takes time. When results are ready, the events to which the research addresses itself may well have changed radically. For example, in the space of a few years, drugs have become a prominent feature of the college scene and have moved down into the high schools; weekly magazines can hardly keep pace with the permutations of the civil rights movement. Dissension on campus has moved at a comparable pace and with as much unpredictability.

Studies of white striking students at Berkeley and San Francisco State suggest that current activists differ in significant ways from the students involved in the Free Speech Movement, the civil rights movement, and Vietnam protests. Both groups, to be sure, share common ideals and goals—for example, a speedy end to the war in Vietnam, and justice as well as law and order. Current activists differ, however, in family and social class background, in personality characteristics, and in concern for and commitment to colleges and universities and to academic values. Many current activists come from working class backgrounds. Others come from conservative political and social backgrounds against which they have rebelled. In many

[8] R. S. Berns, "The Activist Student," paper read at annual meeting of the American Psychiatric Association, Detroit, 1967.

[9] Kenneth Keniston, *Young Radicals: Notes on Committed Youth* (New York: Harcourt, 1968).

cases family upbringing was not characterized by permissiveness and egalitarianism. In a formal academic sense—grades and the like— current activists are not the equal of the activists of several years ago. Moreover, the activists of the Free Speech Movement were committed to the University of California. They wanted it to be a better place. For many current activists, however, the college or university represents only another betrayal of the American dream of individual fulfillment and social justice. For this reason, they have no stake in its survival.

Certain reservations are in order at this point. First of all, strikes and their sympathizers are a very mixed bag. The profile we have just presented applies more accurately, probably, to strike leaders than to more passive strike supporters and sympathizers. The writers interviewed fifteen white leaders of the strikes on the Berkeley and San Francisco State campuses. Five came from conservative Republican homes and six from working class homes. The remaining four students were closer to the activists of the Free Speech Movement. On the other hand, we interviewed a number of students who were involved in various social service projects—for example, tutoring programs for black and Chicano children, teaching English to Chicano and Chinese adults, and the like. These students resembled very closely the activists of several years ago in background and academic interest and per- formance. Most of them were not attending classes but were not otherwise active in the strikes. They were troubled by certain tactics of the strikers—the destruction of property, for example.

Secondly, studying student strikers is no easy task. Many of them regard social scientific research as nonsense or as an establish- ment tool, and they are wary of it. Keniston describes students as the most avid readers of research on students. This is not the case for many militant students. Given this opposition to social research, sampling is a hit-and-miss procedure. Sampling problems are further complicated by the fragmented and transitory nature of New Left membership and leadership. For example, a number of the fifteen leaders we interviewed no longer hold leadership positions.

Dissident student movements in which blacks and other non- white or non-Anglo minorities and New Left groups are prominent are not likely to be gentlemanly affairs. By traditional academic stand- ards, most of the students are not impressive scholars. Respect for traditional academic values and symbols is minimal. The strike situation is essentially modelled on the labor dispute; but the labor-management conflict model has little appeal for most academics and for middle-class liberals. Add to this the anxieties engendered by property damage and physical threats and the complex and confused images of Third World people, blacks in particular, that middle-class whites carry about with them. In retrospect it would have been astonishing had the strikes received appreciable support from faculty and other middle-class liberals.

Many, probably most, of the students involved in the Free Speech Movement, in civil rights demonstrations, and in Vietnam protests received support from family, from appreciable segments of the faculty, and from traditional liberal organizations. A sense of mutuality existed, of reinforcement from society, at least from that segment of society that mattered most to the dissident students. The situation of the striking students at San Francisco State and at Berkeley and of the striking faculty at San Francisco State was different. Support from outside the striking communities themselves was minimal. The sense of worth and integrity that ensues from positive social reinforcement was not forthcoming. As Erik Erikson has pointed out, societies tend to be very hard on elements within the larger society that reject that society. The strikers were thrown back upon one another for support. Encapsulation within the strike situation probably accounts to some extent for misperceptions of power and public opinion that the strikers displayed.

The Silent Majority. Unruly college students are a great boon to conservative political figures. In the state of California, Governor Reagan's popularity, for example, increases whenever campus disturbances dominate newspaper headlines and television newscasts. On campuses, however, right-wing reaction to strikers and demonstrators has not really set in among students. To be sure, at Columbia and at San Francisco State various skirmishes between "jocks" and dissident students occurred and at Berkeley some students insisted upon entering the campus by crossing through massed pickets, the consequence of which frequently was a fist fight. Young Americans for Freedom, however, have hardly swept the campuses. It may be that more right-wing students are enrolled in schools that are not leaders in intellectual life, as Lipset and Altbach suggest.[10] But one hears little of political activity from these campuses. The prevalent conservatism among students expresses itself as lack of interest in politics, as Bay notes (Chapter Three). At Berkeley and at San Francisco State most of the students who opposed the strikes were quite disposed to agree that the strikers had much justice on their side. Indeed, they openly expressed agreement with the ends or goals; their opposition focused rather on the methods of the strikers. Moreover, the non-striking students were very sensitive to the injustices of authority—of police or campus administrators. In the "People's Park" controversy which took place in Berkeley in the spring of 1969, Berkeley students voted overwhelmingly to support the dissident students and the "street people" of Berkeley. It seems that the generation of students now in college can tolerate disorder and confusion without resorting to suppression and repression somewhat more readily than their elders.

Blacks and the Third World. Probably it were well that analysis of the psychology of black and Third World strikers not be attempted by a couple of white academics. We wish only to present two observations. Simple demographic considerations explain a great deal about black and other nonwhite or non-Anglo student movements. The number of black students who are attending colleges and universities is still pitiably small, for example, and last year fully half of these black students were freshmen. This means that black student societies and comparable groups received a large influx of freshman students in the academic year 1968–69. In some cases the majority of their members were freshmen. First-year college students, needless to say, can be more easily stirred by inflammatory rhetoric and more readily aroused to reckless action. In the case of the Berkeley and San Francisco State strikes, in fact, considerable effort was made to enlist the support of high school and even junior high school students as well. A large body of freshmen is likely to influence the leadership of student organizations, to swing it toward more radical positions. It seems not unlikely that larger numbers of black and Third World upperclassmen will lead to a moderation of tactics, if not goals, in the future.

For two women's colleges results are available for black enter-

[10] S. M. Lipset and P. G. Altbach, "Student Politics and Higher Education in the United States," *Comparative Education Review,* 1966, *10,* 320–349.

ing freshmen on the Omnibus Personality Inventory, Form C,[11] for the past five years. Striking differences emerge, when freshmen who entered these colleges in the autumn of 1967 and 1968 are compared with freshmen who entered in the three prior years. For the years 1964–66, the black freshmen score higher than their corresponding freshman classes as a whole on Thinking Introversion (persons scoring high are characterized by a liking for reflective thought and academic activities), Theoretical Orientation (high scorers indicate a preference for dealing with theoretical concerns and problems and for using the scientific method in thinking), and Etheticism (high scorers endorse statements indicating diverse interests in artistic matters and activities and a high level of sensitivity and response to esthetic stimulation). These freshmen score lower than the corresponding freshmen classes as a whole on the Developmental Status and Impulse Expression scales. (These scales are described below.) For the years 1967 and 1968 the test results are reversed. These freshmen score lower than the freshman classes as a whole on Thinking Introversion, Theoretical Orientation, and Estheticism, and higher on Developmental Status and Impulse Expression. Findings for SAT Verbal Scores are comparable. For the years 1964–66 the black freshmen had higher mean scores; for the years 1967–68 they were lower. Presuming that studies on other campuses would produce comparable results, it seems that a dramatic shift has taken place in a very short period of time in the characteristics of black students who are entering colleges. The students who have entered in the last two years have very different educational needs.

BASIC CAUSES

In our analysis, at least four basic factors have joined together to produce the phenomenon of the strike. The first is a worldwide trend—the waning power of authority in general. This trend is manifested in American youth by a significantly higher degree of rebellious independence than characterized college youth of the 1950s. A second factor is an increase in student mobility since World War Two which permits, or even encourages, "migration" of rebellious students to certain campuses. The third cause, according to our analysis, is the curricular crisis in higher education today: liberal education is at a dead

[11] Paul Heist and George Yonge, *Omnibus Personality Inventory* (New York: The Psychological Corporation, 1968).

end. And the fourth factor has to do with the changing roles of people classified as "faculty" and individuals classified as "students" on today's campuses, and especially with the failure of many faculty members to accept the new functions required of them.

Rebellious Independence. In the complacent, quiescent Eisenhower years, one of the authors and several of his colleagues researched personality development among college students. One of the products of our researches was the Developmental Status scale.[12] At almost every college or university where the Developmental Status scale has been administered, seniors score significantly higher than freshmen. Outstanding among the varied traits measured by this scale are critical attitudes toward authority. Webster, in fact, extracted a first factor from the scale which he termed "rebellious independence." Even in the decade of the 1950s, when faculty members and social critics were chastising college students for their lack of verve and their complacency, an increase in rebellious independence during the college years was a widespread phenomenon.

Not only did rebellious independence increase between the freshman and senior years, but each successive entering freshman class —at most institutions that we studied—was likely to have a higher score than its predecessor. Consider mean scores for entering freshman classes at one institution tested in the years indicated: 1953—23; 1955—26; 1957—27; 1959—29 (mean standard deviation = 9). This trend continued on into the decade of the 1960s: 1964—32; 1966—33. Comparable results for successive freshman classes at other institutions emerge from administration of the Developmental Status scale. In American life, the various events or activities that connote or denote adult status tend to take place at increasingly earlier ages. The age at which young people begin to drink alcoholic beverages has declined steadily in recent decades. Use of drugs started among young adults and college students, but the drug scene now envelops the high schools and even the junior high schools.

Decline in respect for authority is obviously an important aspect of student rebelliousness. The waning power of authority is a widespread phenomenon—worldwide, in fact—as witness such phenomena as the autonomous strivings of colonial peoples and the turbulence

---

[12] H. Webster, "Changes in Attitude During College," *Journal of Educational Psychology,* 1958, *49,* 109–117.

within hierarchical churches. Whatever its historical origins, the increase of rebellious independence among students over the last two decades may be documented empirically. Each autumn many colleges and universities admit freshman classes that are less deferent toward authority of all kinds—the family, the church, the state, the school—than their predecessors.

Student Mobility. Although rebellious attitudes toward authority may be increasing generally among American college students, the more rebellious students are likely to cluster on certain campuses. In previous eras, only the rich or very sophisticated students exercised much option in selecting their college or university. An Eastern prep school girl, for example, might choose between Bennington or Sarah Lawrence or a more traditional women's college. A wealthy Californian might choose between Stanford or Berkeley and an Ivy League school. In these days of relative affluence, high mobility, and instant communication, however, such options are widespread. An unconventional and rebellious student who finds few congenial fellow students at his school is likely to transfer to an institution where he is assured of much company. It is no accident that Berkeley and San Francisco State have been the settings for extremely militant student actions. These campuses have attracted large numbers of unconventional and rebellious students, both from the state of California and from the country at large.

It is likely that in the past such personality characteristics as rebelliousness and unconventionality were distributed over college campuses much more evenly than at present. Campuses differed, of course, in such qualities of students as intellectual ability and social class background.[13] Imbalances among campuses in personality characteristics have probably increased as a function of student selectivity in choice of institution. Such "migration" intensifies the consequences of various social trends. Heroin addiction, for example, is a negligible social problem in terms of actual numbers of addicts (although, of course, a terrible personal problem) as compared to the total population of the United States; but concentration of almost all addicts in a few of the

[13] Paul Heist, "Diversity in College Student Characteristics," in J. A. Fishman (Ed.), "The Social Psychology of School to College Transition," *Journal of Educational Sociology,* 1960, *33,* 279–291.

largest cities has resulted in a social problem of considerable consequence.

Liberal Education at a Dead End. The empirical findings for the Developmental Status scale reported above may be matched by results for other scales. On the Authoritarianism scale, for example: 1953—116; 1955—106; 1957—101; 1959—99; 1964—90; 1966—89 (mean standard deviation = 21). Among many traits that are considered to be expressions of authoritarian tendency are compulsiveness, rigidity, intolerance of ambiguity, punitive morality, submission to power, conventionality, cynicism, and anti-intraception. (*Intraception* is defined as the dominance of feelings, fantasies, speculations, and aspirations—an imaginative, subjective human outlook). Scores increase on the Impulse Expression scale: 1953—41; 1955—42; 1957—44; 1959—47; 1965—52; 1967—54 (mean standard deviation = 13). High scorers on the Impulse Expression scale are dominant, aggressive, autonomous, and exhibitionistic, and they express interest in sex, excitement, and change.

Since World War One an important element of liberal education has been introduction of a sense of openness and relativism into the minds of students. Students have learned that official American actions have not always held up well when subjected to moral scrutiny; that all virtue does not reside in Christianity, or Protestantism, or Episcopalianism; that conventional morality is a dubious set of beliefs; that virtue is not always rewarded; and the like. When the majority of freshmen were constricted and authoritarian (as they are still on many campuses), these constituted exciting revelations; and the faculty who provided these relevations were exciting figures. Graduating seniors represented something of a compromise between the complexity of outlook, the relativism, and the sophistication of faculty, on the one hand, and the more traditional or conventional outlook of home environment and family, on the other.

On some campuses these days, however, freshmen are in many ways more relativistic and sophisticated than their faculty. In a number of high schools in the San Francisco region, students read Eldridge Cleaver and Malcolm X. G. B. Shaw and D. H. Lawrence are not shockingly liberating to young people who have read the underground press. Arrests for participating in demonstrations and for using drugs are not uncommon. The lyrics of popular music and folk heroes like John

Lennon or Bob Dylan assault traditional middle-class morality with a vengeance. Much student unrest may be traced to the simple fact that liberal education is no longer "liberating" for many students. The pace of social change has simply outstripped the inner resources of most faculty members. In the long run, resolution of the difficulties that have led to campus turmoil and strikes rests upon the design, development, and implementation of new educational philosophies. This is a cooperative task for students and faculty members together.[14]

Social Change and Role of Faculty. The American college in its twentieth-century form is an institution that is designed to cope with gradual change. After years of debates, discussions, and the rounds of committees, some change in procedures—as, for example, the elective system at Harvard—is introduced into a college or university. During the next twenty or thirty years such a reform is incorporated into the curriculum of the majority of colleges and universities after comparable debates, discussions, and reviews by committees.

At a time of exponential rather than gradual change such a procedure for coping with changes in students or in society simply breaks down. Consider the statement by the strikers at Berkeley and San Francisco State, "These demands are not negotiable." On the surface this is a wildly irrational statement. It appears to be designed to close off discussion or negotiation. Out of sheer bravado it invites confrontation. And yet it conveys a desperate and angry but rational message. The strikers can demonstrate that over the course of the past several years they have made requests for increased admissions of blacks and students of Third World origin and for educational programs for these students in the customary polite academic fashion. And nothing has come of it. These requests go to one committee and then another (almost never does one of these committees have a black or Third World member) and eventually wind up in limbo. To the strikers, routine academic procedures have come to mean simply "a lot of jive" and no action. At a time when the needs of American society require direct and fast action, it is difficult to dispute the accuracy of such a view of academic procedure.

The conflicts between black and Third World students and faculty members are fashioned of the same elements as those between

---

[14] Some suggestions for curricula based on these concerns may be found in Axelrod *et al., op. cit.*

middle-class white students and faculty. In the case of students of minority origins, the intensity of the conflict is heightened and its components emerge more clearly. As traditional liberal higher education has gradually and in recent years more swiftly lost its meaning and significance, the moral foundations of the role of the faculty have been eroded. If faculty members are engaged with students in educational activities that have meaning for both participants, faculty members enjoy a sense of fulfillment. Very simply, they feel they are doing what they should be doing, that their power and their authority are legitimate. As traditional liberal education has gradually lost meaning, the legitimacy of the role of faculty members is being destroyed. A consequence is the resort to power for protection of the role. When a role shifts in a bureaucracy and people take on roles that were not intended with the legality of the original system, concern for the protection of this role by the exercise of power frequently ensues.

Study of the curriculum of almost any college or university is evidence for the exercise of authority that has little basis in legitimate educational concerns. If a senior faculty member has few students who enroll in his classes, it is likely that these classes will appear on the roster of courses required for the degree. A goodly proportion of the curriculum of any college or university reflects the interests of faculty members, often the detritus of graduate school interests of ten, twenty, and thirty years earlier. The extent to which such courses have educational value for students in the sense of contributing to their intellectual or personality development is at best a secondary consideration.

In recent years faculty members have been chastised for their inattention to teaching. Instead of teaching they are researching or consulting. Professional reputation and consulting funds, it is said, have wooed them away from teaching. We suggest that many faculty members are only too happy to abdicate teaching functions because of the moral ambiguity of their roles as teachers. Restoration of legitimacy to the role of faculty member as teacher by development of truly educational philosophies and procedures is the first and essential step required to eliminate consulting and research activities that have little or no educational relevance.

CHAPTER VII

Sources of
Student Dissent

Kenneth Keniston

$\mathbb{R}$arely in history has apathy been replaced by involvement with such startling rapidity as in the current move of American college students away from silence on grave national and international issues toward active protest. The same commencement speakers who, a decade ago, were decrying the lack of commitment in such areas are now warning against unreflective and irresponsible student dissent and disruption.

The upsurge of activism is one of the most puzzling phenomena in recent history. It has captured the attention of mass media—popular magazines, newspapers, and television—inspiring articles of interpretation, deprecation, and occasionally praise. Student dissenters, often distinctively talented, seem to have a flair for using news media effectively to make themselves and their cause visible.

This visibility is the more dramatic because the majority of America's 7,000,000 college students still remain generally uncritical of the wider society, fundamentally conformist in behavior and outlook, and basically "adjusted" to the prevailing collegiate, national, and international order. Dissent is still far from being the dominant mood among them. On a majority of our 2,200 campuses, protest, alienation, and unrest appear to be something that happens elsewhere —except for the merest handful of "kooks" on the local scene. Overt dissent, however defined, is relatively infrequent. Every responsible survey[1] shows apathy and privatism far more dominant than protest. Whatever we say about student dissidents is said about a very small minority of America's college students. On many campuses, dissent is not visible at all.

Where it does appear, it tends to be concentrated largely at more selective, progressive, and "academic" colleges and universities. Richard Peterson's study, *The Scope of Organized Student Protest in*

[1] See, for example, *Newsweek,* March 22, 1965, Campus section; J. Katz, "The Learning Environment: Social Expectations and Influences," paper presented at American Council of Education, Washington, D.C., 1965; M. Reed, "Student Non-Politics, or How to Make Irrelevancy a Virtue," *The American Student,* 1966, *1*(3), 7–10; Richard E. Peterson, *The Scope of Organized Student Protest in 1964–65* (Princeton, N.J.: Educational Testing Service, 1966); J. Block, N. Haan, and M. B. Smith, "Activism and Apathy in Contemporary Adolescents," in J. F. Adams (Ed.), *Contributions to the Understanding of Adolescence* (New York: Allyn and Bacon, 1967).

1964–65, revealed that the political demonstrations found in the larger universities and institutions of higher caliber were almost totally absent at teachers colleges, technical institutes, and nonacademic denominational colleges. Even at those institutions with the greatest number of dissenters, the vast majority of students—generally well over 95 per cent—were not actively involved, but remained interested onlookers or opponents.

From the very beginning of the student civil rights movement, social scientists have been regular participant-observers and investigators of student dissent. A considerable body of research[2] deals with the characteristics and setting of protest. Many studies are topical, centered around a particular demonstration. Others are still in the making. Yet enough evidence has been gathered to permit generalization about the varieties, origins, and future of student dissent in the 1960s. It is this which I wish to evaluate, along with my own research and informal observations, in an attempt to understand the nature of the recent wave of protest in American colleges, its sources, and its future.

A highly inaccurate stereotype of the student activist has emerged as much from the imaginings of the public at large as from his portrayal in mass media. Student protesters of all types arouse deep and ambivalent feelings in nondissenting students and adults—envy, resentment, admiration, repulsion, nostalgia, and guilt. Such feelings contribute both to the selective overattention dissenters receive and to the often distorted perceptions and interpretations of them and their activities.

The stereotypical dissenter, as popularly portrayed, is both a bohemian and a political activist. Bearded, be-Levi-ed, long-haired, dirty, and unkempt, he is seen as profoundly disaffected from his society; often influenced by radical Marxist, Communist, Maoist, or Castroite ideas; an experimenter in sex and drugs, unconventional in his daily behavior. Frustrated and unhappy, often deeply maladjusted

---

[2] For summaries of this research see Seymour Martin Lipset and P. G. Altbach, "Student Politics and Higher Education in the United States," *Comparative Education Review,* 1966, *10,* 320–49; Block, Haan, and Smith, *op. cit.;* J. Katz, *The Student Activists: Rights, Needs and Powers of Undergraduates* (Stanford, Calif.: Institute for the Study of Human Problems, 1967); Richard E. Peterson, "The Student Left in American Higher Education," draft for Puerto Rico Conference on Students and Politics, 1967.

as a person, he is seen as a failure—or, as one United States Senator put it, a reject. Certain academic communities like Berkeley are said to act as magnets for dissenters, who selectively attend colleges with a reputation as protest centers. Furthermore, dropouts—or nonstudents who have failed in college—cluster in large numbers around the fringes of such colleges, actively seeking pretexts for protest, refusing all compromise and impatient with ordinary democratic processes.

According to such popular analyses, the sources of dissent are to be found in the loss of certain traditional American virtues. The breakdown of American family life, high divorce rate, softness of American living, inadequate parents, and above all, overindulgence and spoiling, contribute to the prevalence of dissent. Brought up in undisciplined homes—this popular diagnosis goes—by parents unsure of their own values and standards, dissenters channel their frustration and anger against the older generation, against all authority, and against established institutions.

Similar themes are sometimes found even in the interpretations of more scholarly commentators. Generational conflict is said to underlie the motivation to dissent, and a profound alienation from American society is seen as a factor of major importance in producing protests. Then, too, such factors as the poor quality and impersonality of American college education, the large size and lack of close student-faculty contact in the so-called multiversity are sometimes seen as the latent or precipitating factors in student protests, regardless of the manifest issues around which students are organized. Still other scholarly analysts—usually men now disillusioned by the radicalism of the 1930s—have expressed fear of the dogmatism, rigidity, and "authoritarianism of the left" of today's student activists.

Such stereotyped viewpoints seem to me incorrect in a variety of ways. They confuse two distinct varieties of student dissent. Equally important, they fuse dissent with maladjustment. There are as many forms of dissent, of course, as there are individual dissenters; and any effort to counter the popular stereotype of the dissenter by pointing to the existence of distinct types runs the risk of oversimplification at a lower level of abstraction. It seems to me useful, nonetheless, to suggest that student dissenters generally fall somewhere along a continuum running between two extremes—first, the political activist or protester, and second, the withdrawn, culturally alienated student,

The defining characteristic of what might be called the *new*
activist is his participation in a student demonstration or group activity
which concerns itself with some matter of general political, social, or
ethical principle. Characteristically, the activist feels that some injustice
has been done and attempts to take a stand—to demonstrate or in
some fashion express his convictions. Specific issues under fire range
from protest against a paternalistic college administration's actions to
disagreement with the Vietnam policy of the United States, from indig-
nation at the exploitation of the poor to anger at the firing of a devoted
teacher, from opposition to the Selective Service laws which exempt
him but not the poor to—most important—outrage at the deprivation
of the civil rights of other Americans.

The initial concern of the protester is almost always immediate,
ad hoc, and local. The student who protests about one issue is likely,
to be sure, to feel inclined or obliged to demonstrate his convictions
on other issues as well.[3] But whatever the issue, the protester rarely
demonstrates because his own interests are jeopardized, but rather
because he perceives injustices being done to others less fortunate than
himself. One of the apparent paradoxes about protests against current
draft policies is that the protesting students are selectively drawn from
that subgroup most likely to receive student deferments for graduate
work. The basis of protest is a general sense that the selective service
rules and the war in Vietnam are unjust to others, with whom the student is identified, but whose fate he does not share. A rundown of the
list of causes taken up by student activists reveals that only in rare
cases are demonstrations directed at improving the lot of the protesters
themselves. Identification with the oppressed is a more important
motivating factor than an actual sense of immediate personal oppression.

The anti-ideological stance of today's activists has been widely
noted. Their distrust of formal ideologies and, at times, of articulate
thought makes it difficult to pinpoint the positive social and political
values of student protesters. Clearly they oppose many current American institutions, such as de facto segregation. Clearly, too, most students of the New Left reject careerism and familism as personal values.
In this sense, we might think of them as politically alienated.

But the alienation label seems to me more misleading than

[3] Paul Heist, "The Dynamics of Student Discontent and Protest," paper
read at American Psychological Association conference, New York, 1966.

illuminating, for it overlooks the more basic commitment of most student activists to other ancient, traditional, and credal American values like free speech, citizen's participation in decision making, equal opportunity, and justice. To emphasize the alienation of activists is to neglect that most still retain their basic allegiance to the American creed. Insofar as they reject all or part of the power structure, they do so because current political realities fall so far short of the ideals they see as central to the American ideal. And insofar as they repudiate career-ism and familism, they do so because of implicit allegiance to other human goals seen as more crucial to American life.

One of their ideals is, of course, a belief in the desirability of political and social action. Sustained in good measure by the successes of the student civil rights movement, the protester is usually convinced that demonstrations are effective in mobilizing public opinion, bringing moral or political pressure to bear, demonstrating the existence of his opinions, or at times, in "bringing the machine to a halt." In this sense, then, despite his criticisms of existing political practices and social institutions, he is a political optimist. The protester must believe, as well, in at least minimal organization and group activity; otherwise, he would find it impossible to take part, as he does, in any organized demonstrations or activities. In spite of their search for what they call more truly democratic forms of organization and action—participatory democracy, for instance—activists agree that group action is more effective than purely individual acts. Belief in the value and efficacy of political action is not, of course, equivalent to endorsement of preva-lent political institutions or forms of activity. What the activists are seeking is new forms of social action, protest, and political organization —such as sit-in, participatory democracy, or community organization —which will be more effective and less oppressive than traditional political institutions.

In contrast to the politically optimistic, active, and socially concerned protester, the culturally alienated student is far too pessi-mistic and too firmly opposed to the system to wish to demonstrate his disapproval in any organized public way.[4] His demonstrations of dis-

---

[4] These paragraphs are based on the study of culturally alienated students described in K. Keniston, *The Uncommitted* New York: Harcourt, 1965). For a more extensive discussion of the overwhelmingly anti-political stance of these students, see K. Keniston, "The Psychology of Alienated Stu-

sent are private: through nonconformity of behavior, ideology, and dress, through personal experimentation, and above all through efforts to intensify his own subjective experience, he shows his distaste and disinterest in politics and society. The activist attempts to change the world around him, but the alienated student is convinced that meaningful change in the social and political world is impossible. To him, dropping out appears to be the only real option.

Although alienated students tend to be drawn from the same general social strata and colleges as protesters, their background, both psychologically and ideologically, is often entirely different. They are more likely to be disturbed psychologically; and although they are often highly talented and artistically gifted, they are less committed to academic values and intellectual achievement than are protesters. The alienated student's real campus is the school of the absurd. He has more affinity for pessimistic existentialist ontology than for traditional American activism. For him, it is usually psychologically and ideologically impossible to take part in organized group activities for any length of time, especially if expected to assume any responsibility for leadership. On the rare occasions when such students do become involved at all in demonstrations, they may usually be found in peripheral roles, avoiding responsibility, and being adjudged a nuisance by serious activists.[5]

Whereas the protesting student is apt to accept the basic political and social values of his parents, the alienated student almost always rejects them. He tends, in particular, to see his father as a man who has sold out to the pressures for success and status in American society; he is determined to avoid the fate that overtook his father. Toward their mothers, however, alienated students usually express a

---

dents," paper read at American Psychological Association conference, New York, 1966; and Francis J. Rigney and L. D. Smith, *The Real Bohemia* (New York: Basic Books, 1961); M. Allen and H. Silverstein, *Progress Report: Creative Arts–Alienated Youth Project* (New York: March 1967); William Watts and David Whittaker, *Sociopsychological Characteristics of Intellectually Oriented, Alienated Youth: A Study of the Berkeley Nonstudent* (Berkeley: University of California, 1967), mimeographed; Whittaker and Watts, "Personality and Value Attitudes of Intellectually Disposed, Alienated Youth," paper presented at American Psychological Association conference, New York, 1966.

[5] Hal Draper, *Berkeley: The New Student Revolt* (New York: Grove Press, 1965).

very special sympathy and identification. Too often, these mothers have been oversolicitous and limiting, neglecting to encourage their sons to move toward independence and achievement. The most common family environment of the alienated-student-to-be consists of a parental schism, supplemented by a special mother-son alliance of mutual understanding, maternal control, and deprecation of the father.[6]

Alienated students often constitute, in many colleges, a kind of hiden underground, disorganized and shifting in membership, in which students can temporarily or permanently withdraw from the ordinary pressures of college life. It is a mistake in general, however, to associate the college dropout with the dissenter, whether he is a protester or an alienated student. The opposite is more nearly the truth. Although considerable attention has been given to the presence among student dissenters of a group of nonstudents (dropouts from college or graduate school who congregate near some academic center), the number of students who have chosen to drop out of college for a period solely to devote themselves to political and societal protest activities is little more than a handful. In fact, student protesters seem somewhat *less* likely than nondemonstrators to drop out of college.[7]

Nor is there any evidence that dropping out of college is related to dissent from American society. Several studies[8] suggest, on the contrary, that the academically gifted and psychologically intact student who drops out of college voluntarily has few distinctive discontents about his college or about American society. If he is dissatisfied at all, it is with himself, usually for failing to take advantage of the "rich educational opportunities" he sees in his college. The motivations of

[6] Keniston, *The Uncommitted, op. cit.*

[7] Heist, *op. cit.*

[8] K. Keniston and R. Helmreich, *An Exploratory Study of Discontent and Potential Dropouts at Yale* (New Haven: Yale University, 1965), mimeographed. Several other studies suggest further that the academically gifted and psychologically intact student who drops out of college voluntarily has few distinctive discontents about his college or about American society. See Robert Francis Suczek and E. Alfert, *Personality Characteristics of College Dropouts* (Berkeley: University of California, 1966), mimeographed; Lawrence A. Pervin *et al., The College Dropout and the Utilization of Talent* (Princeton, N.J.: Princeton University Press, 1966); E. O. Wright, "Student Leaves of Absence from Harvard College: A Personality and Social System Approach," unpublished paper, Harvard University, 1966.

students dropping out of college are complex and varied; but these more often seem related to personal questions of self-definition and parental identification—or to a desire to escape relentless academic pressures—than to a special dissent from American society.

Alienated students are especially attracted to the hallucinogenic drugs like marijuana, mescaline, and LSD, precisely because these agents combine withdrawal from ordinary social life with the promise of greatly intensified subjectivity and perception. To the confirmed acid head, what matters is intense, drug-assisted perception. The rest— including politics, social action, and student demonstrations—is usually seen as mere role-playing.

The recent and much publicized emergence of hippie sub-cultures in several major cities—and increasingly on the campuses of many selective and progressive colleges—illustrates the overwhelmingly apolitical stance of alienated youth. For although hippies oppose war and believe in interracial living, few have been willing or able to engage in anything beyond occasional peace marches or apolitical "human be-ins." Indeed, the hippie's emphasis upon immediacy, love, and turning on, together with his basic rejection of the traditional values of American life, inoculates him against involvement in long-range activist endeavors like education or community organization— even against the sustained effort needed to plan and execute demonstrations or marches. To the alienated hippie, American society appears to be beyond redemption, or not worth trying to redeem. But for the activist, no matter how intense his rejection of specific policies and practices, the firm conviction remains that American society is worth saving and can be changed. Cooperation between the alienated and the activists is, therefore, a rarity, whatever occasional agreement on principle there may be between them. Any attempt at cooperation is apt to end with the activists accusing the alienated of irresponsibility, while the alienated are, in turn, more confirmed in their view of activists as moralistic, up tight, and uncool.

No description of a type can ever fit any individual perfectly, of course. But by this rough typology, I mean to suggest that popular stereotypes, presenting a unified portrait of student dissenters, are gravely oversimplified: they confuse the politically pessimistic and socially uncommitted alienated student with the politically hopeful and socially committed activist. Many students, to be sure, fall between these two extremes; some may even alternate between passionate search for intensified subjectivity and equally passionate efforts to remedy social and political injustices. And as I suggest below, even within the student movement, one of the central tensions is between political activism and cultural alienation. To hope to understand this tension, we must first distinguish between the varieties of dissent apparent on American campuses.

The distinction between activist and alienated students as psychological types further suggests the incompleteness of scholarly analyses that see social and historical factors as the only forces that push a student toward one or the other of these forms of dissent. Social and cultural factors are of immense importance, to be sure, in providing channels for the expression or suppression of dissent, and in determining *which* kinds of dissenters receive publicity, censure, support, or ostracism in any historical period. But these factors cannot, in general, change a hippie into a committed activist or an SNCC field worker into a full-time acid head. Thus, the prototypical activist of 1966 is not the same sort of student as the prototypical bohemian of 1956. He is, rather, the politically aware, though frustrated, academically oriented privatist of that era. Similarly, as I will argue below, the most compelling alternative to most activists is not the search for kicks or sentience but the quest for scholarly competence. And if culturally sanctioned opportunities for the expression of alienation were to disappear, most alienated students would turn to private psychopathology rather than to public activism.

Stated more generally, historical forces do not ordinarily transform radically the character, values, and inclinations of an adult in later life. They tend, instead, to thrust certain groups forward in some eras, discouraging or suppressing others. Recent alternation in styles of student dissent in America stems, therefore, not so much from the malleability of individual character as from the power of society to bring activists into the limelight, providing them with the intellectual and moral instruments for action. Only a minority of potential dissenters falls close enough to the midpoint between alienation and activism to constitute a "swing vote," acutely responsive to social and cultural pressures and styles. The rest, in the majority, are characterologically committed to one or another style of dissent.

What are the sources of the recent wave of protest by college students? Certainly there is nothing new about alienation in American life. Bohemians, beatniks, and artistically inclined undergraduates who rejected middle-class values have long been a part of the American student scene, especially at the more selective colleges. They constituted the most visible form of dissent during the relative political silence of American students in the 1950s.

What is distinctive about student dissent in recent years is the unexpected emergence of a vocal minority of politically and socially active protesters on American campuses.[9] It is abundantly clear that no single factor will suffice to explain this phenomenon. At least four seem involved in any one protest: the involved individual's predisposition toward dissent through personal background, values, and motivation; a suitable educational and social setting; a special cultural climate; and a conducive historical situation.

Although much is known of the characteristics of dissidents and the circumstances nurturing activism, much is still unknown. In exploring these areas of ignorance, I make certain hypotheses concerning the sources of student dissent. These are necessarily complex and interrelated, however narrow the definition of an activist. Most narrowly defined, he may be said to be one who works within a group toward basic social or political change, motivated by concern for some ethical, social, theoretical, or political issues. Increasingly, such students espouse a hatred of the war in Vietnam, or acute concern for the plight and portion of black Americans, and an interest in restructuring (or even destroying) the university in its present form.

I use the terms *activist* and *protester* interchangeably, although I am aware that some activists are not involved in protest and that the category of activism embraces certain distinct subclasses,[10] which are rarely distinguished.

---

[9] Student activism, albeit of a rather different nature, was also found in the 1930s. For a discussion and contrast of student protest today and after the depression, see S. M. Lipset, "Student Opposition in the United States," *Government and Opposition*, 1965, *1*, 351–374.

[10] First of the subclasses is those who might be termed *reformers;* that is, students involved in community organization work, the Peace Corps, tutoring programs, VISTA, and the like, but not generally affiliated with any of the

Basic to the make-up of the activist is a protest-prone personality. A remarkably consistent picture of protest-prone individuals emerges from a large and still-growing number of studies,[11] conducted under different auspices, at different times, and about different students. From these, student protesters appear to be generally outstanding students: the higher the student's grade average and the more outstanding his academic achievement, the more likely he is to become involved in any particular political demonstration. Similarly, student activists come from families with liberal political values. A disproportionate number report that their parents hold views essentially similar to their own and accept or support their activities. Thus, among the parents of protesters, we find large numbers of liberal Democrats, plus an unusually large scattering of pacifists, socialists, and the like. A dis-

New Left organizations. Second is the group of *activists proper,* most of whom are or have been affiliated with organizations like the Free Speech Movement at Berkeley, Students for a Democratic Society, the Student Nonviolent Coordinating Committee, the Congress on Racial Equality, or the Vietnam Summer Project. Finally, there is a much publicized handful of students who might be considered *extremists,* who belong to doctrinaire Marxist and Trotskyite organizations like the now-defunct May Second Movement. No empirical study with which I am acquainted has investigated the differences between students in these three subgroups. Most studies have concentrated on the activist proper, and my remarks will be based on a reading of their data.

[11] See M. Aiken, N. J. Demerath, and G. Marwell, *Conscience and Confrontation: Some Preliminary Findings on Summer Civil Rights Volunteers* (Madison: University of Wisconsin, 1966), mimeographed; Richard Flacks, Chapter Five, this volume; D. Gastwirth, "Why Students Protest," unpublished paper, Yale University, 1965; P. Heist, "Intellect and Commitment: The Faces of Discontent," in *Order and Freedom on the Campus* (Boulder, Colo.: Western Interstate Commission for Higher Education and the Center for the Study of Higher Education, 1965); P. Heist, "The Dynamics of Student Discontent and Protest," *op. cit.;* G. Lyonns, "The Police Car Demonstration: A Survey of Participants," in S. M. Lipset and S. Wolin (Eds.), *The Berkeley Student Revolt* (New York: Doubleday, 1965); R. H. Somers, "The Mainsprings of the Rebellion: A Survey of Berkeley Students in November 1964," in Lipset and Wolin, *op. cit.;* William Watts and David Whittaker, "Some Socio-Psychological Differences Between Highly Committed Members of the Free Speech Movement and the Student Population at Berkeley," *Journal of Applied Behavioral Science,* 1966, 2, 41–62; D. Westby and R. Braungart, "Class and Politics in the Family Backgrounds of Student Political Activists," *American Sociological Review,* 1966, *31,* 690–692; J. Katz, *The Student Activists, op. cit.;* O. Paulus, *A Multivariate Analysis Study of Student Activist Leaders, Student Government Leaders, and Non-activists* (cited in Richard E. Peterson, "The student left in American higher education," *op. cit.*).

proportionate number of protesters come from Jewish families; and if the parents of activists are religious, they tend to be concentrated in the more liberal denominations—Reform Judaism, Unitarianism, the Society of Friends. Such parents are reported to have high ethical and political standards, regardless of their actual religious convictions.

As might be expected of a group of politically liberal and academically talented students, a disproportionate number are drawn from professional and intellectual families of upper middle-class status. Compared with active student conservatives, members of protest groups tend to have higher parental incomes, more parental education, and less anxiety about social status.[12] High levels of education appear to distinguish the activist's family even in the grandparental generation.[13] In brief, activists—so far from being drawn from disadvantaged, status-anxious, underprivileged, or uneducated groups—are selectively recruited from among those young Americans who have had the most socially fortunate upbringings.

Basic value commitments of the activist tend to be academic and nonvocational. Such students are rarely found among engineers, future teachers at teachers colleges, or students of business administration.[14] Their overall educational goals are those of a liberal education for its own sake, not specific technical, vocational, or professional preparation. Rejecting careerist and familist goals, activists espouse humanitarian, expressive, and self-actualizing values. Perhaps because of these values, they tend to delay career choice longer than their classmates.

Nor are such students distinctively dogmatic, rigid, or authoritarian. On the contrary, the substance and style of their beliefs and activities tend to be open, flexible, and highly liberal. They incline toward the social sciences and humanities as fields of academic specialization and take their academic commitments seriously, dropping out of college less frequently than most of their classmates. As might be expected, a disproportionate number receive a B.A. within four years and continue with graduate school, in preparation for academic careers.

[12] Westby and Braungart, *op. cit.*

[13] Richard Flacks, Chapter Five, this volume.

[14] James Trent and Judith Craise, "Commitment and Conformity in the American College," *Journal of Social Issues,* 1967, *23,* 34–51.

Survey data suggest that dissatisfaction with educational failings of the impersonal multiversity—however important as a rallying cry—does not, in fact, appear to be a distinctive cause of activism. Since activists generally attend colleges which provide the best undergraduate education available today, they probably have less to complain about objectively in their undergraduate educations than most other students. Subjectively, too, surveys by Somers and by Kornhauser show that most activists share with other American undergraduates relative satisfaction with the quality of their undergraduate educations.

In contrast, they are distinctly dissatisfied with what might be be termed the "civil libertarian" defects of their college administrations. Distrust of University Hall—no doubt prevalent among many American undergraduates—is especially pronounced among student protesters.[15] They tend, also, to be more responsive than other students to deprivations of civil rights, on campus as well as off, particularly when political pressures appear to motivate campus policies they consider unjust. The same responsiveness extends, increasingly, to issues of student power—student participation in decisions affecting campus life. Bans on controversial speakers, censorship of student publications, and limitations on off-campus political or social action are apt to incense the activist, to say nothing of arbitrary "administration without the consent of the administered." It is such actions—primarily perceived as unjust or a denial of student rights by the administration—which agitate the activist, not poor educational quality, neglect by the faculty, or the impersonality of the multiversity.

Most studies of activists have concentrated on variables which are relatively easy to measure: social class, academic achievement, explicit values, and satisfaction with college. But these factors alone will not explain activism. More students possess the demographic and attitudinal characteristics of the protest-prone personality than are actually involved in protests and social action programs. Situational, institutional, cultural, and historical factors, discussed below, obviously contribute to catalyzing a protest-prone personality into an actual protester.

There are also, however, more specific psychodynamic factors

[15] W. Kornhauser, "Alienation and Participation in the Mass University," paper read at American Orthopsychiatric Association, Washington, D.C., 1967; Paulus, op. cit.

which contribute to activism within the broad demographic group so far defined. In discussing them, however, we must leave the ground of established fact and enter that of speculation. Few studies[16] have explored the personality dynamics and family constellation of the activist, and most of these are impressionistic and clinical. Yet certain facts are clear. As noted above, there is some evidence that activists— so far from repudiating or rebelling against explicit parental values and ideologies—are living them out in practice. Flacks goes so far as to suggest that activists may actually be somewhat closer to their parents' values than nonactivists. Any concept of generational conflict or rebellion against parental authority as forces of protest motivation is obviously an oversimplification.

It does seem probable, however, that many activists are concerned with living out expressed but unimplemented parental values. Solomon and Fishman, in their 1963 study of civil rights activists and peace marchers, argued that many of the demonstrators were acting out values in which their parents explicitly believed, but for which they did not have the courage to fight. Similarly, criticism of fathers by protesters appeared to be mostly for failure to practice what they had preached throughout their children's lives. In the personal background of the protester is occasionally a suggestion that the father is less than sincere and even, at times, hypocritical in his profession of political liberalism. Both careerism and familism are favorite butts of activist criticism because of the conflict between these implicit goals and explicit parental values. Protesters may possibly receive both covert and overt

16 For example, Robert Coles, *Children of Crisis* (Boston: Little, Brown, 1967); John Ehle, *The Free Men* (New York: Harper, 1965); Hal Draper, *op. cit.;* Jacob R. Fishman and Frederic Solomon, "Psychological Observations on the Student Sit-in Movement," *Proceedings of the Third World Congress of Psychiatry* (Toronto: University of Toronto/McGill, 1961); Fishman and Solomon, "Youth and Social Action," *Journal of Social Issues,* 1964, *20,* 1–28; Gastwirth, *op. cit.;* Jack Newfield, *A Prophetic Minority* (New York: New American Library, 1966); Patricia Schneider, "A Study of Members of SDS and YD at Harvard," unpublished B.A. thesis, Wellesley College, 1966; F. Solomon and J. R. Fishman, "Perspectives on the Student Sit-in Movement," *American Journal of Orthopsychiatry,* 1963, *33,* 873–874; Solomon and Fishman, "Youth and Peace: a Psycho-social Study of Student Peace Demonstrators in Washington, D.C.," *Journal of Social Issues,* 1964, *20,* 54–73; Howard Zinn, *SNCC: The New Abolitionists* (Boston: Beacon, 1965).

support from their parents because of a secret pride in their children's eagerness to implement the ideals to which they, as parents, have been able to give lip-service only. The ambivalence of the situation must not, however, be overemphasized. More significant, by far, is the solidarity of older and younger generations and its influence in producing the protest-prone personality.

No empirical study has yet tested a second hypothesis of my own concerning the activist-producing family as a source of student dissent. It relates to the significance of what might be called the protest-promoting family, in which the mother has a dominant psychological influence on her son's development. I have already noted that the protester's cause is rarely himself, but the hope of alleviating the oppression of others. As a group, activists seem to possess an unusual capacity for nurturant identification; that is, for empathy and sympathy with the underdog, the oppressed, and the needy. Such a capacity can have many origins, but its most common source in upper middle-class professional families is identification with an active mother, whose own work embodies nurturant concern for others. Flacks' finding that the mothers of activists are likely to be employed, often in professional or service roles, such as teaching and social work, is consistent with this hypothesis. Middle-class women in American society have, generally, greater social and financial freedom to work in jobs which are idealistically fulfilling, as opposed to merely lucrative or prestigious. As a rule, then, it is the mother in such families who actively embodies in her life and work the humanitarian, social, and political ideals that the father may share in principle but cannot, or does not, implement in his career.

Given what we know about the general characteristics of the families of protest-prone students, it also seems probable that the dominant ethos of their families is unusually equalitarian, permissive, democratic, and highly individuated. We might expect these to be families in which children talk back to their parents at the dinner table, free dialogue and discussion of feelings is encouraged, and "rational" solutions are sought to everyday family problems and conflicts. We would also expect that such families would place a high premium on self-expression and intellectual independence, encouraging their children to make up their own minds and to stand firm against group pressures. Once again, the mother seems the most likely carrier and epitome of these values, given her relative freedom from professional and financial pressures.

The contrast between such protest-prompting families and alienating families should be underlined. In both, the son's deepest emotional ties are often to his mother. But in the alienating family, the mother-son relationship is characterized by maternal control and intrusiveness, whereas in the protest-prompting family, the mother is a highly individuating force in her son's life, pushing him to independence and autonomy. The alienated student feels determined to avoid the fate that befell his father; the protesting one merely wants to live out the values his father has not always worked hard enough to practice. Finally, the egalitarian, permissive, democratic, and individuating environment of the entire family of the protester contrasts with the overcontrolling, oversolicitous attitude of the mother in the alienating family, in which the father is usually excluded from major emotional life within the family.

These hypotheses about the family background and psychodynamics of the protester are speculative, and future research could prove their invalidity. But regardless of whether these particular speculations are correct, it seems clear that protest-proneness depends, not only upon the general social, demographic, and attitudinal factors mentioned in most research, but also upon more specific familial and psychodynamic influences.

One activist—however his characteristics may be defined— cannot alone make a protest. The protest-promoting institution has much to do with whether his proneness will ever be mobilized into actual activism. Politically, socially, and ideologically motivated demonstrations are most likely to occur at certain types of college: they are almost unknown on a majority of campuses. The effects of institutional characteristics on protests have been studied by Cowan, Peterson, Sampson, and Brown.[17]

In order for an organized protest or related activities to occur,

---

[17] See John Lewis Cowan, "Academic Freedom, Protest, and University Environments," paper read at American Psychological Association conference, New York, 1966; Peterson, *The Scope of Organized Student Protest in 1964–65, op. cit.;* Edward Sampson, Chapter One, this volume; Donald R. Brown, Chapter Four, this volume.

there must obviously be sufficient numbers of protest-prone students to form a group, with leaders to initiate and mount the protest, and an opportunity for interaction among the students. Thus we might expect —and we indeed find—that protest is associated with institutional size, particularly with the congregation of large numbers of protest-prone students in proximity to each other. More important than sheer size alone, however, is the image of the institution: certain ones selectively recruit students with protest-prone characteristics. A reputation for academic excellence and freedom, coupled with highly selective admissions policies, will tend to lure large numbers of potentially protesting students to the campus. Certain institutions seem, therefore, to act as magnets for potential activists—not so much because of their reputations for political radicalism as because they are noted for their academic excellence. Among such institutions are some of the most selective and progressive private liberal arts colleges, major state universities, such as Michigan, California at Berkeley, and Wisconsin, which have long traditions of vivid undergraduate teaching and high admissions standards,[18] and many of the more prestigious private universities.

Once protest-prone students are on campus, they must have an opportunity to interact, to support one another, to develop common outlooks and shared policies—in short, to form an activist subculture with sufficient mass and potency to generate a demonstration or action program. Establishing honors colleges for talented and academically motivated students is one particularly effective way of creating a critical mass of protest-prone students. Similarly, inadequate on-campus housing indirectly results in the development of off-campus protest-prone subcultures (for example, co-op houses) in residences where student activists can develop a high degree of ideological solidarity and organizational cohesion.

But even the presence of a critical mass of protest-prone undergraduates in an activist subculture is not enough to make a protest without leaders and issues. The most effective protest leaders have, in general, not been undergraduates, but teaching assistants. The presence of large numbers of exploited, underpaid, disgruntled, and frustrated teacher assistants—or other equivalent graduate students and younger

---

[18] Lipset and Altbach, *op. cit.*

faculty members—is almost essential for organized and persistent protest. Advanced students tend to be more liberal politically, for one thing, and more sensitive to political issues than most undergraduates —partly because education seems to have a liberalizing effect, and partly because students who persist into graduate school tend to be more liberal from the start than those who drop out or go elsewhere. Furthermore, the frustrations of graduate students, especially at very large public universities, make them particularly sensitive to general problems of injustice, exploitation, and oppression. Teaching assistants, graduate students, and young faculty members also tend to be in daily and prolonged contact with students, are close enough to them in age to sense their mood, and are therefore in an excellent position to lead and organize student protests. Particularly at institutions which command little institutional allegiance from large numbers of highly capable graduate students, Lipset and Altbach found such students to be in the forefront of the protest movement.

Issues, too, are a necessity. They may be provided by historical developments on the national or international scene, a point to which I will return. But in some instances, as at Berkeley, on-campus issues are the focus of protest. In other cases, off-campus and on-campus issues are fused—as in the recent protests over institutional cooperation with draft board policies considered unjust by demonstrating students. The attitude of the university administration is of central importance in providing such issues. The likelihood of organized protest may be minimized by skillful handling of student complaints, the maintenance of open channels of communication between student leaders and faculty members, and administrative willingness to resist public and political pressures in order to protect the rights of students. Conversely, a university administration is asking for trouble if it shows itself to be unduly sensitive to political, legislative, or public pressures, or treats students arrogantly, ineptly, condescendingly, hypocritically, or—above all—dishonestly.

Thus one reason for the relative absence of on-campus student protests and demonstrations on the campuses of private, nondenominational "academic" colleges and universities, which recruit many protest-prone students, probably lies in the liberal policies of the administrations. As Cowan noted in his 1966 study, liberal students generally attend nonrestrictive and "libertarian" colleges. Given an administration and faculty which support or tolerate activism and student rights, student activists must generally find their issues off-campus. The same ones might conceivably engage in strenuous on-campus protest if confronting an administration unduly sensitive to political pressures from a conservative board of regents or state legislature. There is also some evidence that clever administrative manipulation of student complaints, even in the absence of genuine concern with their rights, can serve to dissipate the potentialities of protest.[19]

Among the institutional factors often cited as motivating student protest are the largeness, impersonality, atomization, "multiversification," and so on, of the university. Yet, as noted above, student protesters do not seem distinctively dissatisfied with their educations. Besides, their outstanding academic achievements and intellectual motivation concentrate them, within any college, in the courses and programs providing the most personal attention: honors programs, individual instruction, advanced seminars, and so on. It is probable, then, that they receive relatively more individual attention and a higher caliber of instruction than do nonprotesters. Furthermore, protests generally tend to occur at the best, rather than the worst colleges, judged from the point of view of the quality of undergraduate instruction. Thus, despite the popularity of student slogans dealing with the impersonality and irrelevance of the multiversity, the absolute level of educational opportunity would appear to be, if anything, positively related to the occurrence of protest: the better the institution, the more likely are demonstrations.

Nor can today's student activism be attributed in any direct way to mounting academic pressure. To be sure, it is most manifest at those selective colleges in which the pressure to perform is greatest,[20] standards highest, and anxiety most pronounced over being admitted to a "good" graduate or professional school. But contrary to the argument advanced by Lipset and Altbach in their 1966 study of student politics and higher education, the impact of academic pressure on activism seems rather more negative than positive. Protest-prone students, with their superior academic attainments and strong intellectual

---

[19] S. Keene, "How One Big University Laid Unrest to Rest," *The American Student*, 1966, *1*, 18–21.

[20] K. Keniston, "The Pressure to Perform," *The Intercollegian*, September 1965.

commitments, seem especially vulnerable to a kind of academic professionalism which, because of the enormous demands it makes upon the student's energies, serves to cancel or preclude activism. Student demonstrations rarely take place during examination periods; protests concerned with educational quality almost invariably seek to improve it, not to lessen pressure. Pressure to perform, undoubtedly affecting all American students, appears to act as a deterrent and not a stimulus to student activism.

What probably does matter is the relative deprivation of student expectations.[21] Student protests over the quality of education may well arise from the academic backlash created by a college which, for instance, recruits large numbers of academically motivated and capable students into a less-than-first-rate educational program. Or one that oversells entering freshmen on the virtues of the college, or reneges on implicit or explicit promises about the quality and freedom of education. Even more important is the gap between expectation and actuality with respect to freedom of student expression. Stern has demonstrated, in his "Myth and Reality in the American College," that most entering freshmen have extremely high hopes regarding the freedom of speech and action they will be able to exercise during college. Most of them learn the facts quickly and graduate thoroughly disabused of their illusions.

But activists—being particularly responsive to these issues, as argued above—are apt to tolerate disillusion less lightly and to take up arms in order to give concrete expression to their dashed hopes. The relative deprivation of civil libertarian hopes appears to be a more potent source of protest than frustration engendered by disillusionment concerning educational quality. It must be recalled that, in both respects, protests have been found to be fewest at institutions of low educational quality and little freedom of student expression. What matters, then, is not the absolute level of either educational quality or student freedom, but the gap between student hopes and institutional facts.

The quiescence of American students during the 1950s suggests that student protests are by no means inevitable, even when a critical mass of interacting protest-prone students gathers in an institution

---

[21] See Brown, Chapter Four, this volume.

providing leadership and issues. Something more is necessary, which might be termed a protest-prompting cultural climate, incorporating broadly cultural factors, attitudes, and values. Protest activities must be seen as meaningful acts, in either an instrumental or an expressive sense. Activists must be convinced that the consequences of activism and protest will not be overwhelmingly damaging to them. One factor which was much discussed during the 1950s and may have militated against student activism was a general belief in the extreme likelihood of its harmful consequences for the individual—blacklisting, FBI investigations, problems in obtaining security clearance, difficulty in getting jobs. Of perhaps even greater importance was a feeling among many politically conscious students that participation in left-wing causes could only reveal their naivete, gullibility, and political innocence without furthering any worthy cause. The prevailing climate was such that protest was rarely seen as an act of any meaning or usefulness.

Today, in contrast, student protesters—although criticized and excoriated by a large segment of the general public—are also (and this is more crucial) actively defended, encouraged, lionized, praised, publicized, photographed, interviewed, and studied by a portion of the academic community. Since the primary reference group of most activists is not the general public, but that liberal segment of the academic world most sympathetic to protest, such support has a disproportionate impact on protest-prone students' perception of their own activities. The active participation of admired faculty members in protests, teach-ins, and peace marches acts as a further incentive to students.[22] Thus in a certain number of American colleges, subcultures have arisen where protest is felt to be both an important existential act—a dignified way of "standing up to be counted"—and an effective method of "bringing the machine to a halt," sometimes by disruptive acts such as sit-ins or strikes; more often by calling public attention to injustice.

An equally significant, if less tangible, cultural factor is the broad climate of social criticism in American society. Parsons and White are among those noting that an enduring theme of American society is the pressure toward "universalism"; that is, an increasing

[22] H. D. Kelman, "Notes on Faculty Activism," letter to University of Michigan Alumni, 1966,

extension of principles like equality, equal opportunity, and fair protection of the law to all groups within the society—and in recent years, to all groups in the world.[23] With an increase of affluence in American society comes impatience with the lack of progress in nonaffluent minority groups. This is true not only of student groups, but of other segments of the population as well. Support for racial segregation was diminishing even before the advent of the student civil rights movement. Similarly, current concern for the "forgotten fifth" was not so much initiated by student activists as taken up by them. Thus they find themselves both caught up in and in the vanguard of a new wave of extension of universalism. Student activists, while usually going far beyond the national consensus, do reflect—as well as help advance—one of the continuing trends in American social change.

A contrasting but equally enduring theme in American social criticism is a more fundamental revulsion against the premises of industrial—and now technological—society. Universalistic-liberal criticism blames our society for not having yet extended its principles, privileges, and benefits to all. The complaint is injustice; the goal is to complete our unfinished business. But alienated-romantic criticism questions the validity and importance of these same principles, privileges, and benefits. In this case, the complaint is materialism and the goal spiritual, aesthetic, or expressive fulfillment. The tradition of revulsion against conformist, anti-esthetic, materialistic, ugly, middle-class America runs through literature from Melville to the Lost and Beat Generations and has been expressed concretely in the bohemian subcultures flourishing in a few large American cities since the turn of the century.

Today, the power of the romantic-alienated position has increased. One response to prosperity is a more searching examination of the technological assumptions upon which prosperity has been based. Affluence is taken for granted, especially by the children of the upper middle class. The drive to "get ahead in the world" makes no sense for students who start out ahead. Life's meaning must be sought elsewhere—in art, sentience, philosophy, love, service to others, intensified experience, adventure. It must, in short, be found in the broadly esthetic or expressive realm.

[23] Talcott Parsons, *The Social System* (Glencoe, Ill.: Free Press, 1951); T. Parsons, *Structure and Process in Modern Societies* (Glencoe, Ill.: Free Press, 1960); Winston White, *Beyond Conformity* (Glencoe, Ill.: Free Press, 1961).

Since neither the universalistic nor the romantic critique of modern society is new, they affect the current student generation *indirectly* as well as directly, because of their influence upon upbringing. Lipset and Altbach indicate that a few of today's activists are children of the "radicals of the 1930s"; and Flacks comments on the growing number of intellectual, professional upper middle-class families who have adopted "deviant" views of traditional American life and embodied them in the practices by which they brought up their children. Some of today's activists are, then, the children of bohemians, college professors, and so on.

Still, in general, parental deviance does not seem a fully convincing explanation. The backgrounds of activists are, indeed, "atypical" in a statistical sense and might, therefore, be termed empirically "deviant." Their parents may, in fact, prove to be distinguished by their emphasis on humanitarianism, intellectualism, and romanticism, and by their lack of stress on moralism, as Flacks indicates. But it is not obvious that such parental values can be termed deviant in any but a statistical sense. Concern with the plight of others, desire to realize intellectual capacities, and lack of concern about the importance of strictly controlling personal impulses—all these values may be thought of as more normative than deviant in the upper middle-class suburban American society of 1966. Even sensitivity to beauty and art is becoming increasingly acceptable. Nor can such socioeconomic facts as affluence, freedom from status anxiety, high educational levels, permissiveness with children, and training for independence be considered normatively deviant in middle-class America. Thus, the sense in which activists are seen as deviant offspring of subculturally deviant parents remains to be clarified.

Another explanation, which seems equally plausible for certain student activists, is the relationship of their activism to the social and cultural conditions promoting high levels of psychological flexibility, complexity, and integration. As Bay argues,[24] social scientists tend to be too reluctant to entertain the possibility that some political and social outlooks or activities are symptomatic of psychological *health*, while others indicate "disturbance." Many of the personal characteristics of activists—empathy, superior intellectual attainments,

---

[24] Christian Bay, Chapter Three, this volume.

capacity for group involvement, strong humanitarian values, emphasis on self-realization—are actually altogether consistent with the hypothesis that, as a group, they are unusually healthy psychologically. Similarly, the personal antecedents of the activist—for example, economic security, committed parents; humanitarian, liberal, and permissive home environments; good education—are those which would seem to promote unusually high levels of psychological functioning.

If this is correct, former SDS president Tom Hayden's words may be a valid commentary on the cultural setting of activism: "Most of the active student radicals today come from middle to upper middle-class professional homes. They were born with status and affluence as facts of life, not goals to be striven for. In their upbringing, their parents stressed the right of children to question and make judgments, producing perhaps the first generation of young people both affluent and independent of mind."[25]

While agreeing with Bay that activists may be more psychologically healthy as a group than nonactivists, I am fully aware of the difficulties entailed by the hypothesis. It is by no means easy to define such concepts as complexity, flexibility, integration, or high levels of functioning; and criteria for positive mental health remain vague and elusive.[26] Then, too, there are obviously many individuals with the same so-called healthy characteristics who are not activists, just as there are many within the group of activists who do have definite psychopathologies. A variety of individuals with highly diverse talents and motivations are bound to be involved in any social movement; global descriptions are certain to be oversimplified. A third consideration is that explanations of activism based upon psychological health and upon parental deviance are not necessarily opposed. They may, in fact, become identical, if we assume that the preconditions for high levels of psychological functioning are both statistically and normatively deviant in modern American society. This assumption seems quite plausible.

Whatever may be the most reasonable explanation of the sociocultural sources of activism, the importance of prevailing attitudes

    [25] Tom Hayden, quoted in *Comparative Education Review*, 1966, *10*, 187.
    [26] Marie Jahoda, *Current Concepts of Positive Mental Health* (New York: Basic Books, 1958).

toward student protest and of the climate of social criticism in America seems clear. In recent years a conviction has arisen—at least among a minority of American college students—that protest and social action are effective and honorable. Furthermore, changes in American society, especially middle-class child-rearing practices, have made our students increasingly responsive to both the universalistic and the romantic critiques of our society. Both strands of social criticism have been picked up by student activists in a rhetoric of protest, which combines a major theme of impatience over the slow fulfillment of American ideals, with a more muted minor theme of esthetic revulsion toward technological society itself. By and large, it is the activists who respond most affirmatively to the first of these; alienated students to the second. But within the student protest movement, the two themes coexist in uneasy tension.

Today's student activists appear to have a special sensitivity to historical events and trends, which do not immediately impinge upon their own lives. To separate what I am calling a protest-producing historical situation from "cultural climate" is largely arbitrary, although I think the difference significant. In other nations, and in the past, student protest movements seem to have been more closely related to immediate student frustrations than they are in America today. The transformationist aspirations of activist youth—utopian, Marxist, universalistic, or democratic—in rapidly developing nations often seem closely related to their personal frustrations under oppressive regimes or over the feudal practices of their societies. Restorationist youth movements—romantic, alienated—appearing in later stages of industrialization seem closely connected to a personal sense of the loss of a feudal, maternal, and organic past.[27] Both universalistic and romantic youth movements in other nations have traditionally been highly ideological, committed either to concepts of universal democracy and economic justice or to particularistic values of brotherhood, loyalty, feeling, and nation.

[27] See Robert Jay Lifton, "Japanese Youth: The Search for the New and the Pure," *The American Scholar,* 1960, *30,* 332–344; R. J. Lifton, "Youth and History: Individual Change in Postwar Japan," in E. Erikson (Ed.), *The Challenge of Youth* (New York: Harper, 1963); R. J. Lifton, "Individual Patterns in Historical Change," *Comparative Studies in Society and History,* 1964, *6,* 369–383.

Today's activists, in contrast, are rarely concerned with improving their own condition and are highly motivated by identification with the oppression of others. Virtually every commentator has underlined the anti-ideological bias of today's student activists. Flacks observes that the historical conditions which have produced protest elsewhere are largely absent in modern America; the student movement in this country differs in important ways from those elsewhere. Today's American activists have, then, no historical perspective in many respects. Only time will tell to what extent the appearance of organized student dissent in the 1960s is a product of national conditions, or the psychosocial effect of a technological affluence which will before long characterize other advanced nations as well; or the result of widespread changes in identity and style produced by psychohistorical factors affecting youth of all nations; for example, thermonuclear warfare, increased culture contact, and rapid communication.

But whatever the historical roots of protest, today's student protester seems uniquely sensitive to historical trends and events. In interviewing student activists, I have been impressed by how often they mention some world-historical event as the catalyst for their activism. Perhaps they witnessed by television the Little Rock demonstrations over school integration—or watched rioting Zengakuren students in Japan protesting the arrival of President Eisenhower. Negro students, in particular, may feel strong identification with the rising black nationalism of recently independent African nations.

Several factors help explain this sensitivity to world events. For one, modern means of communication make the historical world more psychologically available to youth. Students today are exposed to world events and world trends with a speed and intensity which has no historical precedent. Revolutions, trends, fashions, and fads are now worldwide. It takes but two or three years for fashions to spread from Carnaby Street to New York, New Delhi, Tokyo, Warsaw, Lagos, and Lima. In particular, students who have been brought up in a tradition that makes them unusually empathic, humanitarian, and universalistic in values may react more intensely to exposure via television to student demonstrations in Japan than to social pressures from their fellow seniors in Centerville High. Finally, this broadening of empathy is, I believe, part of a general modern trend toward the internationalization of identity. Hastened by modern communications and consolidated by the worldwide threat of nuclear warfare, this trend involves, in vanguard groups in many nations, a loosening of parochial and national allegiances in favor of a more inclusive sense of affinity with one's peers (and nonpeers) from all nations. In this respect, American student activists are both participants and leaders in the reorganization of psychosocial identity and ideology, which is gradually emerging from the unique historical conditions of the twentieth century.[28]

A small but growing number of American students, then, exhibit a peculiar responsiveness to world-historical events—a responsiveness based partly on their own broad identification with others like themselves throughout the world, and partly on the availability of information about world events via the mass media. The impact of historical events—be they the worldwide revolution for human dignity and esteem, the rising aspirations of the developing nations, or the war in Vietnam—is greatly magnified for these students. For their primary identification is not their unreflective national identity, but their sense of affinity for Vietnamese peasants, Negro sharecroppers, demonstrating Zengakuren activists, exploited migrant workers, and the oppressed everywhere. One of the consequences of security, affluence, and education is a growing sense of personal involvement with those who are insecure, nonaffluent, and uneducated.

Active expressions of dissent have, then, become more prevalent because of an interaction of individual, institutional, cultural, and historical factors. No single one of them can explain or help us predict the future of the student protest movement in America. Affluence and education have changed the environment within which middle-class children are reared, in turn producing a minority of students with special sensitivity to the oppressed and the dissenting everywhere. At the same time, technological innovations like television have made available to these students abundant imagery of oppression in America and in other nations. And each of these factors exerts a potentiating influence on the others.

WHAT OF THE FUTURE?

Where is all this leading? Are we likely to produce more protest-prone personalities, more of the institutional settings and cultural

[28] R. J. Lifton, *Protean Man* (New Haven: Yale University, 1965), mimeographed.

climate which foster dissent, and a historical situation facilitating activism? I suspect that a qualified yes concerning personality, institutions, and history may mean that, in the future, if the cultural climate remains the same, student activism and protest will continue to be visible features on the American social landscape.

Consider first the factors that promote protest-prone personalities. In the coming generation, there will be more and more students who come from the upper middle-class, highly educated, politically liberal professional backgrounds, from which protesters are selectively recruited.[29] We can expect that a significant and perhaps growing proportion of these families will have the universalistic, humanitarian, equalitarian, and individualistic values found in the families of protesters. The expressive, permissive, democratic, and autonomy-promoting atmosphere of these families seems to be the emerging trend of middle-class America. Older patterns of "entrepreneurial-authoritarian" control are slowly giving way to more "bureaucratic-democratic" techniques of socialization.[30] Such secular changes in the American family would produce a growing proportion of students with protest-prone personalities.

Institutional factors are of primary importance, as I have argued, insofar as they bring together a critical mass of suitably protest-predisposed students in an atmosphere where they can interact, create their own subculture, develop leadership, and find issues. The growing size of major American universities, their increasing academic and intellectual selectivity, and the emphasis upon "quality" education— such as honors programs, individual instruction, and greater student freedom—all seem to promote the continuing development of activist subcultures in a minority of American institutions. The increasing use of graduate student teaching assistants in major universities points to the growing availability of large numbers of potential leaders for student protests. Admittedly, a sudden increase in the administrative wisdom in college deans and presidents could reduce the number of available on-campus issues; but such a growth in wisdom does not seem imminent.

[29] Donald Nelson Michael, *The Next Generation: The Prospects Ahead for the Youth of Today and Tomorrow* (New York: Vintage, 1965).

[30] Daniel R. Miller and Guy E. Swanson, *The Changing American Parent* (New York: Wiley, 1958).

In sharp contrast to all this, maintenance of the cultural climate required for continuation of activism during the coming years seems far more problematical. Much depends on the future course of the war in Vietnam. Continuing escalation of the war in Southeast Asia will convince many student activists that their efforts are doomed to ineffectuality. For as of mid-1967, anti-war activism has become the primary common cause of student protesters. The increasing militancy and exclusivity of the Negro student civil rights movement, its emphasis on Black Power and on grass-roots community organization work (to be done by Negroes) is rapidly pushing white activists out of civil rights work, thus depriving them of the issue upon which the current mood of student activism was built. This tends to turn activists away from domestic issues toward an increasingly single-minded focus on the war in Vietnam, as does the downgrading of the war on poverty, the decline of public enthusiasm for civil rights, and the increasing scarcity of public and private financing for work with underprivileged sectors of American society. Yet at the same time, increasing numbers of activists overtly or covertly despair of the efficacy of student attempts to mobilize public opinion against the war, let alone hope to exert a direct influence upon American foreign policies. Continuing escalation in Southeast Asia has also begun to create a more repressive atmosphere toward student and other protesters of the war, as exemplified by the question, "Dissent or Treason?" A movement of activists back to full-time academic work is already apparent.

A crisis is thus being produced among activists by the war in Vietnam, coupled by the rejection of white middle-class students from the vestigial black Civil Rights Movement. That crisis is manifest by a "search for issues" and intense disagreement over strategy and tactics. Diminution of support for student activism tends, at the same time, to exert a "radicalizing" effect upon those who remain committed activists—partly because frustration itself tends to radicalize the frustrated, and partly because many of the less dedicated and committed activists have dropped away from the movement. Many find it difficult to turn from civil rights or peace work toward "organizing the middle class," as suggested by alienated-romantic critics of technological society. Activists tend, on the whole, to remain more responsive to universalistic issues, such as peace and civil rights, than to criticisms of society which are primarily expressive or esthetic. Besides, the practical and organizational problems of middle-class organization are over-whelming. It seems to me that the following and efficacy of the student movement would diminish considerably, if it were forced to turn away from universalistic issues, such as civil rights and peace, to a romantic critique of the "quality of middle-class life." Were this to happen, observations based on student activism of a more universalistic variety would have to be modified to take into account a more radical, yet more alienated, membership. Thus, escalation or even continuation of the war in Vietnam, particularly over a long period, will reduce the likelihood of student activism.

Yet other trends in American culture, hopefully more per-manent, argue for a continuation of protests. The further extension of affluence in America will probably mean growing impatience over society's failure to include the "forgotten fifth" in its prosperity. As the excluded and underprivileged become fewer in number, pressures to include them in American society will grow. Similarly, as more young Americans are brought up in well-to-do homes and subcultures, many will undoubtedly be moved to question the value of monetary, familistic, and careerist goals, looking instead toward expressive, romantic, experiential, humanitarian, and self-actualizing pursuits to give their lives meaning. Barring a major world conflagration, criticism of American society will probably continue during the next decades, intensifying on two grounds: first, that it has excluded a significant minority from its prosperity; second, that affluence in itself is empty without humanitarian, esthetic, or expressive fulfillment. Both trends would strengthen the climate conducive to continuing activism.

Finally, protest-promoting pressures from the rest of the world will doubtless increase in the coming years. A growing international unrest—especially in developing nations—is the portent of the esteem revolution, growing aspirations in the impoverished two-thirds of the world, and the spread of universalistic principles to other nations. If young Americans continue to be unusually responsive to the unfulfilled aspirations of those abroad, international trends will touch a minority of them deeply, inspiring them to overseas activities like the Peace Corps and efforts to "internationalize" American foreign policies, besides stimulating acute sensitivity to the frustrated aspirations of other Americans. Similarly, continuation of the current American policy of supporting anti-Communist, but often repressive, regimes in developing nations will tend to agitate American students further, particularly when it is in support of those regimes which are anathema to student activists abroad. Pressures from the probable world situation are apt, then, to support continuance of student protests in American society. The trend would be fundamentally reversed only if activists were to become convinced that protests were ineffectual or social action impossible. This is not to say that protesters are likely to become a majority among American students; but we can expect a slowly-growing minority of the most talented, empathic, and intellectually independent of our students to take up arms against injustice both here and abroad.

Tension between romantic-alienated and universalistic-activist styles of dissent will probably increase in the future. I would anticipate a growing polarization between those students and student groups who turn to highly personal and experiential pursuits like drugs, sex, art, and intimacy, and those who redouble their efforts to change American society.

That is why I have emphasized here the contrast between the two types of dissenting student, two types of family background, and two sets of values which inspire dissent from post-industrial American society. I have discussed, on the one hand, students I term alienated, whose values are not political, but romantic and esthetic. They are most responsive to romantic themes of social criticism, rejecting our society because of its dehumanizing effects, its lack of esthetic quality, and its failure to provide spiritual fulfillment to its members. And they are relatively impervious to appeals to social, economic, or political justice.

On the other hand, I have discussed politically involved activists, their values universalistic and humanitarian. Such students object to our society, not because they oppose its basic principles, but because it fails to implement these principles fully at home and abroad.

How and whether the tension between alienation and activism is resolved seems to me of the utmost importance. In recent years, activists have been ascendant, and the alienated have been little involved in organized political protests. But it is an ascendancy which might conceivably be reversed. Frustration, disillusionment, and repression—compounded by the activists' own lack of organization and failure to define long-range objectives—may cause them to withdraw from active social concern into a narrowly academic quest for professional competence. A considerable reservoir of the most talented young Americans would thus be lost to our society and to the world. The field of dissent would be left to the alienated, whose intense quest for personal salvation, creativity, meaning, and revelation dulls their perception of the public world and inhibits attempts to better the lot of others.

If tomorrow's potential activists can feel that their actions are effective in molding public opinion and, more important, in effecting needed social change, the possibilities for constructive change in post-industrial American society are virtually without limit. Without some shared sustaining vision of the society and world they are working to promote, most will return, disheartened, to the library, while a few will move on to the barricades and from there to the prisons.

Chapter VIII

Two Revolutions

Edward E. Sampson

$\mathbf{I}$n addition to the striking impact of the technological revolution in modifying our ways of life, there exists today two interdependent human revolutions, each a responsive spinoff of our technologically advanced society. I refer to these as the Third World's revolution for justice and the Fourth World's revolution for quality.

The residues of slavery combined with the injustices of ghettoized contemporary life provide more than ample background for adopting a militant ideology that calls upon the rhetoric, symbolism, and tactics embodied in the very phrase, Third World Liberation Movement. The jargon of the Cold War gave us the First World of the "free" nations, the Second World of the iron curtain countries, and the Third World, those largely populated but economically and technologically depressed developing nations. Unaligned politically with either the free or the unfree first two worlds, these Third World nations provided ready targets for the wooing advances of the United States, Russia, and, eventually, for mainland China.

The colonial situation, as it had existed prior to the emergence of the Third World as independent nations, covered the entire spectrum of relationships, including the political, the economic, and the social. Politically, the colonizers, though numerically in the minority, held the positions of power, especially in the form of military strength, and made decisions that governed the lives of their colonies. Economically, the colonizers developed the colonies to serve the needs of the "mother country," exploiting the resources, human and natural, for their own gain. It was argued, of course, that once heathen peoples, living crudely in mud huts and ravaged by disease, had been saved by the colonizer. But saved for what? To be more useful workers in the colonizer's economic arrangements.

Social relationships between the colonizer and the colonized took on the form of a master-slave relationship. From the perspective of the colonizer, *his* people were lazy but happy, superstitious, tending to excesses; they required careful surveillance much as one would care for a child in order to prevent him from doing harm to himself. And from his perspective, more often than not, the colonized identified

192

with the colonizer, saw himself through the other's eyes as an incompetent childlike creature, and wished above all else to be "white."

Today in the United States, a small but growing number of militant blacks, joined with militant groups of Mexican-Americans (Chicanos) and other peoples of color (for example, a small number of Asians and American Indians), have defined their situation vis-à-vis the majority white American society in terms of the Third World colonizer-colonized model and see the remedy for their people in terms of this same model.

Rather than attempting here to document the objective validity or invalidity of the model (there are both similarities and some discrepancies which would be uncovered in any careful documentation) suffice it to point out (1) that how a man defines his situation significantly affects the way he relates to that situation and (2) there are in fact several parallels between the situation of the blacks in this country and the colonial situation worldwide. Their colony has been and now more than ever *is* the black ghetto deep within the central city. Into the ghetto stream the white colonials to conduct business in their shops, taking money out, bringing little benefits back into the ghetto subcommunity. Out from the ghetto stream the black housecleaners, janitors, or manual laborers, off to work in the homes, backrooms, and factories of the white owners. Black works for white while controlling little or nothing of his own. Skin bleaches, hair straighteners, light skin, and white features define the good and the beautiful. Pride in race, pride in culture, and pride in self wither and die with barely a whimper in this atmosphere of lovely white.

To break the master-slave or colonizer-colonized cycle in the Third World model requires a sharp move toward political, economic, and social independence. No longer does slave face master; no longer does slave define master's way as good; no longer does slave permit himself to see the world through master's eyes. Black is beautiful; Afro-American culture has a status and dignity of its own. To make it in white society, black will not convert himself to white, but rather will remain fully a black.

On the college campus, where much of the noise and vigor of the Third World's Movement has been felt, major demands have focused upon curricular changes: black studies colleges or departments established by blacks, run by blacks, teaching black history and the black experience. The argument is not simply that history, for example, has omitted the black man's contribution, but, more importantly, that the entire perspective of a white, derived as it is from a society with the residues of slavery serving as blinders, can never capture the life and culture of the black. And furthermore, rather clearly, when the colonized reaches for his freedom, he rightly distrusts the relationship which awaits him should he allow the colonizer to assist him. Autonomy in this case clearly means no whites allowed. Pride in self and race do not come to the person simply because he is allowed to study his own history, sociology, or psychology, but rather, pride has its locus in being the captain of one's own soul: that is, in the self-determination of one's life and education.

The whites who had been involved in civil rights work just prior to the Black Power movement encountered this reversal when they found themselves cast out of the movement. No whites allowed. "Reverse racism!" went up the cries. "Segregation in black!" more cries to be heard. Yet, in the context of the Third World model, one cannot help but understand the basis for distrust of white involvement in black activities. For the black, whenever the white came around, good intentions and all, the relationship of superior to inferior, of master to slave or colonizer to colonized, was experienced. And shouting that this is not so, or not intended, does not remove the deeply etched scars on which this experience is based.

On many college campuses, where psychology and ideology, or so it is argued, are not employed in determining curricular matters, there is often great resistance to the Third World's demands for black studies departments set up by blacks and administered autonomously by blacks. It is perversely humorous to watch some of the white faculty, who define what is and what is not legitimate academics, tell the demanding black students that there is no real subject matter unique to the "black experience." For the black, used to hearing white definitions of his reality, this is but one further example to add to his 300-year-long ledger. Two key sources of professional resistance have been revealed. In the first, the professor fears that permitting black students to structure their own curriculum will open the flood gates to general student participation in curricular matters. In the second, although the professor glibly talks about quality control and maintaining an ivory-tower institution free from political or community involvement, essentially he is worried that black studies, like "relevant" white studies (that is, radical history and politics), will turn his campus into an anti-establishment force for change, thereby disrupting its presently highly political pro-establishment stance. In either case, clearly, each of these threatens the entrepreneurial fiefdoms that many faculty have established for themselves. One does not give up power and privilege without a battle; many campuses are witnessing these battles.

FOURTH WORLD

In order to gain some perspective on the Fourth World's movement, it will be helpful to distinguish between single-edged and double-edged views of contemporary society and the proper place of the individual in it. Into the single-edged category, I would place the recent writings of Clark Kerr, former president of the University of California, and Zbigniew Brzezinski, a professor of political science at Columbia and a well-known government adviser.[1]

In an article entitled "The University and Utopia," Kerr boldly took to task all those who urged a change away from what he felt to be the inevitable direction of development of higher education. Those utopian theories, he argued, have little to do with the modern age in which we live, one in which the multiversity must necessarily service the needs of a technological society:

> The cry for community, the cry for integration of thought and action, are cries that call backward to a smaller, simpler world. The revolutionary visions of today are of the old, not the new, of ancient Athens and medieval Paris and not of modern New York. It is sad commentary when the new revolutionary goal is the old past, not the future. . . . The standard model for the University is not the small, unified, autonomous community. Small intellectual communities can exist and serve a purpose, but they run against the logic of the times. . . . The longing for community, for this fantasy, this pie-in-the-sky, can actually impede efforts to make better that which must be. . . . The campus consistent with the society has served as a good introduction to society—to bigness, to specialization, to diffusion of interests; to problems, to possibilities.[2]

[1] Clark Kerr, "The University and Utopia," *The Daily Californian,* May 11, 1967, pp. 7–9; and Zbigniew Brzezinski, *New Republic,* June 1, 1968, pp. 23–25.

[2] Kerr, *op. cit.,* pp. 7–9.

Brzezinski contributed his own rather fascinating account of revolution and counterrevolution, but as he put it, "not necessarily about Columbia!" He maintains that America today is in its post-industrial era; it is becoming a *technetronic society:* "this is a society in which technology, especially electronic communications and computers is prompting basic social changes."[3] With this as the direction of our future, Brzezinski argues that any revolutionary process that is valid and significant, that is, a *true* revolution as opposed to what is in actuality a counterrevolution, must be historically relevant. It must be oriented toward this technetronic future. Counterrevolutionary movements—he cites the peasant uprisings in response to the industrial era as one example—respond to the past rather than to the future. For Brzezinski, student uprisings are counterrevolutionary; we hear in them, "the death rattle of the historical irrelevants."[4]

Fascinating to ponder. Both Kerr and Brzezinski paint a single-edged portrait of the future of American society and the inevitable role of the university in this future. Furthermore, those who do not accept the inevitability of this future are to be cast aside as being historically irrelevant dissidents. Even more fascinating is the basic assumption which both share, namely that malleable man must bend to fit the needs of an apparently immutable technetronic social organization. An alternative assumption argues that man has a certain degree of malleability, but within clear limits; he has basic needs to be met and can bend only so far in fitting himself to a social structure (cf. Etzioni's discussion of this point).[5] Social structure and organization, in this view, must be reshaped in order to fit better with man's needs and to permit him to live healthfully and creatively. The malleables in this alternative formulation are the structures and institutions of the technetronic age rather than the vital core of human existence.

For the double-edged perspective on modern society, we turn our historical gazes backwards to the mid-nineteenth and early twentieth century to examine briefly the writings of Alexis de Tocque-

[3] Brzezinski, *op. cit.,* p. 25.
[4] *Ibid.*
[5] Amitai Etzioni, "Basic Human Needs, Alienation and Inauthenticity," *American Sociological Review,* 1968, *33,* 870–885.

ville and two sociologists, Max Weber and Georg Simmel.[6] Each of these authors noted the two-sided sword that was man's future as his bondage to traditional society gave way to modernism with its own form of bondage.

For de Tocqueville, democracy, with its emphasis on secularism and equalitarianism, marked the bright future for man freed from the oppression of his life in the old regime. Max Weber, whose writings have significantly influenced contemporary sociological and psychological thought, described modern Western society in terms of the bureaucratization and rationalization of life. Weber's bureaucracy is the ideal typical model of all social organization of the modern era. The driving force behind this era is rationalization; that is, "the conversion of social values and relationships from the primary, communal and traditional shapes of modern life."[7] A rationalized existence is one which is guided by the advanced methods of science and technology toward the most organizationally efficient attainment of scientifically selected goals.

Georg Simmel saw the direction of history as being toward modernism and what he called *metropolis*. Metropolis for Simmel is the objectified society of the mind rather than the heart. In metropolis, man's mind becomes more calculating, precise and regimented; his attitude becomes one of protective reserve; he becomes sophisticated and blasé.

On the positive side, de Tocqueville's equalitarian democracy, Weber's rationalized bureaucracy, and Simmel's objectified metropolis have all freed man from the bondage of his traditional life. His loyalties in this modern society shifted from their traditional focus in the family and community to relationships based on political and legal grounds: a move away from *Gemeinschaft* and toward *Gesellschaft*.

On the other edge of this same sword, however, each of these authors and social critics recognized the disastrous consequences to

[6] Alexis de Tocqueville, *Democracy in America* (New York: Oxford University Press, 1947); Max Weber, *The Theory of Social and Economic Organization*, A. M. Henderson and T. Parsons (Trans.) (New York: Oxford University Press, 1947); Georg Simmel, *The Sociology of Georg Simmel*, K. H. Wolff (Trans.) (Glencoe, Ill.: Free Press, 1950).

[7] Robert Nisbet, *The Sociological Tradition* (New York: Basic Books, 1966).

the individual and humane relationships which would result. Such terms as dehumanization, alienation, impotency, routinization, and so on, capture a sense of the life that awaited contemporary man. De Tocqueville described the power of democracy as being one which ". . . does not destroy, but it prevents existence; it does not tyrannize, but it compresses, enervates, extinguishes, and stupefies a people. . . ."[8]

Max Weber, while in one breath arguing for the high-level efficiency that the impersonal and rationalized system of bureaucracies provides for dealing with the complex technological problems of the future, was compelled to point out the other inevitable consequences that excessive bureaucratization and rationalization would produce. "Rationalization threatens . . . to become, not creative and liberating, but mechanizing, regimenting, and ultimately, reason-destroying."[9] Likewise, Simmel suggested that the fragmentation of one's life in metropolis defied man's bent towards a unity and totality of existence.

Clearly, for de Tocqueville, Weber, and Simmel, this other edge of technological society is focused upon the factor of life's *quality*. Similar themes can be found in the works of contemporary authors and social critics, who have noted how the structure and institutions that have evolved in modern industrial and post-industrial societies— cutting thereby across national boundaries—have created conditions which frustrate essential human needs, which threaten to extinguish the humane and creative potential that is man's heritage and hope, and which fuel the varieties of protest that mark the American and international landscape.[10]

What is to become of man in the technetronic age? Are those who now protest against the presumed negative outcomes of this age to be cast aside as being historically irrelevant? Or, perhaps is it not more likely that these humanistic protest movements, still small in absolute number, nevertheless hold the revolutionary position of his-

[8] De Tocqueville, *op. cit.*, p. 319.

[9] Nisbet, *op. cit.*, p. 249.

[10] See, for example, Paul Goodman, *Growing Up Absurd* (New York: Random House, 1960); Edgar Z. Friedenberg, *Coming of Age in America* (New York: Random House, 1965); Kenneth Keniston, *The Uncommitted: Alienated Youth in American Society* (New York: Harcourt, 1965); and Herbert Marcuse, *One-Dimensional Man* (Boston: Beacon Press, 1964).

torical relevance? The responses of the under-thirty's social movements, in my opinion, reflect a keenly instinctive grasp of man's essential human needs and values. They are manned by our most intelligent and most aware young citizens, by those most in touch with today's realities.[11] They represent a sensitivity to the tragedy of a life based too much on the themes of quantity; their efforts orient us toward a world in which the quality of life becomes central. Can their protestations be as Brzezinski would have us believe, the final gasping death rattle of the historical irrelevants? Or, perhaps in their shouts and demonstrations, we see reflected man's continuing efforts to recapture a hold on his destiny and shape his life and his world as an active agent rather than as a pawn.

This Fourth World is one primarily of the young, the affluent, the white, the educated, the middle and upper-middle classes. Theirs is a slowly emerging, still relatively small subclass that occurs primarily in those societies that have reached their proper historical point; one in which affluence settles the quantity question, but one in which the very conditions requisite to producing and maintaining that affluence have brought into focus the felt concerns of life's quality. Thus, this is a revolutionary movement that is most marked among the affluent classes of societies which are most technologically advanced. That this movement should be most marked among the young, the intelligent, the sensitive, the collegian taught to think critically about his life and his world; that it comes at a time when Sputnik and the space race pushed science and technology to the fore and left man's problems far behind or only as some technological spinoff of the program, until at last he spoke up angrily—should also come as no surprise. The young and sensitive are quicker to spot, often intuitively, the key contradictions and sore spots of their society. They fought for civil rights and opposed the war in Vietnam long before these were such popular causes. They tend to be more imaginative and more innovative in seeking the solutions required to produce necessary social change. They are less captured in worn ruts, applying old formulas to new problems. Typically, they are more willing or able to take risks, venture forth with greater daring, think the unthinkable. Many also

[11] See Christian Bay, Chapter Three, this volume; and James W. Trent, Chapter Two, this volume.

tend to be more optimistic and hopeful than the prematurely cynicized post-thirty group. They have a vision of a better tomorrow. Some even have the audacity to imagine that through their efforts change can be brought about.

THIRD AND FOURTH WORLDS

There are both parallels and distinct differences, even conflicts between the Third and Fourth World revolutionaries. At times coalitions are formed and cooperative ventures undertaken; yet at other times, one group (usually the Fourth) seeks an ally in the other, and finds little interest.

A return to our initial analogy involving the colonizer and the colonized will serve to highlight a rather striking reversal in relationships between these two diverse groups. In the typical colonial situation, the colonized identifies with the colonizer and wishes to be just like he is. In breaking that pattern, as noted, the militant blacks have rejected white society and things white as models for their identification. Yet, so too have the white radicals, members of the Fourth World. Black is beautiful, white is pale, colorless, and ugly, for both black and white radicals alike. The paradoxical situation is that the white who occupies the colonizer or socially "up" position, is himself actively striving to break away from this position and this kind of relationship with others; in turn, he has come to identify himself with black and other Third World cultures. Though his background and education allow him to become part of the established power elite, he wishes to relate more as an equal, and so clothes himself in sackcloth and wanders among the less fortunate. That he can never attain real entry into the black world or is rebuffed in his efforts leaves the Fourth Worlder even further alienated. He does not wish to relate to others from the one-up stance that his color and privilege allow; he cannot become black and relate as a true member of that group. A marginal man between two worlds, he casts about in search of a place for himself. Many manifestations of his efforts are seen. In his clothing, his language, his mannerisms, his musical tastes, dance forms, style of personal expression, and so on, these white affluent Fourth Worlders emulate the Third World. To be black means to have *soul*. To be white, by contrast, means to be plastic, unreal, and too abstractly mental. And it is soul that the Fourth Worlder seeks for himself. Soul in his music, in his dance, in his life.

Nowhere is this reversal in identification more apparent than in the folk heroes of the Fourth Worlder. In the writings and life of Malcolm X, Martin Luther King, Huey Newton, Eldridge Cleaver, Che Guevara, Fidel Castro, or the likewise alienated existential writers, he finds his cultural heroes. Not in George Washington, Abe Lincoln, or for that matter, for the deeply radical Fourth Worlder, in the Kennedys or Gene McCarthy. His heroes are the oppressed Third Worlders around the world engaged in their struggle for independence.

In terms of the tactics of protest and in the efforts to evolve a self-conscious protest movement, once again, we see the Fourth Worlders seeking guidance from the activities of the Third World. From silent acceptance, to nonviolent protest, to spontaneous violence and increasingly to tactics of organized hit-and-run guerilla warfare: this is the sketchpad outline of the Third World's efforts as they are being followed by the militant Fourth Worlders.

The turn to hit-and-run tactics, defined as violent by those in positions of authority, is not a tactic positively sought as part of the program of most of the Third and Fourth World groups. Rather, like so many of their actions, it is a *reaction* to the inaction of those in power or those who no longer are willing to listen to the complaints of the youthful protesters. When regular channels have been tried and exhausted, or have been closed, or have been opened to conversation without communication, in despair, groups take to the streets to use the only source of power remaining, the power to disrupt. A somewhat similar conclusion has been reached by one of the task forces preparing a report for the President's National Commission on the Causes and Prevention of Violence.

In addition to the identity reversal, still another paradox exists in the relationship between the Third and Fourth World groups. In the eye of the public, after hundreds of years in the socially "down" position, Third World upheavals of protest are granted a significant degree of legitimacy. Even conservative politicans recognize the need for Third World groups to be given greater access to the affluence and material advantages of this society. Theirs is a legitimacy based both on fear and on the understanding that the deprived group should share in the society's general affluence. The fear-factor is part of the folklore of white folks who sense there to be a real possibility for a Negro uprising in retaliation for their years of deprivation. When a black threatens, whites sit up and take notice, for he "ain't just a jivin'," he means business: and deep down, we all know why he is serious.

The Fourth World's protest, on the other hand, is met with increasing puzzlement and little real fear; thereby it is granted lesser legitimacy, especially in the eyes of the public at large, but also to a certain extent in the eyes of the Third World community as well. After all, or so it is argued, these kids have had the best of everything and have a great future awaiting them, so what's their complaint? In the eyes of the Third Worlder, the Fourth World student has voluntarily given up many of those things which he himself wants. Furthermore, the white has substantial choice within the system, as compared with his own limited options. Any time he wants to, he can shave his beard, cut his hair and return happily to the fold. So when the white opts out of the system, it comes as somewhat of a puzzle, even to the Third Worlder.

As far as the public itself goes, there is hardly any access to or compassion for the plight of the Fourth Worlder. In terms of the criteria of quantity—affluence, the material goodies of life, and job opportunities in the several precast molds offered up to him—the Fourth Worlder has little to complain about. In terms of these indices he is overprivileged, so therefore, why the protest! Recently onto the Berkeley campus there came a group of high school students representing their version of underground or guerilla theater. They put on several skits in the plaza. In one scene, a young kid tells his parents that he really does not want to own a Cadillac. Puzzled, hurt, and angry, they accuse him of being un-American: "Why it's un-American not to want a Cadillac. What are you trying to do, destroy America!"

Yet, of course, just these very criteria of quantity and material success are those against which the Fourth Worlder's protest is directed. But since others do not easily identify with these kinds of frustrations, in their eyes his protest lacks true legitimacy; thus, the reasons for the Fourth Worlder's revolt is sought elsewhere. He is often seen to be complaining as part of some conspiracy directed by outside agitators. Note, in passing, how during the slave period in this country much the same kind of theory was held. The masters believed that the life of their slaves was far better here than in Africa, thus they should be happy. Any slave uprising, therefore, could in no way be a reflection on the faulty system of slavery itself, but rather must necessarily reflect the intrusion of "outside agitators" on an otherwise happy people.

Another reason that the Fourth World's protest seems "illegitimate" is that its motives are often attributed to a soggy mentality, seeking to destroy only for the sake of destroying. Those very persons who during the FSM at Berkeley lauded the idealism of the protesters —who then were and now are fighting for a greater role in determining the course of their education and the nature of their university —are now convinced that the continuation of student protests reflects a nihilistic attitude and has very little basis in legitimate complaints. In fact, the longer the protests continue and the louder they get, the more do former supporters drop by the wayside, deciding that "these kids are just protesting for the sake of protesting; all they want to do is destroy an imperfect but good institution." If you complain once, perhaps twice, it is idealism; but three, four, five times; nihilism.

The paradox of legitimacy: if you are short on material wealth and you protest, we all understand; but if you seek a better quality for a material-abundant life, we who think in terms of quantity see in your protest only nihilism, illness, or conspiracy.

REFLECTIONS ON THE REVOLUTIONS

The pursuits of the Third and Fourth World's movements, though increasingly directed toward the universities and colleges, are reflected more broadly as well across generations and institutional boundaries.

Three significant themes have emerged. These can be recognized in the directly militant protest form they take on the campus or in the surrounding community as well as in the more typically quiet ways in which even those of the silent majority have been swept up in the changing currents of modern times: (1) individualism; (2) power and control; (3) anti-rationalism.

Individualism. It is the age of anarchy, where doing one's own thing has become the watchword of those who would rebel, if only momentarily, from doing their duty to God, organization, and nation. But not really. For in the increasingly well-programmed, one might say *overorganized,* life most persons now lead, anarchy becomes more a symbolic whisper, an inching sideburn, a flashy tie, a daring moustache. If this be anarchy, if this be a real return to individualism, then surely we should call foul and claim a quick refund on our too feeble efforts.

Nevertheless, efforts to express individuality and uniqueness are reflected in styles of appearance, clothing, music, art, dance, and drama. Everyone today is a dancer. Where you put your foot, when, and how matters less than the fact that you feel free enough to express yourself to the rhythmic beats. Most of the dancing styles themselves seek to emulate the beats and forms of Africa—yet another instance in which white America copies black. And if everyone today is a dancer, so too is everyone an author, playwright, moviemaker, artist. The emphasis is upon individual expression. When but in this era could Susan Sontag write a work "against interpretation" and thereby capture the *Zeitgeist* of an era?

On the negative side, however, are those high *Kultur* critics who feel that the arts and great culture have suffered by this influx of fully expressive but untrained, undisciplined amateurs. They bemoan the unfettered individual expressions that occur without evaluation, without critique, without authoritative appraisal, let alone without interpretation. For these critics, this emerging revolutionary age is one in which the motto, "doing one's thing," has legitimized nearly everything as art and culture and thereby, they feel, has reduced art to nothingness. Harold Wilensky's study of mass society and mass culture reaches much the same conclusion. After close analysis of his data, he states, ". . . what *is* new, unique to our time, is a thorough interpenetration of cultural levels; the good, the mediocre, and the trashy are becoming fused in one massive middle mush."[12]

The theme of individualism has found its way into organizational behavior as well as into human relationships in general. Anyone who has ever attended a meeting of a New Left political group will fully realize the anti-organizational bias which exists. And this bias extends to running the meeting itself.

Power and Control. What position do we occupy with regard

[12] Harold Wilensky, "Mass Society and Mass Culture: Interdependence or Independence?" *American Sociological Review,* 1964, *29,* 173–197.

to affecting the course of our life? Are we *origins,* able to effect a change, or merely *pawns,* small pieces to be moved about by those truly in control? With large size and complexity of social organization, man is removed increasingly from the centers of power in decision making. Often, he senses that decisions have been cranked out by an impersonal entity—the organization—rather than by any one responsible person. Today there is the Rule by Nobody, as Hannah Arendt has recently noted.[13] If Nobody rules, then Nobody is responsible. So when a grievance exists, one goes to the streets until that Nobody emerges and becomes a Somebody to deal with. No more vivid example of this faceless bureaucratic Rule by Nobody can be found than in the recent People's Park controversy in Berkeley. A vacant lot near the campus owned by the university, eventually to be used for residence halls, was made into a user-developed park by persons who lived in the area. Many weeks after grass, trees, and flowers had been planted and children's playground equipment set up, the university, with the aid of several hundreds of police and over 2,000 National Guardsmen, built a fence to keep the people out of their property. The entire Berkeley community was caught up in literal warfare: shootings, one killing, several maimings, clubbings, gassings, mass arrests, and the removal of constitutional rights to speech and assembly marked the Berkeley war zone. How would the heavily guarded fence come down and the issue about the use of the land finally be settled? Who was in charge? Not the chancellor, who took responsibility for building the fence but on those rare occasions when he was visible, said he could not have it nor the police and military forces removed. Not the mayor, city manager, and city council of Berkeley, who found their town under occupation by forces over which they had no control. Not the faculty, who could only pass resolutions urging that peaceful ways be rapidly found to settle the issue. Apparently, not even the Board of Regents, some of whose members said that the chancellor could remove the fence any time he wished and so washed their hands of the whole affair; others of whom felt the university had no business in running a community park and so tossed it back to the city council. The hot potato of the People's Park issue was tossed gingerly from

[13] Hannah Arendt, "Reflections on Violence," *The New York Review of Books,* February 27, 1969, pp. 19–31.

one person and agency to another; no one would hold it long enough to take firm responsibility for settlement. With bureaucratic rule by Nobody, then, is there any wonder that the streets become the chosen locale for forcing Somebody finally to emerge and take charge? Is there any wonder, either, that students and others demand their rights to participate in decision making so that future disasters will not have to take place before Somebody finally emerges?

On the college campus, the cry from Third and Fourth Worlders alike is for "increasing, meaningful participation." Where once the focus of this passion to contribute to one's educational life centered on the standard extracurricular rules of campus living, the focus has increasingly shifted toward directly curricular matters. Where once the "enemy" whose power was to be grabbed consisted of the administration, in matters curricular, the "enemy" who will give up power only grudgingly, if at all, consists of the faculty.

On the Berkeley campus, the success of the Fourth World's demand for increased power in curricular matters, which started during the 1964 FSM, reached a downswing during the Eldridge Cleaver controversy of 1968. After the FSM, the faculty had established a legitimizing body within the Academic Senate—called the Board of Educational Development (BED)—which could fairly rapidly set up experimental courses, cutting through the normal red-tape delays. In their turn, the students established their own group, the Committee for Participant Education (CPE), designed to initiate courses which the BED could review. After several years of feeling each other out, a reasonably adventurous arrangement had evolved linking the BED with CPE. In this manner, in fact, a quasi-underground college program developed, offering a wide range of courses having "relevant" content and being taught by persons selected by the students and reviewed by the faculty BED.

But then one day, the CPE decided that it wished to have a course about Eldridge Cleaver and the Black Panther Movement, with Cleaver as one of the primary lecturers in the course. Going through normal channels, they received BED approval. Things were ready to roll, when the Board of Regents—who have constitutionally delegated, absolute power—in response to an outraged public ruled that the Cleaver course was a no-no. In that one action, the regents managed to undercut the faculty's power over curricular matters and as importantly to create a chilling atmosphere for further meaningful student involvement. No future BED, having been stepped on once in a way that created a statewide educational crisis, would ever again want to consider *that* kind of student-initiated course.

Not to be permanently done-in, however, the students of CPE returned the very next quarter with another plan—their last hope. Here they would call upon the good services of individual faculty members using their prerogative of granting independent study credit to gain legitimate credit for student initiated courses. And this time, the students selected Tom Hayden, a founder of SDS, as their major course lecturer. Expectedly, the cry of foul went up, but this time from the faculty even more loudly than the public or the regents.

Whether the faculty as a body realize it or not, the militant students at least seem rather aware that the name of the game is "political power." By this is meant nothing other than the fact that organizational structures which look static and unyielding, claiming that tradition and professional expertise produced the control configuration one sees, really got that way out of multiple skirmishes and battles between persons and agencies with often conflicting interests and values. Recognizing this, the students realize that they will only get a share of the pie if they organize themselves into a meaningful political force on their campus and keep up the pressure until negotiations are forthcoming. What they may not realize quite as well, however, is that those who have the power are not simply going to give some of it up out of the kindness of their warm little hearts. Thus, the battles over power and control which we have seen emerging on the college campus will continue for some time to come.

Both on the campus and off, there are certain aspects of broad-based participation in decision making that are important to examine, if only briefly. First, participation serves to legitimize the decisions that are made. This is in contrast to the consequences of today's almost too efficient system of bureaucratic democracy, in which the legitimacy of the constituted authority is increasingly being questioned. Second, participation leads to a collective sense of responsibility and involvement. This is to be contrasted with the general state of collective apathy and the let-George-do-it philosophy which still characterizes the majority of people in our technetronic society. The university that would withhold from its students meaningful involvement in their own governance, a truly educational experience in itself, is preparing them more to play a continued role of frustrated and apathetic do-nothing bystander than of responsible participant-citizen. The institution should be a training ground for a new and better society of involved citizenry and not a continuing school for frustration and eventual withdrawal. Third, participation leads to a sense of community, or to use the terms of the sociologist, Emile Durkheim, to a form of collective representation. Thus, participation serves a socially integrative function, especially important in a society that lacks the unifying ties of community.

Anti-Rationalism. Though man is a being with passions and emotions as well as reason and intellect, the extremes of rationalized existence, as Weber noted, make his feelings on the one hand irrelevant and on the other, an obtrusive error factor: feelings and emotions come to be seen as noise in the otherwise smooth cybernetics of modern life.

Furthermore, as Talcott Parsons has noted,[14] with each leap forward in our intellectual sophistication, especially as regards the nature of man and his institutions, we uncover two troublesome psychological side effects. Each academic "psyching out" gives one the feeling that just that much more of his freedom has been limited. Freud's impact on society, for example, carried with it the message that man's motivations could at long last be understood. And with such understanding comes the feeling that one's freedom to be unknown and unpredictable is limited.

A second and related psychological side effect of the advance of formal knowledge is the sense that one has lost his unique dignity as man. By taking his place among the other knowns of the universe, man can no longer view himself uniquely. One of the consequences of Darwin's theory was to place man and animals into the same evolutionary sequence, thereby depriving man of his unique status. Likewise, the rapid advances in automation, and computer science, and the mechanistic approaches in psychology rob man still further of his own sense of human dignity.

Not surprisingly, therefore, given the preceding developments,

[14] Talcott Parsons, "The Position of Identity in the General Theory of Action," in C. Gordon and K. Gergen (Eds.), *The Self in Social Interaction* (New York: Wiley, 1968), pp. 11–23.

we find ourselves caught up today in a reactive return to the non-rational over the rational, the affective over the cognitive, the mysterious over the known, the experiential and direct over the analytic and abstract. In the broader community, one finds the almost frighteningly rapid growth of sensitivity training groups, Esalen-type sensory awareness programs, Synanon trips and games, encounter groups, meditation cults, and so on almost endlessly. In most of these efforts, which cater it seems primarily to the white, affluent middle and upper middle classes—one might say to the overorganized, bureaucraticized uptights of modern society—the emphasis is upon instinctual or emotional release. It is rare to find any concern with intellectual understanding; but rather, all seems to focus on the release of feelings, the expression of feelings, the true open, honest, unabashed encounter with the other person. Concerted efforts are made to divest the person of his societal, organizational roles and identities—those aspects of modern living that tend to fragment the person—and get down to the basic, holistic human nitty gritty.

In human relationships, the effort, typically unsuccessful, is to move from an I-It contact with others (which soon becomes an It-It relationship between two objects) to an I-Thou bond. Imagine the reaction evoked in students when they witness the typical meeting of a faculty body or for that matter any governmental body—a bevy of elder statesmen gathered to try their hand at playing with Robert's Rules of Order. To the winner goes very little but the knowledge that he played the game well that week: but for the academic, this is sufficient reward. The I-It atmosphere abounds so thickly that the student visitors in the back row can taste it. Why, they wonder, don't these men just come right out and say what they feel? Why don't these men just talk straight? Out of order! Definitely. Out of order!

In the university, the anti-rationalistic, more humanistic trend is reflected in many important ways. There is a concerted effort to restore morality and values into the increasingly amoral academic community. The secularization and rationalization of life that characterizes the twentieth century has produced a group of seekers in search of those new institutions in which values and principles of morality are both expressed and, more importantly, are lived in fact. In their study of religion in America, Rodney Stark and Charles Glock suggest that those seeking such values are turned away at the institutional church's door.[15] Thus they turn elsewhere, some toward the more mystic religions of the East; others toward the university.

The university, where one might hope to find enduring values, even those of scholarship and the pursuit of truth, too often fails miserably. The university, in fact, has become the leader in the super-rationalized trend from which these young seekers are seeking escape. With near total dispassion and without even a confession to being value-laden, the academician tries to lead his students to follow in his style. But the student sees in him a man of reason but little of value; a man of the head, but without soul. He sees in him a hypocritical detachment from the web of societal life. The university turns out to be the most rationalized of all bureaucracies, too often promoting a dehumanizing experience rather than fostering the humane values for which presumably it once stood. The academician turns out to be the essence of societal rather than communal man. He is seen to be more in pursuit of the buck, of status, stardom, and fame than of anything so apparently mundane as truth and wisdom. The student is himself seeking a new way, a new quality of life and is ever hopeful of finding an institution in which and persons in whom the new way is reflected. It has not been in the halls of academe that the student seeker has found this illusive moral man. In essence, the young seeker finds values and a morality in the institutions, but rather than their being a remedy to the rationalized sterility around him, they exist in as severe a form as on the outside. Values and moral choices enter the academician's and the institution's world, but these turn out to be the same values of personal achievement and self-aggrandizement that abound in everyman. But, as Clark Kerr said, the campus does serve as a good introduction to society.

WILL WE MAKE IT?

Social change, it seems, is not to be accomplished smoothly, peacefully, or without conflict. And this is especially the case when that change calls for a radical reversal in the direction of a society and a substantial overhaul of the society's organized structures. Those with a vested interest in their society as it presently exists have good reason to be concerned about the demanding pressure of the Third

---

[15] Rodney Stark and Charles Glock, "Will Ethics Be the Death of Christianity?" *Transaction*, 1968, *5*, 7–14.

and Fourth World groups. The university, in particular, serving today as it does as the major port of entry into the society, is appropriately enough the prime target of these revolutionary movements. The university as we now know it, serving increasingly one major role (as Kerr has noted) and one major segment of society, will necessarily look much different in the years ahead when the dust finally settles.

The question is not really whether or not the themes embodied within the Third and Fourth Worlds' movements carry the essential message of tomorrow. For they do. But rather, the question is really the as yet unanswerable one, whether or not we will make it into that future without the disastrous turmoil of internal warfare that some writers have predicted: where black faces off against white, young militant against old, with no innocents claiming they are merely the observers of the silent majority waiting until the ashes cool. The drama today is unfolding on the college campus. How it is resolved there is no small matter. There will be revealed in smaller scale the options available to the entire society. One can only hope that the college will provide leadership to direct and guide us on the long journey that lies ahead.

Individualism and Higher Education

Harold A. Korn

The events of the 1960s are unique in the history of higher education. Never before have the avowed goals of undergraduate education been in such accord with the expressed needs of students. Yet never before have the traditional liberal arts goals been so hard to implement as in the present social context. Add to this paradox the failure to satisfy such human needs as a sense of personal freedom and a sense of purpose, and you can begin to imagine the profound implications these shortcomings have for the future of society.

The college experience is an arena in which youth have much faith—a faith too often misplaced. The discrepancy between expectation and reality is responsible, in no small degree, for the education crisis, despite the congruence of stated goals and needs. The very quality of life in our technological age depends largely upon our ability to resolve this crisis. Higher education has only two alternatives: it can either reexamine and restructure its fundamental operating procedures, or it can passively accept the line of least resistance. The price of passivity, however, is the eventual disappearance of those human values which advanced education professes to promote and, of course, the concomitant loss of the faith of youth in the worth of higher education.

The crisis revolves around society's effort to transmit to the leaders of the future a humanitarian spirit through institutional means. It can be understood from two perspectives: a historical perspective and a behavioral science perspective. The historical reveals those enduring values for which Western man has been groping; the behavioral helps evaluate intricate processes governing his activity. By combining the two perspectives we can discover what man seems to want and why he is so often thwarted in his efforts to satisfy those wants.

Human development is influenced by everything from child-rearing practices to faith in current political processes. The established patterns for expressing these influences are now being challenged and modified at nearly all levels of complexity. Kenneth Boulding uses the expression *integrative system* for the network of interrelationships among these influences. When working smoothly, the system provides cohesion and direction. When it begins to break down, a whole array of social disorders arises—protest, repression, general malaise.

213

Significant sectors of the integrative system of our society show signs of maladaptive functioning. Widely diverse groups of individuals are, as a consequence, losing faith in the validity of certain social institutions. The interplay between the structure of such institutions and their impact upon individual lives is our primary concern here. By balancing the declared purpose and actual functioning of social institutions against the needs of our times, we can begin to see the direction of desirable change.

This chapter first outlines some of the major ambiguities in what may well be the predominant social philosophy of our culture, individualism. The second section analyzes certain characteristics of that emerging social philosophy which can best be termed the *youth culture*. Finally, we examine the reform efforts of institutions of higher learning and suggest a new perspective with a better chance of bringing those efforts in line with student needs.

AMBIGUITY OF INDIVIDUALISM

The avowed goal of a liberal education has long been the development of the intellectual life of the individual, with emphasis upon self-knowledge and a critical understanding of culture. The sharp contrast between this ideal and the impersonal, highly specialized, and fractionated experience of most college students is alarming. Such a discrepancy between the promises of any one institution and what it actually delivers depicts, in microcosm, the central dilemma of the day—the relative helplessness of the strongest and wealthiest nation in the world in the face of many social crises. Why is this so?

A clue is suggested by the anomaly that the nation's enormous success in certain endeavors is continuously being offset by frustration in others. The degree of success may quite possibly depend upon responsiveness to the changing needs of the times. It appears that those social institutions most directly concerned with human development have been the least adaptive in the past fifty years. The American system of higher education, in particular, has changed its basic operating procedures remarkably little, in spite of enormous growth. One possibility, to be explored here, is that this pehnomenon of unequal responsiveness to changing needs can be explained in terms of the prevailing ideology of individualism and man's resistance to any threat to basic beliefs.

Americans' implicit faith in the principles of individual freedom and equal opportunity has always been basic to their philosophy. Natural abundance and material success have confirmed that faith. Social institutions, coupled with the dynamics of the national economy, have promised realization of the ideal. As long as the integrative system was working effectively, freedom and opportunity were taken for granted.

One of the strongest of all strands in the integrative network of American society has been the philosophy of individualism. It has drawn support from both the Protestant ethic and the French Enlightenment and found a natural environment in which to flourish where frontiers were continually unfolding. In it lay the source of much of America's past strength—and her present crisis. At least two basic forms of individualism prevail in contemporary culture. Traditional rugged individualism emphasizes self-sufficiency, self-denial, and competitive achievement. Another type centers, as well, on respect for the individual, but the emphasis is upon expansion of human consciousness and depth of experience. The focus here is upon development of a broad range of responsiveness to experience—one's own and that of others. Confusion and ambivalence about the meaning of individualism go back through the recorded history of Western man. Early Christianity stressed the supreme worth of the individual in relation to others. Service to fellow man was predominant in its philosophy. Self-centered individualism did not get a toehold until the Reformation. Throughout the history of Christianity, the individualist and collectivist elements have at different times had the more dominant influence. With the Reformation, the individualist element, which had been overshadowed by the authority of tradition and the organization (the church), came once again to the fore.

The Reformation's emphasis upon individual responsibility interacted with and reinforced the social and economic forces leading to the contemporary era. From then on, concern over self-sufficiency and individual responsibility became the key political philosophy of democratic institutions. What it amounted to was essentially a statement of the right to be free of interference in the pursuit of individualism. So effective was freedom from restraint as a vehicle for economic expansion that those voices speaking for humane causes went unheeded. Concern for the welfare of man and the rights of others has contributed much to our intellectual development; little to social philosophy and institutions.

It is the rugged individualism slant which has dominated American thought, although both types of individualism have had their advocates through the years. Individual worth appears to be paramount in both ideologies. Yet in actual practice they produce wholly different organizations and experiences of reality. Until recently, those social institutions based upon an underlying philosophy of rugged individualism have been able to satisfy the needs of our political and economic system.

This is not to say there were no attendant evils. Inherent in the orientation were human exploitation and greed—even ulcers for the successful. Yet the philosophy did contribute something of value to the integrative system. Not all could taste the fruits of success; yet they had a sense of purpose and the tantalizing promise of equal opportunity. The very success of American society made it natural for assumptions concerning man's individualistic nature to permeate free enterprise economics, religious institutions, and the educational system. It all seemed to fit nicely into a political structure based upon the premise of individual liberty and the pursuit of happiness.

It did fit, not because the social institutions actually encouraged such goals, but because there was enough psychological space and actual opportunity for individuals to tolerate constraint while being promised freedom. Throughout history, societies have developed institutions which exercised a controlling function over individual citizens. In nearly all, however, the idea of freedom was not part of the integrative network. The socializing influence of American institutions was tolerated in America, where both freedom and individualism were taken for granted, because it was not too intrusive. Mass communication media did not exist, prolonged schooling was not required, big government did not account for a huge part of the gross national product. You went to church on Sunday and remembered what was useful for getting ahead the rest of the week. Human misery was ignored and condoned, because it was not powerful enough to make itself heeded.

The integrative system that served America's needs during the past two hundred years is no longer functional, because the nation is faced with wholly different problems. The social institutions with which we still try to provide stability are anachronistic on two important and interrelated counts. For one thing, they are still permeated with a philosophy of rugged individualism. Yet dramatic changes in nearly all sectors of society would suggest questioning that principle as a successful strategy of life. Even more fundamental, perhaps, than man's implicit or explicit philosophy of life is the second factor—the way he adapts to change, particularly at the accelerated rate of present-day society. History teaches us that man's flexibility has enabled him to adapt to every new change as it appears. Yet it also reveals enormous resistance along the way. In maturity, man tends to hold on tenaciously to habitual ways of seeing and doing, lacking the child's ability to adapt. So breathtaking is the rate of change in today's America that we have lost the adaptive mechanism effective during transitional periods spread over generations.

Conditions of a post-industrial age, like the rate of social change, demand that institutions respond quickly to emerging needs. The general prevalence of social unrest is indicative of their failure to keep pace. And it is the principle of rugged individualism which must, in no small part, bear the blame. Through the years it has led to certain assumptions being taken for granted. People were expected to solve problems by themselves; if they failed, it was because they did not try hard enough. Sinners were supposed to find an individual faith which would lead to salvation; if they failed, they were forever damned. Students were expected to do well in school; if they did poorly, the fault was their own. Businesses failed because men did not have enough drive or ambition.

In most American social institutions, the emphasis was placed on the individual's responsibility for his own success. Little attention was given to defining the criteria of success or fixing a degree of social responsibility. Perhaps the most tragic and forceful illustration of that failure is the condition of blacks in our society. Yet the phenomenon is pervasive.

Contemporary social problems demonstrate what behavioral scientists are just beginning to understand: that placing responsibility for the use of freedom and the pursuit of happiness solely in the hands of the individual ignores the complex relationship between man and the social system of which he is a part. Emphasis upon individual responsibility as the predominant social philosophy tends to overlook, for instance, the impact of the family during childhood. Yet this may be the most significant of all influences upon the mature man. The "child self" is part of every adult. Peter Madison has treated this subject in considerable detail in his *Personality Development in College*.[1]

So, too, does this predominant American philosophy deny man's dual nature as both a rational and an emotional human being. The emphasis upon individual responsibility, by which men were prepared for the relatively simple world of the nineteenth century, ignored the relevance of both external social constraint and internal feeling. Yet it did, in the early days, encourage a somewhat constructive response to the social system by offering alternative life-styles which did not call for jumping educational hurdles. Little subtlety or sophistication was required to understand the meaning of life in those days. Under the prevailing philosophy, a human life might be lost, but it did not, as today, pose a series of threats to the entire human race.

Although man was as much influenced by his environment in frontier days as now, he could exercise a degree of control over his life which is impossible today. Dependence upon one's fellow man is now evident at every level of life. From those who bring food into the heart of the city to those who decide whether we have enough nuclear warheads, interdependence is a way of life.

It is not physical survival alone over which we have lost control. Control of psychological survival has been even more drastically diminished. A growing sense of the importance of this realm clashes, by its very nature, with the philosophy of rugged individualism, which tends to deny it. Dependence upon others must take into account ways and means of communicating with them to meet current needs. It calls for taking into account their wishes and wants. Tolerance and understanding replace power and self-righteousness as effective dimensions of human interaction. The very criteria of success are becoming more and more psychological. No longer can it be measured, as in the past, in terms of a self-sufficient farm, a profitable small business, or for a professional man, the respect of a small circle of admirers.

[1] Peter Madison, *Personality Development in College* (Reading, Mass.: Addison-Wesley, 1966).

Living and working closely with others can pose a severe challenge to identity—and to self-esteem, which must be evaluated today within the context of a complex set of social relationships. Yet even those institutions which are primarily concerned with human development—the home and the school—have not prepared us to deal with the new challenges in a genuinely adaptive fashion. Neither the child-rearing practices of the American family nor the teaching practices of the educational system have been able to free themselves of the philosophy of rugged individualism. Despite the efforts of John Dewey and Benjamin Spock, development in both areas is better suited to another era. Things would be even worse were it not for man's ability to learn from his own experience.

Our sense of impotence in attempting to solve current social problems grows out of a curious paradox, illustrated by two prevailing views of social ethics. For the purpose of analysis, one of these may be called the business-technology ethic; the other, the love–human-growth–religion ethic. The ideology of individualism no longer pervades both. Surprisingly, it is the business-technology slant which has changed to meet current needs. Herein lies the paradox. The long-range planning and organization utilized by major corporations to achieve their goals are proving the worth of cooperative endeavor. Although the submerging of individualism within corporate life can itself become a problem, few would deny the effectiveness of the overall effort.

Institutions primarily concerned with an ethic of human development are, on the contrary, still dominated by an ideology of individualism which subverts their effectiveness and too often produces disorder and frustration. The church, schools, even the so-called helping professions, tend to emphasize solely the responsibility of the individual, thus denying the powerful impact of the environment as a whole. Such a denial is not, of course, the sole cause of ineffectiveness. Another may be found in inadequate examination of their own methods by those trying to foster the love-growth philosophy. Yet the modes of operation of social institutions will inevitably reflect their dedication to the principle of self-sufficiency, with a consequent belittling of the psychological realm.

America's best corporations, while emphasizing profit and overall productivity, still tend to reflect a certain intuitive knowledge of human nature and the complexities of present-day society which is all too often lacking in those *social* institutions explicitly devoted to human development. We are inclined to stand so much in awe or anguish over industry's technological advances that we ignore its achievement in the organization of human effort for the purpose of attaining complex goals. Some of the more innovative efforts to understand human interaction have grown out of research in business organizations. Schein and Bennis[2] have made a study of many of the issues raised here in the abstract, attempting to come to grips with them in a practical manner.

It appears that those social institutions primarily responsible for human development have too often failed to secure a functional relationship between ideology and achievement. Witness the discrepancy between the philosophy of a liberal education and the actual situation in liberal arts colleges. Witness, too, the gap between the philosophy of brotherhood, inherent in most religions, and the tenuous interpersonal relationships apparent in even a single congregation. Witness the failure of the mental health professions to reach so many in need.

The contrast between the impotence of the human development ethic and the relative success of the ethic in contemporary technology and business reveals two salient distinctions. These relate to environmental control and a functional recognition of the complexity of human motivation. Any attempt to abstract the essential difference between the human-development and business-technology ethics reveals the contrast between a systems approach and one focused upon the individual. The former is a way of recognizing that performance in any one of a series of successful stages is dependent upon performance in others. Such interdependence necessitates careful analysis of every step in a sequence. Its relationship to other stages must be painstakingly spelled out.

The suggestion that human development can be encouraged through such a systematic analysis of goals and procedures is often met with aversion by those subscribing to the ideology of individualism which permeates the human development ethic. Yet absence of a "systems approach" does not in itself mean that no system is operative

[2] Edgar H. Schein and W. G. Bennis, *Personal and Organizational Change Through Group Methods* (New York: Wiley, 1965).

in their own methods. What *is* missing is that careful evaluation of goals and the effectiveness of techniques which is characteristic of systems analysis. As a consequence, contemporary methods fail to meet the avowed goal of promoting maximum human development. That the social system is in trouble is becoming increasingly apparent. Its dilemma is amply documented in everything from the daily newspaper to various scholarly appraisals.

What we have been trying to say here is, in brief, that American society has reached a new point in its development and is in desperate need of fresh conceptions concerning the goals of social institutions. The new age is characterized by organizations, both private and governmental, which have a pervasive influence upon our day-to-day lives. Unfortunately, the dramatic shift in the way our economy and our government work has not been accompanied by comparable change in other sectors of society. Those social institutions most directly concerned with human development have been least responsive to change. We have suggested that a fundamental source of their resistance to change grows out of a philosophy of individualism, rooted in past centuries. Although the ideology of an alternative aspect of individualism exists, the institutions we would most expect to adhere to it do not have a structure which encourages this more humane and realistic type of individualism.

RESISTANCE TO CHANGE

Man's capacity to suffer pain is the key to his physical survival. He withdraws from fire, builds shelters from the cold, produces food to reduce hunger. When it comes to the experiencing of psychological pain, however, man's adaptive response is far less clearly defined. Adaptation may initially involve still greater pain and result in avoidance of the experience. Individual differences are pertinent in this area: What may produce anguish in one can be accepted with aplomb by another. Yet there comes a time when significant numbers of individuals find certain aspects of their psychological life intolerable. We have suggested above that American society is entering just such a period.

While withdrawal from physical pain is intuitively understood by all, certain kinds of psychological pain are more difficult to comprehend. They are difficult for several reasons. First is the pervasive denial of the psychological realm which is the heritage of our cultural commitment to rugged individualism. A second, somewhat related factor has to do with the emotional "style" of those in pain and its impact upon others not similarly affected. Another difficulty is connected with the psychology of man's belief systems concerning himself and society and his capacity to modify those beliefs.

American college students, collectively, have, during the last few years, begun to experience unusual psychological pain and disaffection in connection with their daily experience. What they have long endured with apathy, cynicism, or escapism has suddenly become intolerable. While the war in Vietnam is the energizing force of student discontent, it would be a grave error to deny an underlying malaise.

To some it is wholly incomprehensible that American youth, reared in affluence, can now be troubled by the very society which produced it. They can find no explanation other than that these youths have come under the influence of a foreign and competing ideology. Yet a careful consideration of what most of these students are seeking reveals their dedication to the very ideals which are so vital a part of the American heritage—principles expressed in the Declaration of Independence and the United States Constitution. Perhaps it is the relative affluence of their upbringing which has given them time to take those principles seriously and render them more than lip service.

Their very idealism has caused large numbers of college students to find something wanting in our institutions of higher education. Only now are we beginning to realize that these institutions, which have always fancied themselves the place for fostering idealism and transmitting enduring values, are, in fact, but agents of the philosophy of rugged individualism.

Staggering alternatives confront society as it moves ever further from the relative simplicity of the early twentieth century, when man could still feel he was his own master. At the dawn of the twenty-first century, he finds himself, as an individual, relatively powerless. It is inevitable that we become a nation of organizations and supraorganizations. Yet even within this kind of structure, diametrically opposed alternatives are available to institutions of human development. They can concentrate upon encouraging man's unique characteristics or they can move toward mass production of individuals satisfied to be impersonal contributors to an impersonal system. How we respond to the youth of today will, in part, determine which path society will take.

Expectation of turmoil and extravagance during adolescence is familiar through both literature and experience. It is somehow understood that growth and development involve the painful process of finding oneself. What is not so clearly understood is that growing up in a society which has a fragmented integrative structure places an unusual kind of stress upon the young. The psychological pain of the youth of America must be understood as evidence of and reaction to a difficult transitional period in society.

We have taught them to believe in their own worth as individuals and promised an opportunity to continue their growth. We have stimulated belief in the democratic process and faith in those institutions which preserve and implement such values. Yet those very institutions are burdened by an ambiguous social philosophy and technological progress heretofore only dreamed of.

Despite occasional episodes of chaos and the pervasive confusion of American society, it would be naive to deny the enormous power and intrinsic stability of the institutions under attack. Such a combination of power and stability makes the youth culture more thorn than dagger. Repressive action could remove the discomfort. Or it could be accepted as a warning signal of danger ahead. Faced with psychological pain, societies, like individuals, can act to ignore the validity of that pain or can use it as a source of constructive growth.

Few would deny that changes are needed in our social institutions. Scholarly journals, like other communication media, are filled with exhortations from all shades of the political spectrum. What is missing is adequate consideration of man's inherent resistance to changing his way of seeing the world. Yet this problem is fundamental to any evaluation of student activism in the university setting.

Higher education is clearly a vital part of technological society. Its capacity both to generate and to transmit the spirit of a search for truth must be safeguarded. The search differs in certain important respects from the production of knowledge. For it involves a commitment to examine all phases of society critically, even those bearing upon fundamental assumptions. If higher education, as a social institution, is to become genuinely committed to the search for truth, it must itself be open to critical evaluation and change. Students—at least the present generation—are providing the stimulus for this reevaluation.

Reactions to independence and a demand for change at the group, or institutional, level reflect a paradox which continually plagues the individual. Put starkly, he must forever choose between personal growth and what passes for security. One reason today's youth find it so hard to trust anyone over thirty is their discovery that so many in that age group are wholly unable to change their fundamental perception of the world. And that perception is markedly different from their own perspective.

Growth—or at least change—is inevitable at the societal level. Yet at the level of the individual, it is possible to live out a lifespan with relatively little change. Some understanding of the processes affecting an individual's choice between growth and security can lead to a better comprehension of the present crisis facing higher education. These will be evaluated here as they apply to current issues, in the hope of providing a possible clue to educational reform.

Nearly thirty years ago, Erich Fromm made a penetrating analysis of a paradoxical characteristic in man's nature. In his now-classic *Escape from Freedom*,[3] he showed how the history of Western civilization records not only man's search for freedom, but also his struggle to evade that freedom. Fromm's analysis deals with the basic goals of society; hence, indirectly, with its expectations for educational institutions. In discussing man's ambivalence about his own freedom, he helps delineate the central issue in the contemporary crisis facing higher education. That issue is how to encourage individual freedom of inquiry, at the same time helping one to tolerate the insecurity associated with freedom.

Fromm implicitly assumes a sharing of his basic premises, thus failing to seek ways of convincing any whose freedom may be threatened by his analysis. This sort of failure-to-communicate hampers the relationship of even a liberal administrator and the activist student. The problem goes far beyond the crisis of confrontation and becomes the central issue in all liberal education. Without taking into account the intrinsic difficulty of communication between individuals who do not share a common frame of reference, the most

[3] Erich Fromm, *Escape from Freedom* (New York: Holt, 1941).

brilliantly conceived lecture and most superbly organized curriculum must fail.

For many decades, but particularly within the last, a growing body of relevant evidence, theory, and informed speculation has come from the behavioral sciences. From it we can better understand Fromm's insight into man's conflicting attitudes toward freedom; from it, derive ideas for effectively communicating that insight. Behavioral scientists have their own technical terms for describing this realm of inquiry. Two primary concepts are important for our purpose here. One focuses upon man's nature as an information-seeking organism, for whom the cycle of search and discovery is intrinsically satisfying. This characteristic is more apparent, unfortunately, in young children than in adults. Too often it is severely constrained by the time of entering college. The other concept focuses upon the need to find some meaning or order in life so that its events can be predicted or interpreted. A certain structure must be put upon information, whether baseball scores or philosophical insight, before it acquires a central significance. Any belief system, once established, is exceedingly difficult to modify. This type of adaptive functioning may have served the human species adequately when the pace of social change was slower. It is no longer so appropriate.

There is a subtle and complex interaction between these two potentialities of man. Its true significance lies in neither the intrinsic satisfaction he gains from seeking new information nor the security found in organizing it into some complex philosophical or scientific system. It rests, rather, upon the realization that once man has arrived at a certain ordering of his life, any threat to this order seems to endanger his very survival. Anxiety and hostility are the natural responses to such a threat.

There is infinite variety in the type of information people seek and their ways of organizing it. For most, the kind and quality of information considered essential to survival is not apt to be subject to dramatic challenge. The physical world is remarkably predictable— and consequently, reassuring. The interpersonal world of family, friends, and career may be equally predictable for those willing to stay within certain well-defined organizations of thought and belief. It is here, however, that man's two systems of security begin to work against each other. For those who can accept unquestioningly the goals and constraints of family, church, and country, a sense of security and meaning are readily available. But the problem is compounded for those who can no longer find established cultural institutions coherent enough to provide genuine meaning to their lives. The security of such individuals is threatened by their compulsion to seek new organizations of meaning, new cultural institutions, a new way of life.

This search demands an ability to tolerate anxiety—an anxiety stemming from the loss of established patterns of security and support. It is apparent in both the thinking and the behavior of the group of students who become activists. Such anxiety-laden thought and deed are distinct from the goals these students profess. Both behavior and goals can become sources of threat to the Establishment. But each threat is of a different magnitude; each calls for a different response.

It is essential to understand that the activist is not only disturbing, but disturbed. In the sense that he is different he is disturbing—unidentified with the mainstream. But he is disturbed as well—disturbed by the discrepancy between what is promised and what actually transpires. He takes seriously the ideas forming the language of promises. If those promises are broken, he cannot forgive. The activist—unable to find satisfaction in conventional sources of information and ways of organizing it—must seek security in another way. Security and search become fused and nonconformity becomes a way of life. Once nonconformity has become organized as a system of both search and security, any attempt to change this orientation becomes a major threat to the individual.

A vicious cycle of escalation is involved in the relationship between the activist and any given segment of society which he touches. Of particular concern here is the reaction of nonconformists to the educational establishment. Most arrive at the institution of their choice predisposed to take ideas and promises seriously. They are predisposed, as well, to a fusion of the twin potentialities of search and security. Although in the minority, they are precisely the kind of student the faculty has said it was seeking. Yet as they begin to take the promises of the college catalogue seriously, they are disappointed and rebuffed. Precisely because ideas and ideals are so integral a part of the security of these students, their thoughts and actions begin to bear the stamp of anxiety as they begin the search for ways of implementing their hopes and aspirations.

It is this aspect of activist behavior which drives even a would-be sympathetic administrator or member of the faculty to respond as if his own security were threatened. The activist is at times driven to desperate acts and simplistic thinking, as if his very survival depended upon a single act or slogan. His anxiety and associated irrationality threaten the Establishment's belief in the need for reason. That commitment to rationality, in which higher education takes such pride, may itself be based upon an emotional need for security. The very existence of the university seems threatened when students find an issue for confrontation. The anxiety-produced behavior of the radicals is then matched by that of the people in authority. They, too, often resort, in a panic, to desperate acts and trite slogans to protest the apparent threat to the Establishment.

As the cycle occurs repeatedly, the anxiety of both groups increases; the threat escalates. The radical is forced into a more nonconforming posture than ever. The anomaly of the situation is that his particular need for security demands change. As his acts of desperation increase, the thinking of those in authority, as well, becomes more confused and hostile. Their role in perpetuating the cycle of action and reaction is no less than that of the dissenters, however loud their cry for reason. This does not deny the need for rationality. An open society must be a lawful one based upon wisdom and reason. It does, however, point up the danger of resorting to excessive rationality, which is little more than a mask for fear. When that happens, wisdom is lost.

Institutions of higher education must, then, seek more than ever before the means of becoming responsive to the needs of students. Activists are at the top of the iceberg of discontent which characterizes American youth. Their individual psychology is such that they are in the minority, change being of greater value to them than conventional forms of security. This commitment to change might even become the basis of a new creative element which society so desperately needs.

The challenge higher education must face is the need to find some way of developing these creative energies into socially productive forces. Before suggesting a new approach to meeting that challenge, let us take a look at past efforts at reform in the nation's institutions of higher learning.

Any effort to make the humanitarian and liberal arts goals of the university more viable must be based upon an understanding of two key reform efforts of the past. Most pervasive in altering the structure of the undergraduate curriculum was the introduction, in 1869, of the elective principle, for which the chief spokesman was Charles William Eliot of Harvard. It was a direct response to the changing demands of society in the years immediately following the Civil War and an implicit recognition of certain characteristics of human behavior. The second path of reform was aimed at finding a way to sustain the spirit of a liberal education. It was not so clearly motivated by internal and external sources and has, in fact, been forced to fight a losing battle against the specialization growing out of the elective principle.

Frederick Rudolph, in his classic history of the American college and university, has analyzed the dramatic change in American higher education following the Civil War:

> The country was wealthier than it had ever been before, and the colleges were in a sense getting their first large crop of students who could afford to waste their own time and their father's money. Moreover, their career orientation was less certain than that of earlier generations. Perhaps a job was waiting in the family business, or at least somewhere in business, for which the course of study itself was not a particularly pointed preparation, as need it still was for the ministry, law, and medicine. Now, what mattered for so many young men was not the course of study but the environment of friendship, social development, fraternity houses, good sportsmanship, athletic teams. The world of business was a world of dealing with people. What better preparation could there be than the collegiate life outside the classroom—the club room, the playing field, where the qualities that showed what stuff a fellow really was made of were bound to be encouraged? As the decades passed, college-going became for many a social habit, a habit which was sustained by an ever-increasing standard of living and which was encouraged by the clear evidence

that college men made more money than non-college men and that money almost everywhere was the instrument of social elevation. In all of this, the classroom was not terribly important.[4]

Such a lack of congruence between the needs of students and goals of the undergraduate curriculum has a long history. It was inevitable in a country motivated by powerful anti-intellectual forces. Yet in spite of the social forces marshaled against them, institutions of higher learning did make periodic efforts to close the gap between student needs and educational goals. President Eliot of Harvard was not only a man of strong personal commitment to quality in education, but he had, as well, a sense of what a changing society required. His frontal attack upon the old faculty psychology was far ahead of the times. Until then, it had been one of the strongest foundations of the prescribed course of study.

Eliot's adherence to a psychology of individual differences, then led him to suggest how the elective-principle might meet the problem of student motivation. "The elective system," Eliot said, "fosters scholarship, because it gives free play to natural preferences and inborn aptitudes, makes possible enthusiasm for a chosen work, relieves the professor and the ardent student of the presence of a body of students who are compelled to an unwelcome task and enlarges instruction by substituting many and various lessons given to small lively classes, for a few lessons many times repeated to different sections of a numerous class."[5]

The elective principle was intended to bring student and professor together in a study of common interest. The hope was that variety of course content would meet the diversity of student motivation and need. Clearly this was a step in the right direction for the young men of a fast-growing society dominated by an ideology of freedom and individualism.

It was even more a step in the right direction for institutions of higher education, which were just beginning to play a significant role in a thriving economy, small though it was in comparison to the

[4] Frederick Rudolph, *The American College and University* (New York: Knopf, 1962).

[5] Rudolph, *op. cit.*

present. College professors, interested in both research and service, needed the freedom to present their own ideas and teach what was of interest to them. And the elective principle, although couched in the language of student need, helped serve that end. It was, in fact, an ideal vehicle for the expansion of higher education into its contemporary form. Development of a university-dominated system of education was thus a natural outgrowth of a society dominated by a philosophy of rugged individualism. And in the making, higher education's more humane potential was inevitably sidetracked.

The main thrust of its growth has been, instead, in the direction of research, on campus; off campus, toward greater influence in the world of industry and government. Still, periodic attempts have been made to focus attention upon individual human growth. A liberal education, though variously described, is basically concerned with the student as a person—dedicated, in principle, to helping him respond to his experiences intellectually, emotionally, and imaginatively. Efforts to implement this goal have been hampered by the inherent difficulty of going against the predominant social philosophy and the specialized interests of the faculty. Yet that is not sufficient explanation for the inability of reformers to see beyond their own rhetoric and come to grips with the enormous difficulties involved in encouraging human beings to utilize their growth potential.

An analysis of the efforts of various institutions to vitalize the liberal spirit within their own curricula reveals certain pitfalls in which they have become trapped. Attention here is focused upon the most prestigeful institutions, which set the pattern for others. Daniel Bell, in *The Reforming of General Education*,[6] provides an illuminating acount of the efforts made by Columbia, Harvard, and Chicago. All attempted to re-align the growing emphasis upon specialization in the undergraduate curriculum. All attempted to adapt institutional goals to the needs of their time. Yet none reflected a truly sophisticated comprehension of student need.

Bell says of Columbia University's orientation course in Contemporary Civilization, introduced in 1919:

[6] Daniel Bell, *The Reforming of General Education* (New York: Columbia University Press, 1966).

For a program that has had such extraordinary influence, general education at Columbia was the result of a curious mixture of parochial, sociopolitical and philosophical motives. Within Columbia College, if I have read the history correctly, there were three impulses: the college's struggle against the German tradition of the university, with its "professional" emphasis . . . ; the abandonment of a sterile classicism symbolized by the Latin entrance requirement, which aped the English model; and the changing character of the student body, particularly as the children of immigrants began to predominate intellectually, if not in numbers, in Columbia College.[7]

While Columbia, in the post-World War One era, evolved a two-year program of general education which included science, humanities, and contemporary civilization, the University of Chicago was experimenting during the 1930s with an even more daring departure from the constraints of specialization. The stimulus for reform was, in no small measure, the leadership of the university's president, Robert M. Hutchins. In Bell's words again:

There were, one can say, five basic intentions underlying the general education program of the College of the University of Chicago. The most sweeping was the attempt to break the traditional lock step pattern of American schools. . . . The second basic conception of the Chicago plan was a completely prescribed curriculum for all students, no matter what their vocational plans, intellectual interests or capacities, and backgrounds. The intention was to define a common body of materials in the various fields of knowledge which should be mastered by any person who considers himself educated. . . . The heart of the Chicago plan—the third basic conception of the college—was the organization of all knowledge into a comprehensive number of fields which would give the student not the sum of factual knowledge in that field but its basic organizing principles. . . . The fourth element of the Chicago plan was the creation of an autonomous college faculty whose sole duty would be to teach the general courses. . . . The fifth element . . . was the development of comprehensive examinations at the end of the year courses . . . by an independent examinations staff. There were two reasons for independent examination: to test competence in a general field of knowledge on an objective basis and to place the student in an easier relationship with the instructor, since

[7] Bell, *op. cit.*

the instructor was not the assigner of academic rewards and penalties. . . .[8]

The Harvard report, entitled *General Education in a Free Society,* was published in 1945,[9] partly in response to the troublesome problems confronting American schools during World War Two. Bell says of it: "Such problems as 'why we fight,' the principles of a free society, the need to provide a consistent image of the American experience, the definition of democracy in a world of totalitarianism, the effort to fortify the heritage of Western civilization, and the need to provide a 'common learning' for all Americans as a foundation of national unity, were the factors that shaped the thinking of the Redbook."[10]

The main thrust of the recommendation was its emphasis upon the unifying force provided by a study of the classics and history. Within but a few years of its writing, many of the basic assumptions of Harvard's Redbook were laid open to question by developing events.

These three reform efforts have, to some degree or other, served as the models for present-day liberal or general education. Emphasis varies from institution to institution. It may, as at Harvard, be placed upon exposing the student to the mind of a great man. Or as at Chicago, stress organization of the existing body of knowledge according to certain schemes of classification. Whatever the emphasis, such efforts at reform have failed generally to consider the impact of college upon students. Looking to the faculty to solve problems of general education is a bit like expecting highway engineers to evaluate regional problems of transportation. The engineers' preoccupation with the automobile has, in fact, much in common with the faculty's preoccupation with curricula and methods of instruction. Their pride in curricular reform is understandable, given the counterpressures for specialization and service-geared courses. Yet in the long run, any subject-oriented reform is bound to be self-defeating, just as building bigger and better highways leads only to more cars on the road. The

[8] Bell, *op. cit.*
[9] Harvard Committee, *General Education in a Free Society* (Cambridge: Harvard University Press, 1945).
[10] Bell, *op. cit.*

fundamental issue is whether institutions of higher education are seriously interested in the goals of a liberal education for their students. On the face of it, that interest appears to be secondary to what the faculty wants for itself.

Among the societal forces operating today, which point toward the need for a truly liberal education, the most inescapable stimulus comes from the students themselves. Somehow the combination of heretofore unknown affluence and myriad social problems has nurtured a generation of students who are both thoughtful and angry. It is a generation born of a society just beginning to face the implications of a post-industrial age. The new social structure calls for an ability to respond to change. It demands, too, an understanding of the role of planning in all facets of life, without sacrifice of personal identity. For this new age there must be a new philosophy. The binding social habits and predominant principles of the past are no longer adaptive. It is a time of disruption with more need than ever before to teach individuals to know themselves in the true Socratic sense.

The central deficiency in nearly all efforts at reform in higher education results from a failure to follow through on implications of what a liberal education is all about. An institution must commit itself, not only to helping the student develop his intellect through an open-minded and critical evaluation of the fruits of civilization, but also to helping him grow as an individual. A fundamental contradiction in nearly all liberal arts curricula rests in expecting students to comprehend philosophies, belief systems, and the products of human experience which are in some cases completely alien to them. Too often, classroom emphasis is limited to stressing some aspect of the intellectual content of the material.

A study of the history of Western civilization may, for instance, expect the student to group the history of ideas or analyze the interrelationship between the historical events and the art of a certain period. What is left out is an attempt to relate the intellectual content of the material to the student's own intellectual and personal development. All too often a student with no intrinsic interest in history can, under such a system, coast through the course, learning what seems important to the teacher but never becoming genuinely challenged by different points of view.

College teaching has somehow come to be a process whereby

an expert imparts knowledge. Yet through it a student is expected to be liberated and his intellectual development cultivated. The process denies in the abstract what everyone knows in practice: that it is enormously difficult to encourage anyone to examine his own belief system in anything resembling an open-minded or critical fashion. It is a difficulty which may provide a key to the problem of faculty interest. By training and often by disposition, professors tend to be more interested in their subject matter than in the intellectual and personal development of their students. The whole system of higher education has been set up to reinforce this pattern.

The discrepancy between faculty goals and student needs may have been tolerable in the past, when students were less idealistic than now, and society's need less urgent for individuals who could cope with enormous social complexities. The situation is vastly changed today. And given the ineffectualness of universities' past efforts at self-evaluation and change, a speedy resolution of the difficulty can hardly be anticipated.

The Berkeley crisis of 1964 and succeeding events might be expected to make reform efforts more realistic. Yet recent faculty studies give little evidence that much has been learned about student needs and the process of encouraging intellectual development. In fairness, it must be admitted that proposed changes in the governance of the university are coming closer to the avowed goals of higher education. Various experimental programs are being conducted. Exciting new courses and bold residence programs have been initiated, sometimes being brought together in an experimental college. But where are programs which adequately take into account the student's ambivalence about his own growth? The full force of the college experience is still not being utilized to further his intellectual and personal growth.

To meet the needs of students in a manner consistent with the philosophy of a liberal education, at the same time satisfying the manifold commitments of the multiversity, calls for bold new organizational alternatives. A possible alternative is outlined here. This proposal envisions creation of a wholly new organizational structure uniting two distinct segments of the university in a common effort toward a common goal. It would combine administrative units having primary responsibility for what is euphemistically called student affairs with those research efforts of certain academic departments which are designed to gain a deeper understanding of the problems of student and university.

Too often, the high-minded goals of members of the student personnel profession become bogged down in a maze of housekeeping and disciplinary functions. Indeed, these sometimes appear to have become their primary duties. And too often their day-to-day struggle with a whole array of human problems is out of touch with ongoing teaching and research. Would it not, then, be a natural marriage to bring the two together in a new administrative structure?

By giving student affairs a research emphasis, several things would be accomplished automatically. Most significant would be an integration of the research interests of certain segments of the faculty with the growth and development of students. The actual organization of such an administrative structure would, of course, vary from institution to institution. But the goals would be the same, and it seems wholly reasonable to expect a community of scholars to approach human problems with all possible sophistication and insight.

A reorganization of this sort would show students that their intellectual and personal development was, in fact, being taken seriously by the university. Students themselves can be expected to play an active role, both in research programs designed to increase understanding of the impact of college, and in the numerous services now handled by university administrators. The new structure would capitalize upon their enormous energy and desire to be productively engaged. These attributes, channeled toward intellectual growth and competence, would no longer be relegated to the never-never land of the extracurricular.

Such a proposal is in no way intended to deny the enormity of the problems to be solved or the paucity of knowledge available in many areas. It does seem, however, that much can be gained through such an approach. It is time to treat the discrepancy between the current emphasis of most institutions of higher learning and the actual needs of students as a problem to be solved through research. In that way we can begin to bring the university into better alignment with its own stated goals.

CHAPTER X

Recent Research:
A Brief Review

Harold A. Korn

T̲hat higher education is facing a time of crisis and of change is generally conceded, but there agreement ends. Finding solutions to the problems is complicated by competing, often antagonistic views. This chapter, focused on recent literature and research on the student in higher education, attempts to clarify the problems, identify relevant conceptual and methodological approaches, and raise questions concerning the most effective path to constructive change. The period from June 1965 to October 1968 is reviewed, with occasional reference to earlier studies.

Higher education programs usually refer to those activities which take place outside the formal curriculum. These activities are performed or supervised by members of the student personnel services profession. Traditional program emphases need critical reappraisal in light of current needs of students. *Student development* refers to a point of view which is consistent with the goals of the traditional liberal arts philosophy. It goes an important step further, however, in recognizing that the affective domain of behavior must be explicitly taken into account along with the cognitive domain. Unless both these areas of behavior are recognized in the teaching of the curriculum and in the activities of the extracurriculum, the goals of a liberal education cannot be achieved.

This chapter attempts to demonstrate the relationship between the findings of the behavioral sciences and the practices of student personnel services. It also attempts to center the attention of behavioral scientists upon the pressing, day-to-day problems of the campus community.

HIGHER EDUCATION AS A SOCIAL SYSTEM

Higher Education and Contemporary Society. One hundred years ago students were the most effective agents of campus reform. Rudolph, in making this point, also suggested that earlier students were able to use colleges as instruments of their maturation; now the university serves professors more effectively than students.[1]

---

[1] Frederick Rudolph, "Changing Patterns of Authority and Influence," Fifth Annual Institute on College Self-Study (Boulder, Colo.: Western Interstate Commission for Higher Education, 1965).

One of the few issues remaining unchanged in the hundred-year span Rudolph sought to understand is the yearning of students for a sense of purpose and fulfillment. For decades, higher education programs have been philosophically committed to help students develop. Yet as Koile put it, the profession has been "Forever the Bridesmaid."[2] The student personnel profession's relatively minor influence on the functioning of higher education must be understood in the context of higher education's role in society. Some perspective on what has been happening in our society is necessary even though some may question the relevance of history and social criticism to scientific research.

In the past hundred years, higher education has moved from a numerically small and only marginally powerful social institution to the center stage of what economist and social critic Galbraith calls the New Industrial State.[3] The Academic Revolution, born of our complex technology's increasing demand for specialized talent, was examined in detail by Jencks and Riesman.[4] They argued that the prestige and power of graduate schools have led to the stifling of liberal arts goals by their discipline-centered programs. Although specialization and bigness are not inherently antithetical to human values and personal development, they tend to be inversely correlated.

The threat of technology to the human condition has attracted the attention of numerous social critics: Ellul, Marcuse, and Mumford are among the most articulate.[5] Becker in his provocative analysis of the current educational dilemma, *Beyond Alienation,* has presented an imaginative set of alternatives for curriculum reform based on the "New Moral View of the World."[6]

It is necessary to move from the abstract discussion of the

---

[2] Earl A. Koile, "Student Affairs: Forever the Bridesmaid," *NASPA Journal,* 1966, *4,* 65–72.

[3] John Kenneth Galbraith, *The New Industrial State* (Boston: Houghton Mifflin, 1967).

[4] Christopher Jencks and David Riesman, *The Academic Revolution* (New York: Doubleday, 1968).

[5] Jacques Ellul, *The Technological Society* (New York: Knopf, 1964); Herbert Marcuse, *One-Dimensional Man* (Boston: Beacon Press, 1964); Lewis Mumford, *The Myth of the Machine* (New York: Harcourt, 1966).

[6] E. Becker, *Beyond Alienation* (New York: Braziller, 1967).

conditions of contemporary man to a detailed analysis of how our social institutions influence the lives of individuals. In the past, the emphasis has too often been on understanding society or understanding the individual, rather than on their mutual interaction. A few men of vision, however, have offered a perspective on this interaction; an outstanding example is Sanford's analysis of higher education.[7]

Systems Perspective. In the last decade, the systems perspective has been gathering enthusiasts because it offers, in schematic form, both conceptual frameworks and methods of inquiry adequate to the task of understanding exceedingly complex phenomena. Boguslaw defined a systems perspective as a way of recognizing that performance in any one of a series of successive stages is dependent upon performance in other stages. This interdependence requires that every stage in a sequence be carefully analyzed and its relationship to other stages be painstakingly spelled out.[8] Churchman argued that the technology of systems science can be used to humanize education by forcing a precise and detailed description of the existing educational system so that actual operations and output can be evaluated relative to goals.[9]

In *Integrating the Individual and the Organization,* Argyris explored ways of achieving organizational effectiveness and individual development.[10] His discussion of the unintended consequences of certain organizational procedures and the individual's quest for secret means of not conforming to the organization or of covertly changing it is pertinent to higher education.

Katz and Kahn, in *The Social Psychology of Organizations,* presented a new approach to study of behavior within organizations. They utilized open systems theory to stress the necessary dependence of any organization upon the individuals who are members of the

[7] Nevitt Sanford, (Ed.), *College and Character* (New York: Wiley, 1964). This book is a brief version of *The American College.*

[8] Robert Boguslaw, *The New Utopians: A Study of System Design and Social Change* (Englewood Cliffs, N.J.: Prentice-Hall, 1965).

[9] C. W. Churchman, "Humanizing Education," *The Center Magazine,* 1968, *1,* 90–93 (Santa Barbara, Calif.: Center for the Study of Democratic Institutions, 1968).

[10] C. Argyris, *Integrating the Individual and the Organization* (New York: Wiley, 1964).

organization—and most important, their willingness to perform as members.[11]

THE SYSTEM IN TROUBLE

Academic Performance and Real-Life Success. The Grade Point Average (GPA) is to the educational world what Gross National Product (GNP) is to the economic world. GPA and GNP are convenient indices which take on properties bordering on the mystical. A careful analysis of the consequences of using both indices so pervasively in evaluating success could lead to significant changes in the way social institutions are organized.

Berle introduced a companion concept to Gross National Product called the Gross National Disproduct.[12] He examined whether creation of GNP might involve as much frustration as satisfaction. The point is important as a commentary on the value dilemmas of society and as an indication of how a nationally accepted index of success may hide more than it reveals.

GPA has been as uncritically accepted in the educational world as GNP has been in the economic world. Some institutions have responded to student pressure by changing from letter or numerical grading to a system of descriptive adjectives. Others have experimented with pass-fail criteria. What has not been adequately recognized, however, is the need to examine the purposes, the interrelationships, and hidden consequences of grades or any set of performance criteria.

Lavin, in *The Prediction of Academic Performance,*[13] provided a thorough introduction to this complex issue. He analyzed studies to determine the validity of ability, personality, and sociological factors as predictors of GPA. None accounted adequately for the variance in GPA; seldom was more than 50 per cent of the variance accounted

[11] Daniel Katz and R. L. Kahn, *The Social Psychology of Organizations* (New York: Wiley, 1966).

[12] A. A. Berle, Jr., "What GNP Doesn't Tell Us," *Saturday Review,* 1968, *51,* 10–12.

[13] David E. Lavin, *The Prediction of Academic Performance: A Theoretical Analysis and Review of Research* (New York: Russell Sage Foundation, 1965).

for. A multivariate approach is necessary to predict GPA, multivariate in the broad sense of including various measures of the social environment. Such an approach should encompass student-teacher relationships and the influence of informal peer-group norms upon academic achievement.

GPA, however, is a very ambiguous and questionable criterion. Hoyt approached the problem of grades from the perspective of how adequately they predict future success. He concluded, after an extensive review, that college grades have no more than a very modest correlation with adult success, no matter how success is defined. He also provided a valuable analysis of the meaning of college grades and the whole problem of evaluation in higher education. Hoyt suggested the use of a profile of student growth and development instead of grades. In a later study, Hoyt also considered the problem of forecasting success in specific colleges.[14]

Implicit in the philosophy of a liberal education has always been a commitment to the development of the entire individual. Despite this commitment, grades are used almost exclusively to measure success of the individual and indirectly, of the system. However, as Holland and Richards have demonstrated, academic potential and achievement have very little relationship to other kinds of nonacademic potential and socially important performance.[15] Richards and Lutz found that nonacademic accomplishments, such as leadership, could be assessed with moderate reliability and could be predicted.[16]

The College Dropout. In a nation increasingly committed to the ideal of higher education for all, an inevitable danger lies in lack

---

[14] Donald P. Hoyt, *The Relationship Between College Grades and Adult Achievement: A Review of the Literature,* American College Testing Program Research Report No. 7 (Iowa City: American College Testing Program, 1965); and *Forecasting Academic Success in Specific Colleges,* American College Testing Program Research Report No. 27 (Iowa City: American College Testing Program, 1968).

[15] J. L. Holland and J. M. Richards, "Academic and Non-Academic Accomplishment: Correlated or Uncorrelated?" *Journal of Educational Psychology,* 1965, *56,* 165–174.

[16] J. M. Richards and Sandra Lutz, *Predicting Student Accomplishment in College from the A.C.T. Assessment* (Iowa City: American College Testing Program, 1967).

of congruence between the individual and the system. Manpower demands of our technological society, a sharp increase in the number of teenagers, and commitment to advanced study have forced some states to develop master plans for higher education. Knoell described the efforts made in New York and California to adopt a social institution designed for the elite to the needs of a democracy.[17]

The lack of congruence between the needs of the individual and the demands of a system of higher education is evidenced by the number of dropouts. At one time or another, 50 per cent of the college population drop out; however, this percentage includes those who transfer or later return to the same school. The issue of "the college dropout and the utilization of talent" was carefully explored in a book by that title, edited by Pervin, Reik, and Dalrymple. Dropping out, they indicated, may be as beneficial to one student as it is detrimental to another. Yet an inescapable social attitude against it persists: individuals who cannot conform to the usual pattern of a four-year college curriculum are treated with disdain.[18]

Ford and Urban broadened the perspective on the utilization of talent by suggesting that "the phenomenon of the college dropout implies a basic flaw in our entire educational structure. . . . We need to invent forms of education that are appropriate for those who are not highly effective as symbolic learners."[19] Heist, in examining problems and needs of creative college students, found that students identified as creative leave college more often or just as often as those who are not so identified.[20]

The Black Student. For black students, the discrepancy between individual needs and institutional requirements reaches tragic proportions. For the white student the curriculum appears to have face

[17] Dorothy M. Knoell, "Free Choice vs. Planned Accommodation: Contrasting State Approaches to Student Input," in Clarence H. Bagley (Ed.), *Research on Academic Input* (New York: Association for Institutional Research, 1966).

[18] L. A. Pervin, L. E. Reik, and W. Dalrymple (Eds.), *The College Dropout and the Utilization of Talent* (Princeton, N.J.: Princeton University Press, 1966).

[19] D. H. Ford and H. B. Urban, "College Dropouts: Successes or Failures?" in Pervin, Reik, and Dalrymple, *op. cit.*, p. 106.

[20] Paul Heist, *The Creative College Student: An Unmet Challenge* (San Francisco: Jossey-Bass, 1968).

validity; the average white student has been taught to believe that he should find the history of Western Civilization, English literature, and the like, interesting. Many black students find this an unwarranted assumption and are demanding more courses that emphasize Afro-American culture. Yet some educators find hope intrinsic in the very problem. "These ghetto youth," Bush indicated, "challenge traditional and accepted academic procedures, inspire the middle-class students to venture beyond pat answers and normal study patterns, and cause professors to reevaluate present teaching methods."[21]

In *Study of Negro Students at Integrated Colleges,* Clark and Plotkin found that GPA was related to fathers' occupations. Further, black students had a lower dropout rate than whites at the same colleges.[22] Bradley found that American College Test (ACT) scores were not equally predictive of GPA for black and white students in predominantly white state colleges and universities in Tennessee. He saw the problem in terms of a need for interracial education at elementary and secondary school levels.[23]

McClain studied the personality characteristics of black college students in the South. Using Cattell's Sixteen Personality Factors inventory, he found marked differences between black and white students in dominance and other aspects of personality development.[24] Boney, exploring a remedial approach to the problem, proposed a model for assertion training in academic situations.[25] The efforts and frustrations of white institutions to recruit black students were graphically described by Sabine. He quoted, for example, a conversation which took place on a basketball court, detailing how the

[21] Dixon Bush, "Disadvantaged Students at College: A New Dimension," *College and University Bulletin,* 1967, *19,* 2–3.

[22] Kenneth B. Clark and L. Plotkin, *The Negro Student at Integrated Colleges* (New York: National Scholarship Service and Fund for Negro Students, 1963).

[23] Nolan E. Bradley, "The Negro Undergraduate Student: Factors Relative to Performance in Predominantly White State Colleges and Universities in Tennessee," *Journal of Negro Education,* 1967, *36,* 15–23.

[24] Edwin W. McClain, "Personality Characteristics of Negro College Students in the South: A Recent Appraisal," *Journal of Negro Education,* 1967, *36,* 300–325.

[25] J. Don Boney, "Some Dynamics of Disadvantaged Students in Learning Situations," *Journal of Negro Education,* 1967, *36,* 315–319.

recruiter talked to a prospective black student while he was practicing set-ups.[26]

Just as the system of higher education must be understood within the framework of contemporary society, so must the black student be understood in the context of that society, which has for so long ignored him. A book of essays edited by Parsons and Clark spelled out the dimensions of the Negro-American experience.[27] At the present time the most significant dimension can be described in terms of the polar concepts *integration* and *separatism*. The long-sought integration into the mainstream of American society now seems to many black Americans too slow and too filled with disappointments. A sense of identity and a basis for self-respect are now being pursued in terms of the development of a visible Afro-American culture. Higher education, unprepared to deal with the culturally disadvantaged student in its traditional curriculum, is now being bombarded with demands for a new kind of curriculum. In one sense, higher education's response to the challenge presented by the black students will be the key to its readiness to respond to a wide variety of problems.

Psychological Needs and Impersonality. The dreams, accomplishments, and failures of mankind are the subject matter of a liberal education. Many students expect that exposure to the wisdom of the past and the accumulated knowledge of the present will promote their personal development. When this fails to happen, they become apathetic, rebellious, or alienated. Pervin considered the reality and nonreality in student expectations of college, and found that students unrealistically expect the college to emphasize abstract understanding or social welfare.[28]

Katz and Associates presented the results of a five-year longitudinal study of changes in students at Stanford and the University of California at Berkeley. The study included semiannual interviews for selected samples of 250 students, analysis of freshman-senior per-

[26] Gordon A. Sabine, "Michigan State's Search for More Negro Students," *College Board Review*, 1968, *69*, 11–14.

[27] Talcott Parsons and Kenneth B. Clark, *The Negro American* (Boston: Houghton Mifflin, 1966).

[28] Lawrence A. Pervin, "Reality and Nonreality in Student Expectations of College," *Journal of Psychology*, 1966, *64*, 41–48.

sonality scales, and a variety of case studies. The researchers, in finding little impact of college on student development, concluded that the answer to the present dilemma lies in changing the curricular offerings and other components of the educational environment. The authors proposed that the student and his development be made the focus of education, rather than the accumulation of course credits. This would involve keeping a profile of the student's development, not merely a transcript of his grades.[29]

Trent and Medsker studied ten thousand high school graduates to determine what impact attending college or going to work has on individuals. The authors concluded: college seems to foster the growth of autonomy and intellectual disposition of its graduates only in comparison with those of their peers who had less college or none at all. Evidence collected from questionnaire and interview items suggested that most college graduates are apathetic to intellectual inquiry and social issues.[30]

Both the Katz and the Trent and Medsker studies focused on how higher education is thwarting the psychological needs of many students. Some of these needs are seemingly mundane and have to do with such things as having work assignments made relevant and not merely hurdles to be jumped. Other needs are thwarted by administrative philosophies like *in loco parentis,* which are antithetical to late adolescents' wish for freedom. If attention is paid to these system details which distress the student, perhaps student motivation can be changed from fighting the system to more active cooperation with the system.

Once changes are made in the ways students are thwarted, it is possible to move into the realm of what man can become if he is encouraged to use his full human potential. That higher education should be centrally involved in this endeavor was clearly articulated by Sanford and Freedman.[31] Kauffman and his associates, in their succinct

---

[29] Joseph Katz and Associates, *No Time for Youth* (San Francisco: Jossey-Bass, 1968).

[30] James W. Trent and Leland L. Medsker, *Beyond High School* (San Francisco: Jossey-Bass, 1968).

[31] Nevitt Sanford, *Where Colleges Fail* (San Francisco: Jossey-Bass, 1967); and Mervin B. Freedman, *The College Experience* (San Francisco: Jossey-Bass, 1967).

explication of this position, described the psychological needs of students in higher education and proposed a broad, heuristic theory of human development. They argued that "the quality of human relationships in higher education must be improved not simply because it will enable students to spend happy and more fulfilling years in college or because many of the present conditions in higher education are intolerable, but primarily because, unless the trends toward giantism and dehumanization are reversed, the college will not be able to educate even the technician."[32]

Student Unrest and Radical Students. It is both ironic and inevitable that students are the ones forcing a reexamination of the system of higher education. Ironic, because the presumed wisdom and knowledge of student personnel professionals and related behavioral scientists have not had the same impact. Inevitable, because students suffer most from the inequities of the system and are in a position to gain most while risking little. Potter, a student, gave some insight into the students' rhetoric: "If my tone is not detached," he wrote, "it is because I find with my compatriots one source of concern—a world in which men so easily detach themselves emotionally from the things they create."[33]

Keniston, analyzing the power of this "youth culture" to effect change, attributed some of its potential force to contradictions inherent in society. Great economic wealth permits development of a class of students and young adults free to pursue idealistic goals. Yet the very factors producing this wealth also incur conditions antithetical to human values, inciting idealists to seek change.[34] Flacks also found student protest based on deep discontent among certain high-status youth.[35]

How this youth culture evolved from the student apathy of the

[32] J. E. Kauffman *et al., The Student in Higher Education* (New Haven: Hazen Foundation, 1968), p. 58.

[33] P. Potter, "Student Discontent and Campus Reform," Fifth Annual Institute on College Self-Study (Boulder, Colo.: Western Interstate Commission for Higher Education, 1965), p. 71.

[34] Kenneth Keniston, *Young Radicals: Notes on Committed Youth* (New York: Harcourt, 1968).

[35] Richard Flacks, "The Liberated Generation: Roots of Student Protest," *Journal of Social Issues,* 1967, *23,* 52–75. See also his chapter (Chapter Five) in the volume.

1950s is explored by Sampson in the first chapter of the present volume. That activist students are intelligent and productive seems to be generally agreed.[36] Yet there is no clear explanation of why students are activists in the sixties when their "brothers" were not in the fifties. Major variables appear to be the Vietnam war and civil rights legislation. While student protesters are by no means in the majority, Gales found that 80 per cent of 400 students randomly selected and interviewed at Berkeley favored the goals of the Free Speech Movement. Yet those students did not all agree with the FSM methods of attaining their goals.[37]

Activists find all social institutions wanting, but they concentrate upon institutions of higher learning. A long tradition of academic freedom makes higher education particularly vulnerable to an accusation of abridging students' constitutional rights. Williamson and Cowan, surveying a representative sample of American institutions of higher education, found students' freedom of expression subject to a variety of definitions.[38] Problems posed by these varying definitions were analyzed by Armacost.[39]

A focal point of student discontent is university governance. A penetrating analysis and a far-sighted set of proposals were recently put forth by the Faculty Student Commission on University Governance at the University of California. Two major themes were explored: (1) promoting a greater degree of open discussion in a spirit of mutual trust; and (2) decentralization of decision-making powers to smaller campus units sharing common purposes.[40]

STUDENT GROWTH

Studying the Impact of College. Feldman and Newcomb made a substantial contribution to the study of college students by

[36] Joseph Katz and Associates, *op. cit.*

[37] Kathleen E. Gales, "A Campus Revolution," *British Journal of Sociology,* 1966, *17,* 1–19.

[38] E. G. Williamson and J. Cowan, *The American Student's Freedom of Expression* (Minneapolis: University of Minnesota Press, 1966).

[39] Peter Armacost, "The American Association of University Professors and the Association of American Colleges Statements of Student Freedoms: A Comparison and Discussion of Viewpoints," Proceedings of the National Association of Student Personnel Administrators (Seattle: The Association, 1966).

[40] Caleb Foote, Henry Mayer, and Associates, *The Culture of the University: Governance and Education* (San Francisco: Jossey-Bass, 1968).

reviewing extant literature on the impact of college. They posed the following question: Under what conditions have what kinds of students changed in what specific ways? They concluded that an increase in open-mindedness, decrease in conservatism concerning public issues, and a growing sensitivity to esthetic and inner experiences take place during college. Newcomb and Feldman warned against the pitfalls of cross-sectional studies and advocated use of longitudinal data. They also examined in some detail the tendency to mask individual changes by presenting results only in terms of mean differences. These authors concluded that college experience, at the very least, accentuates changes inherent in the developmental patterns of individuals.[41]

A fundamental problem for studies using objective personality scales to measure change centers on the validity of such measures. Korn used a cluster analysis technique to study empirical dimensions in the structure of individual scales. (The Social Maturity and Impulse Expression Scales from the Omnibus Personality Inventory were used.) The multidimensional structure of such individual personality scales compounds the difficulty of interpreting what changes in mean scores actually represent.[42]

Conceptual confusion surrounding concepts of personality development and socialization is a basic problem in studying change during college. The use of so-called personality scales to measure change resulting from college experience inadvertently implies change in basic dimensions of personality, whereas the change may actually be the result of the socializing influence of prevailing peer-group attitudes. Unfortunately, behavioral scientists who use socialization as a primary theoretical construct do not use personality constructs in their theories, and vice versa. Relating these two approaches to understanding human behavior could be a fruitful new area of research on college students. Brim and Wheeler made a valuable contribution by delineating how socialization occurs after childhood.[43] Madison used the study of personality in college students to examine new theoretical

[41] Kenneth A. Feldman and Theodore M. Newcomb, *The Impact of College on Students* (San Francisco: Jossey-Bass, 1969).
[42] Harold A. Korn, "Personality Scale Changes from the Freshman Year to the Senior Year," in Joseph Katz and Associates, *op. cit.*
[43] O. G. Brim and S. Wheeler, *Socialization After Childhood: Two Essays* (New York: Wiley, 1966).

constructs in personality theory. Using extensive in-depth interviews, he explored the consequences of one's "child-self" in continuing to influence decisions of later life.[44]

Critical Thinking, Open-mindedness, and Resistance to Change. A basic assumption of the liberal arts curriculum is that critical thinking and open-mindedness are qualities of human behavior which can be encouraged. A further assumption is that these qualities of human behavior are eagerly sought by students and faculty. There is an extensive literature in the behavioral sciences which indirectly bears on these assumptions. It is remarkable, however, that these basic assumptions have not been directly tested. It is equally remarkable that behavioral scientists, who have been most directly concerned with these dimensions, have not seen fit to study the great natural experiment created by the liberal arts curriculum.

A pioneering study relevant here was the analysis by Newcomb and his associates of the long-term results of a Bennington College education in the 1930s. Using a combination of interviews and questionnaires, the researchers found that social awareness, a major objective of the Bennington curriculum, persisted twenty-five years later. The persistence of these attitudes was related to the social environments these women created for themselves. By choosing husbands, friends, and co-workers with similar social philosophies, these Bennington women reinforced throughout their lives the attitudes developed at college.[45]

Unfortunately, few studies have focused directly on the influence of the college experience upon open-mindedness and critical thinking. Rokeach moved away from an emphasis on authoritarianism to a more inclusive view of the nature of belief systems and how they are influenced.[46] This area of research has important implications for higher education because it focuses on the human tendency to hold onto any established belief system. It may be that students do indeed want to examine critically their own belief systems. It should be

[44] Peter Madison, *Personality in College* (Reading, Mass.: Addison-Wesley, 1966).
[45] Theodore M. Newcomb *et al., Persistence and Change: Bennington College and Its Students After Twenty-Five Years* (New York: Wiley, 1967).
[46] Milton Rokeach, *Beliefs, Attitudes, and Values* (San Francisco: Jossey-Bass, 1968).

acknowledged, however, that to do so may be a painful emotional experience; students will find ways to avoid becoming genuinely open-minded and self-critical.

The student personnel professional who is concerned with finding ways to foster critical thinking and open-mindedness can make a genuine contribution to the liberal education of students. Korn, for example, called for collaboration between professors who could teach content and other professionals who could take into account the various sources of resistance which students bring to the liberal arts curriculum.[47] Thoresen discussed several techniques for exploring this kind of collaborative effort. He used video tape in the classroom and a study of the characteristics of nonparticipants in discussion sections to focus attention on dimensions of the affective domain in higher education.[48]

NEW APPROACHES, TRADITIONAL GOALS

Innovative thinking and some experimentation have evolved from seriously questioning the system of higher education. A recent Western Interstate Commission for Higher Education institute resulted in a volume of essays which surveyed much of the recent effort to personalize higher education.[49] Cluster colleges and experimental programs are two broad categories of innovation.

Cluster Colleges. In an effort to combat the impersonality of the multiversity, smaller semi-independent units called cluster colleges are being created. Martin indicated, however, that even cluster colleges were developing along disciplinary lines. He called for programs focused on urban problems and set in strategically located city buildings.[50]

[47] Harold A. Korn, "Counseling and Teaching: An Integrated View," *Journal of College Student Personnel,* 1966, 7, 137–140.

[48] Carl. E. Thoresen, "Oral Non-Participation in College Students: A Study of Characteristics," *American Educational Research Journal,* 1966, 3, 198; and "Video in the College Classroom: An Exploratory Study," *Personnel and Guidance Journal,* 1966, 45, 144–149.

[49] W. J. Minter (Ed.), "The Individual and The System," Seventh Annual Institute of College Self-Study (Boulder, Colo.: Western Interstate Commission for Higher Education, 1967).

[50] Warren Bryan Martin, *Alternative to Irrelevance: A Strategy for Reform in Higher Education* (Nashville, Tenn.: Abingdon Press, 1968).

The promise inherent in the idea of cluster colleges is evident; equally clear are the problems of implementing the idea, as summarized by Kells and Steward.[51] These problems run the gamut from petty departmental jealousies to fundamental questions relating to philosophy of education. Astin, a participant in the Conference on the Cluster College, focused attention on the need to experiment with the composition of student bodies participating in a cluster college program. He called for longitudinal evaluative studies which could systematically assess the impact on students of different types of cluster colleges.[52]

The cluster college setting is ideal for putting into action what has been learned about the influence of peer groups on student development. Ideas found in Newcomb and Wilson, an excellent introduction to the study of college peer groups, might be implemented in cluster colleges.[53] Newcomb stressed the importance of an internal organization in the college leading to formation of meaningful student-faculty groups, involving both their personal and academic lives.[54]

Experimental Programs. The other thrust for experimentation and change finds expression in a variety of experimental programs. Nixon, a student who helped develop the Experimental College at San Francisco State College, found that one significant effect of the program was that students became alert to the possibility of change. No longer did they blindly assume that education had to be presented as they were receiving it in their classrooms.[55]

A product of student protest at the University of California at Berkeley was the report of the Select Committee of the Academic

[51] H. R. Kells and C. T. Steward, "The Conference on the Cluster College Concept: A Summary of the Working Session," *Journal of Higher Education,* 1967, *38,* 359–363.

[52] A. W. Astin, "The Conference on the Cluster College Concept: Students," *Journal of Higher Education,* 1967, *38,* 396–397.

[53] Theodore M. Newcomb and E. K. Wilson (Eds.), *College Peer Groups* (Chicago: Aldine, 1966).

[54] Theodore M. Newcomb, "The Contribution of the Interpersonal Environment to Students' Learning," *NASPA Journal,* 1967, *5,* 175–178.

[55] James Nixon, "The Learner's View About Personalizing Higher Education," in *The Individual and The System,* Seventh Annual Institute on College Self-Study (Boulder, Colo.: Western Interstate Commission for Higher Education, 1967).

Senate, informally known as the Muscatine report.[56] It called for a variety of reforms in structure and organization of the university, including establishment of a Board of Educational Development with power to create new instructional programs and bypass the established university machinery.

Axelrod, finding that the "problem" is often formulated prematurely in new programs, proposed a curricular plan which "attempts to help the student free his mind of the very middle-class bias which determines, more often than not, how a societal problem is perceived and hence formulated."[57]

McKeachie called for further research on the characteristics of college teachers with particular reference to their capacity to see course material from the student perspective.[58] Acker, Danskin, and Kennedy illustrated how knowledge of student characteristics could determine the structure of the curriculum. They found that the entering students in the College of Agriculture expected and needed course work that would tie in with their past experiences and future goals.[59]

At a time when students demand relevance, "games" may appear out of place. Yet Boocock and Schild offered convincing arguments for using simulation games in learning.[60] Issues and processes from real life can be abstracted, permitting students to examine the consequences of different strategies in decision making.

DIRECTIONS FOR THE FUTURE

A systems perspective requires that we examine the consequences of all actions in light of avowed goals. When the student

[56] University of California, Berkeley, Academic Senate, *Education at Berkeley: Report of the Select Committee on Education* (Berkeley: Regents of the University of California, 1966).

[57] Joseph Axelrod, "An Experimental College Model," *Educational Record*, 1967, *48*, 327–337.

[58] Wilbert J. McKeachie, "Significant Student and Faculty Characteristics Relevant to Personality in Higher Education," in *The Individual and the System*, Seventh Annual Institute on College Self-Study (Boulder, Colo.: Western Interstate Commission for Higher Education, 1967).

[59] D. C. Acker, D. G. Danskin, and C. E. Kennedy, Jr., "Student Characteristics in Curriculum Planning," *Journal of College Student Personnel*, 1967, *8*, 381–384.

[60] Sarane S. Boocock and E. O. Schild (Eds.), *Simulation Games in Learning* (Beverly Hills, Calif.: Sage, 1968).

personnel profession considers both the ineffectiveness of past actions and the unsolved current problems, a dramatic reappraisal of the professional role seems inevitable. The urgency of problems facing higher education and the paucity of relevant knowledge available from behavioral sciences demonstrate that a program of action research is vital. Sources of student unrest must be dealt with by developing programs which come to grips with impersonality and the perceived irrelevance of large parts of the curriculum. Such programs must be established in ways which permit critical evaluation of factors contributing to program success and failure. Fairweather has made an interesting start at setting up a community-wide program of social innovation and has described a system for evaluating its success.[61] Webb and his associates described a number of ways for obtaining unobtrusive measures of social behavior which may be useful in evaluating change.[62]

The need to respond to pressing immediate problems is surpassed by the even greater need to develop a sociopsychological theory adequate to the task of increasing understanding of the structures and processes of higher education. This is akin to saying we need a science of human behavior encompassing the far-ranging problems of higher education. Greater recognition of the complexity and scope of the problem is needed in research on higher education. A number of studies have not been considered in this review because they lack scope, although in many ways they are more typical of what is generally found in the journals. Far too many studies are limited to correlating the assessment variables of a certain instrument with some other criterion. No question is raised concerning the validity of the assessment measure, the meaningfulness of the criterion, or the significance of the question being pursued. Because of this lack of critical appraisal, there is seldom replication of the study by other researchers and most often the work is not even followed up by the original researcher. Even more rare are experimental studies where significant variables are systematically varied.

Although it may be relatively easy to say that certain kinds of

[61] G. W. Fairweather, *Methods for Experimental Social Innovation* (New York: Wiley, 1967).

[62] E. J. Webb *et al.*, *Unobtrusive Measures: Nonreactive Research in the Social Sciences* (New York: Rand McNally, 1966).

studies should be discouraged because their only contribution is to the bibliography of the author, it is much more difficult to say what studies should be done. At this stage in the development of the behavioral sciences, no one can claim a corner on truth. It is possible, nevertheless, to point to major research projects which, despite being very different in character, are models of what research efforts should be. One excellent example is the path charted by Astin and his colleagues, who have developed a research program and accompanying methodology to describe graphically what is actually going on in many sectors of higher education.[63] Their evidence suggests that traditional indices of institutional quality do not measure variables which contribute to student achievement. Such empirical evidence must be sought to provide a clear picture of what is actually happening. Problems associated with this empirical research strategy were described by Creager and Astin and by Astin.[64]

Another style of research cannot be so easily characterized, for it deals with what should be as well as what is. Implicit in any discussion of what ought to be are both a statement of values and a theory for translating them into action programs. The recent work of Bloom challenged many fundamental assumptions about the educational process by advocating "learning for mastery." Suggesting that most students can master most material, he expressed the need for the entire educational system to become student oriented—to accept the burden of finding ways and means of becoming effectual, instead of covertly blaming students unable to learn from the traditional prescribed procedures.[65]

[63] Alexander W. Astin, Robert J. Panos, and John A. Creager, *A Program of Longitudinal Research on the Higher Educational System.* ACE Research Reports 1, No. 1 (Washington, D.C.: American Council on Education, 1966); Astin, Panos, and Creager, *Implications of a Program of Research on Student Development in Higher Education.* ACE Research Reports 2. No. 2 (Washington, D.C.: American Council on Education, 1967); and Astin, *The College Environment* (Washington, D.C.: American Council on Education, 1968).

[64] John A. Creager and Alexander W. Astin, "Alternative Methods of Describing Characteristics of Colleges and Universities," *Educational and Psychological Measurement,* 1968, *28,* 719–734; and Alexander W. Astin, "Criterion Centered Research," *Educational and Psychological Measurement,* 1964, *24,* 807–822.

[65] B. S. Bloom, *Learning for Mastery,* Report of the UCLA Center for

These research efforts by Astin and Bloom can be viewed as two kinds of inputs to a systems approach to higher education. As the picture of what is actually happening in higher education becomes clearer, and as agreement grows on what should be happening in higher education, counseling will be faced with the enormous challenge of implementation. The role of the student personnel profession will become clearly defined, because it alone has the potential for acquiring the needed comprehensive knowledge of individual student characteristics and the commitment to create a campus environment conducive to mastery learning. By combining the student development point of view with the educational philosophy implicit in the concept of mastery learning, higher education can find a path out of its current crisis.

For additional references on these and related topics, see the following bibliography.

ADDITIONAL REFERENCES

AXELROD, J. "An Experimental College Model," *Educational Record,* Fall 1967, 327–337.

AXELROD, J. "The Student and the Grading System," in Paul Heist (Ed.), *The Creative College Student* (San Francisco: Jossey-Bass, 1968).

BARATZ, STEPHEN S. "Effect of Race of Experimenter, Instructions and Comparison Population Upon Level of Reported Anxiety in Negro Subjects," *Journal of Personality and Social Psychology,* 1967, *7,* 194–196.

BARTON, A. H. *Organizational Measurement and Its Bearing on the Study of College Environments* (New York: College Entrance Examination Board, 1961).

BARTON, A. H. "Studying the Effects of College Education," in K. Yamamoto (Ed.), *The College Student and His Culture* (Boston: Houghton Mifflin, 1968).

BOOCOCK, SARANE. "Toward a Sociology of Learning: A Selective Review of Existing Research," *Sociology of Education,* 1966, *39,* 1–45.

BOWERS, J. E. "A Test of Variation in Grading Standards," *Educational and Psychological Measurement,* 1967, *27,* 429–430.

BUCKLEY, WALTER (Ed.). *Modern Systems Research for the Behavioral Scientist* (Chicago: Aldine, 1968).

CLARK, KENNETH B. "Higher Education for Negroes: Challenges and Prospects," *Journal of Negro Education,* 1967, *36,* 196–203.

DAVIS, SHELDON A. "An Organic Problem-Solving Method of Organiza-

the Study of Evaluation of Instructional Programs 1, No. 2 (Los Angeles: University of California, 1968).

tional Change," *Journal of Applied Behavioral Science*, 1967, *3*, 3–20.

DREGER, R. M. and MILLER, K. S. "Comparative Psychological Studies of Negroes and Whites in the United States: 1959–65," *Psychological Bulletin Monograph Supplement*, 1968, *70*(3), Part 2, 1–58.

DRESSEL, PAUL L. "Factors Involved in Changing the Values of College Students," *Educational Record*, 1965, *46*, 104–113.

DRESSEL, PAUL L. "A Look at New Curriculum Models for Undergraduate Education,"*Journal of Higher Education*, 1965, *36*, 89.

DRESSEL, PAUL L. and LEHMAN, I. J. "The Impact of Higher Education on Student Attitudes, Values and Critical Thinking Abilities," *Educational Record*, 1965, *46*, 248–259.

GALBRAITH, JOHN K. "Facing Political Reality: How the University Can Protect Itself," *College Management*, 1967, *2*, 32–36.

HARRIS, C. (Ed.). *Problems in Measuring Change* (Madison: University of Wisconsin, 1963).

HARRIS, J., and REITZEL, JOHN. "Negro Freshman Performance in a Predominantly Non-Negro University," *Journal of College Student Personnel*, 1967, *8*, 366–368.

HARRISON, E. C. "Improving Negro Colleges," *Phi Delta Kappan*, 1967, *48*, 296–298.

JUOLA, ARVO E. "Illustrative Problems in College-Level Grading," *Personnel and Guidance Journal*, 1968, *47*, 29.

PALLET, J. E., and HOYT, D. P. "College Curriculum and Success in General Business," *Journal of College Personnel*, 1968, *9*, 238–245.

PERVIN, LAWRENCE A. "The College as a Social System," *Journal of Higher Education*, 1967, *38*, 317–322.

PLANT, W. T. "Longitudinal Changes in Intolerance and Authoritarianism for Subjects Differing in Amount of College Education Over Four Years," *Genetic Psychology Monographs*, 1965, *72*, 247–287.

THORESEN, C. "The Systems Approach in Counselor Education: Basic Features and Implications," in *Counselor Education and Supervision* (in press).

WEBB, SAM C. "The Relations of College Grades and Personal Qualities Considered Within Two Frames of Reference, "*Multivariate Behavioral Research Monographs* 1967, *67*, 2.

Index

A

Academic performance vs. real-life success, 240–241

Academic Senate (Berkeley) and student activists, 12

ACKER, D. C., 252

Activism, 44, 159–190; and academic pressure, 177–178; as acting out of family values, 172–174; activist-administration relationship, 9–11; at Berkeley, 12, 143–149, 205–207, 251–252; black student demands, 193–195; cultural climate as factor, 178–179; extent of, 29–33, 159–160; factors in, 92–96, 102–103, 168–185; future trends, 185–190; among graduates, 32–33; and major field of study, 39–41; mass media coverage, 14–17; political backlash, 150; public's attitude toward, 13–14; as revolt against technology, 180; revolutionary vs. reform types, 25–29; at San Francisco State College, 143–146, 148–149,

257

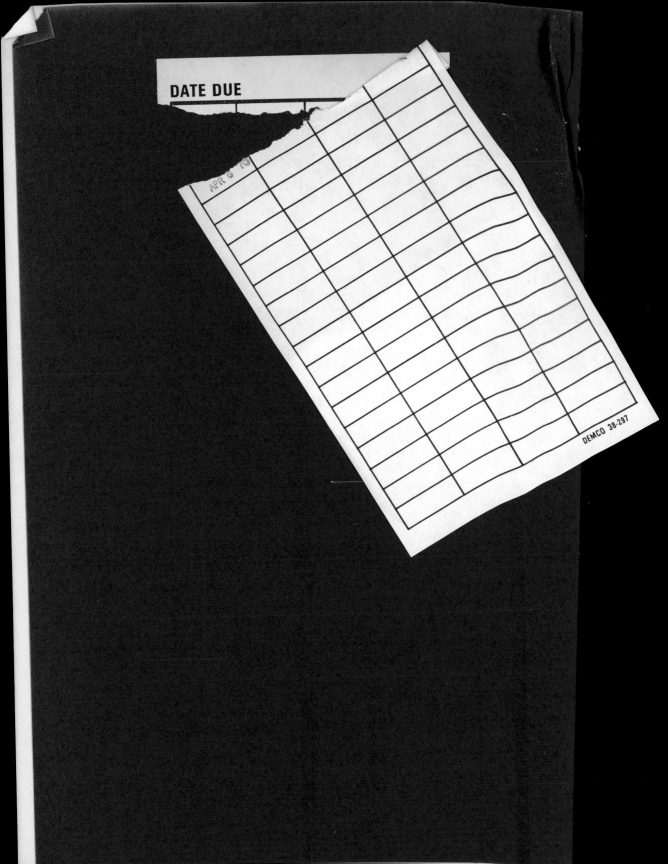